ETHOS

Ethos

CONNECTING WITH VALUED TRAITS

Don Pierce

Heartwood Path

Contact:
Heartwood Path
info@heartwoodpath.com
805-689-7042
www.heartwoodpath.com

ISBN/SKU: 979-8-9857352-8-4
EISBN: 979-8-9857352-9-1

To my closest long-term friends: Jerry, Duke, Tommy, Neil, Mark, Marc, and Steve.

Contents

Read This First

Although anyone may find the practices, challenges, and under-standings in this book to be useful it is made available with the understanding that neither the author nor the publisher are engaged in presenting specific medical, psychological, emotional, sexual, or spiritual advice. Nor is anything in this book intended to be a diagnosis, prescription, recommendation, or cure for any specific kind of medical, psychological, emotional, sexual, or spiritual problem. Each person has unique needs and this book cannot take these individual differences into account. Each reader is encouraged to engage in a program of treatment, prevention, and cure only in consultation with a licensed, qualified physician, therapist, or other competent professional.

Introduction

Wholeness adds a sparkle each time someone displays a valued personality trait. It is a community that determines these values, along with the individuals in it. At the primary entrance of the town—any community, really—I imagine a twinkling two-story roadside crossword puzzle with the heading: "These Positive Character Traits Give Our Community It's Ethos—it's shine, and it's spirit as reflected in its aspirations." This book is called **Ethos** because it is about the valued character traits glimmering on this imaginary large outdoor attraction, whereon both vertically and horizontally the following words glow brightly at night: integrity, honesty, loyalty, respectfulness, responsibility, humility, compassion, fairness, forgiveness, authenticity, courageous, and generosity. Another town's similar sign might have different words, such as politeness, kindness, lovingness, optimism, reliability, conscientiousness, self-discipline, ambition, encouragement, consideration, and thoroughness. Without bathing in the glow of such qualities, a town's people will not be happy enough to work together to regenerate nature locally. That's what **Ethos** is about: how the spirit of a community is shown in the combined radiance of the valued characteristics of its people. We suggest you jump in and do the activities here. If questions arise or you want support, go to www.heartwoodpath.com for previous books in this series or guidance.

We are honored that you are about to bring the shine of your good qualities to the Heartwood Path. Proceed by moving to the next learning station, a waypoint we call "Valued Traits."

1

Valued Traits

BUILD YOUR CHARACTER
APPROPRIATELY

Before going into action fast (as you will learn to do in Heartwood Path Book Six), before going far (as you will learn to do in Book Eight), before going together as a couple (as you will learn to do in Book Nine), and before going long (as you will learn to do in Book Seven), one has to procure valued traits. Without such attributes, which cannot be formed properly without ethos, one's future actions are likely to be counterproductive, unpopular, or unwise. Ethos—the characteristic spirit of a community as manifested in its collective beliefs and aspirations—puts one on the right track.

Ethos is, at times, a ghostly aspect of the mind. Ethos is a frame of mind. In its positive state, ethos is like a genius with talent. It is a mood, an atmosphere, and a disposition. It is a person's or group of persons' positive character and good nature. It generates humor, wit, and intelligence. Positive ethos fosters wisdom and understanding. It spans both reason and enchantment. Ethos, in its positive light, shines as leadership and brilliance. It is a person's or community's background, medium, pattern, atmosphere, and environment. Tendency, temper, and inclination come from ethos (Webster's Online Dictionary).

We all know (our recurring signal for attempted levity) that there are Heartwood Path books entitled **Logos** and **Ethos**, but do you know why there is not one entitled **Pathos**? Because we don't want to become *Aristolitarian*. Although you are asked to occasionally do some empathetic humming to nature and to conduct other odd rituals, along the Heartwood Path there are no witch doctors to hold your hand. The *voodoociary* responsibility, therefore, is yours and yours alone (continue when your roll-on-the floor laughing subsides).

The United States Sports Academy defines character as "the application of qualities...within the appropriate level of focus cognitively, emotionally, and with practice of getting it right" (Farley, USSA Website). How are these traits, those valued by the community, developed?

Part of the answer lies in putting together the right characteristics for the individuals in a community. A program called CHARACTER COUNTS! lists the Six Pillars of Character that one can use to develop positive and valued traits:

"* Trustworthiness—Be honest. Don't deceive, cheat, or steal. Be reliable—do what you say you'll do. Have the courage to do the right thing. Build a good reputation. Be loyal. Stand by your family, friends, and fellows (human and non-human).

* Respect—Treat others with appreciation. Follow the Golden Rule; or, better yet, the Platinum Rule (do unto others as they want to be treated). Be tolerant of differences. Use good manners, not bad language. Be considerate of the feelings of others. Don't threaten, hit, or hurt anyone. Deal peacefully with anger, insults, and disagreements.

* Responsibility—Do what you are supposed to do. Persevere. Keep on trying! Always do your best. Use self-control. Be self-disciplined. Think before you act. Consider the consequences. Be accountable for your choices.

* Fairness—Play by the rules. Take turns and share. Be open-minded. Listen to others. Don't take advantage of others. Don't blame others carelessly.

* Caring—Be kind. Be compassionate and show you care. Express gratitude. Forgive others. Help people in need.

* Citizenship—Do your share to make your school and community better. Cooperate. Stay informed. Vote. Be a good neighbor. Obey laws and rules. Respect authority. Protect the environment" (Michigan Youth Development, Online Website).

The initial development of valued traits and getting one's mind right through methods described above is the crucial precursor to protecting the environment that is not normally included in the list of methodologies used by environmentalists. Despite this omission, psychological improvements are crucial because every action, good or bad, is preceded by a thought. While it is critically important to expand one's perspective and to "become the change you want to see in the world," insignificant change will occur unless one uses valued traits to move effectively into action.

To Good Character . . .

HumaNatureConnect Activity

Start-up Protocol

If this is not a day when you prefer to spend time in nature without an agenda, do the Heartwood Path Start-up Protocol found in the Appendix. Then return here to do the remaining portion of this activity:

Developing Valued Traits

Go to a natural place, the wilder the better, find an attractive natural being, see if it retains its attractiveness for at least ten seconds, and, if it remains attractive, assume that this is a sign that you have the natural being's consent to use it in this activity. While admiring your chosen natural being, appreciate it with your inhalations and give it gratitude with your exhalations. Doing so will give you the optimal functioning that will be helpful as you do this activity. Do these Preliminary Action Steps and the rest of the Start-up Protocol at the beginning of each HumaNatureConnect Activity.

After obtaining your chosen natural being's consent and setting up your optimal functioning, use the twenty-ninth natural sense—the sense of play, sport, humor, pleasure and laughter—to develop valued traits. From the vantage point of your attractive natural being, look for examples of an aspect of nature using play or pleasure to learn, to create, to feel challenged, to pass time, to become calm and focused, to be a spectator, to win a competition, to be cooperative, to have fun, and to be joyful. Hum tones that resonate (echo) how you and your chosen natural being, how your chosen natural being and its environment, and then how you and the environment share vibratory frequencies (feel) about: using play as a way to connect, using play to foster creativity; using play as an antidote to loneliness, alienation, anxiety, and depression; using play as a teacher of perseverance; using play to become happy; using play as an improver of social skills; using play to enter into a state of flow characterized by a balance of opportunity and challenge; and using play in a form that has no loser. After clearing your mind through humming outdoors with your chosen natural being and surrounding environment, interpret how the experience and spontaneity of sport—human and animal—allows for responses to situations that affect and reflect character development. In your interpretations, think about intrinsic individual uniqueness; extrinsic good/better/best; systemic fairness; and, most importantly, how balancing these intrinsic, extrinsic, and systemic value dimensions leads to greater richness of character. Ask yourself, for example: How is the environment that surrounds your chosen attractive being unique, how is it good, best, or better relative to other environments, and how is it fair. After answering such questions regarding the environment, answer these questions about yourself. Write down how the environment and yourself are similarly or dissimilarly unique; good, better, or best; and fair. To aid with these assessments, hum a tone that, according to your own sensibilities, resonates with you and the environment's uniquenesses, hum a tone that, according to your own sensibilities, resonates with you and the environment's goodnesses, and hum a tone that, according to your own sensibilities, resonates with you and the environment's fairness. Determine what messages or interpretations, if at all, you can glean from the humming. Answer, the best you can, the following question: How does balancing these value dimensions add to your character? Rather than measuring the quantitative attributes of yourself and the environment, focus more on your own humming-amplified qualitative feelings about you and the environment—the feelings that come with the echo as you hum seemingly resonant tones. Also, ask yourself: Does winning mean everything? Does losing have no value? (Farley, USSA Website).

Follow-up Protocol

For best results, write down your impressions of this activity in your journal using the Heartwood Path Follow-up Protocol found in the Appendix. Afterwards, consider sharing your interpretations with others.

Heartwood Path Axioms

Key Assertions From Waypoint 5.1

5.1.1.

Build your character.

5.1.2.

Without a good disposition and positive character, one's future actions are likely to be counterproductive, unpopular, or unwise.

5.1.3.

Psychological improvements are crucial because every action, good or bad, is preceded by a thought.

Nocturnal Pilgrimage 5.1

For best results, write down your impressions of each night's dreams in your journal using the Heartwood Path Dreaming Time Protocols found in the Appendix. Afterwards, consider sharing your Dream Tending with others.

If you have difficulty recalling your dreams you ought to . . .

"get into the habit of asking yourself this question the moment you awaken: 'What was I dreaming?' Do this first or you'll forget some or all of your dreams, due to the interference from other thoughts. Don't move from the position in which you awaken, as any body movement may make your dream harder to remember. Also, don't think about the day's concerns, because this too can erase your dream recall" (LaBarge & Rheingold, 1990, p. 37).

The Natural Laws

Enough said about dreams for the moment. Let us now turn to another good use of nighttime hours: developing your character while also receiving what you want from life. In this space at each waypoint, we will present some of the natural laws that keep the universe operating smoothly. Use these laws to bring about important positive changes in your life. Make progress on your journey of growth and improvement during the evening hours by determining how each of these laws apply to your life. After you make the correspondences, work on finding remedies for any current or likely future dilemmas. Use the first line after the title of each waypoint as a foresightful entry on your list of possible prudent solutions.

The First Law Doubles As The Golden Rule:

The Natural Law Of Mutuality

"...as ye would that men should do to you,
do ye also to them likewise."—Luke 6:31

Leave negativity behind. Share the goodness in your heart with everyone you encounter. Treat others the way you want to be treated yourself. Good deeds for others bring goodness to you in return. At a minimum, direct your smile towards others.

Pertinent And Instructive Gems From My Dream Tending Journal

I dreamt that I was a clerk

serving a customer who came to the counter

at my printing company.

This lady wanted to make copies of pictures from her niece's wedding.

She tried to interest me in that event but,

in the interest of being efficient,

I turned the conversation back to the printing order.

She came in smiling but prepared to leave looking unfulfilled,

despite her full box of copies.

Lesson Learned: You can be efficient with things and artificial systems but not with people.

There is a need for me and everyone else to develop traits that:

1. facilitate the enmeshment of the individual into the community,
2. foster the creation of meaningful relationships,
3. help with survival needs, and
4. stimulate the mind while being engaged in service activities.

With this and your impressions of today's lesson in mind, sleep and dream. Be sure to tend to your dreams, as instructed in previous Heartwood Path books.

When ready to take the next step to a restored nature of happiness, by turning your attention to the next learning station, entitled "The Assembly." Make sure you go to a place without advertisement as you go outdoors for the next activity. Advertising makes one want to indulge. The pleasures of doing so quickly fade and take us away from the kind of true satisfaction that doing HumaNatureConnect Activities affords. The nature you are seeking in these activities, according to Selhub and Logan, can ...

"improve cognition by mechanisms involving mood and stress, and also distinctly through taking the weight off voluntary attention and inhibitory demands" (2012, p. 69).

2

The Assembly

EXPERIENCE THE ENDURING STREAM

In attempting to experience the all-pervading flow of the universe, do not look primarily at formed things, for the "enduring stream," as it has been called, is copious information encoded in . . .

"the central organizing force governing our bodies and the rest of creation. The enduring stream, humanity, and the rest of creation, are, at the most elemental level, charges. Every being is a "coalescence of energy in a field of energy connected to every other thing in the world" (McTaggart, 2002, p. xiii).

The pulsating energy field that McTaggart and I call the "enduring stream" is "the central engine of our being and our consciousness, the alpha and the omega of our existence" (McTaggart, 2002, p. xiii). To be consistent with the most advanced science, which is consistent with our purposes in this course, know that everything that is visible is not only a physical being, nor is it just a collection of chemical reactions, but at the root level, each being is a bundle of energetic charges encoded with information.

Being a charge is much more than the spark one can see when one bites down on Evergreen Lifesavers with lips open in a totally dark cave. The charges that make up you and I and all beings are not separate events. They are, instead, pre-real in that they are particles that exist in all-possible states, meaning they have no coherence and are in a state of flux until you or I come along and observe them or measure them. This fact of physics means that you and I and everyone else are central to the process of making the pre-real an actual set energy/thing. Before there is a person's conscious observation everything is a mixed-up, seething sea of energy. After conscious observation, the sea of energy is disturbed enough to coalesce a portion of its energy into what appears to be a being. Even after this disturbance, there is still a connection of every thing to the whole of the sea of energy that I call the "enduring stream" and scientists are beginning to call "the Zero Point Field" (McTaggart, 2002, p. xvii). What this central role in evoking matter means is that what we do and what we think and observe matters because, among other things, doing so makes matter. Without our participation, the world would be uncertain and unpredictable, "a state of pure potential, of infinite possibility" (McTaggart, 2002, p. 11). That may sound good, but in truth it's a mess. Like many of my clients' bedrooms, a lot is in there but nothing is ever in its place—not for long, anyway. The next time someone suggests that it is time to clean up my car I'm just going to say that the randomly placed set of contents is in a "state of pure potentiality," in a state of "infinite possibility." From this potentiality stems much of my positive results.

Find the momentum in a Zero Point Field and you can't find the position, and find the position and you cannot find the momentum. Still, we can trust our consciousness because it is our consciousness that evokes everything.

The Zero Point Field offers a scientific explanation for the Chinese notion of Chi and the Christian belief in the Holy Ghost. It also explains why it is important for you not to fixate on the physicality of your chosen natural attractive beings, but to instead work to attune yourself also to their energies and the energy of, at least, their surrounding environments. The natural being you choose will not likely physically utter words, but it does inherently come from and make information. This information flows on the waves of rhythmic and musical sounds, mostly inaudible, that flow inward and outward to you and from you and your chosen being.

"One of the most important aspects of waves is that they are encoders and carriers of (virtually limitless) information" (McTaggart, 2002, p. 26). Coming from nature, this information is bound to be highly intelligent. Part of our assignment as eartHearts—those working to complete the Heartwood Path—is to tap into this information, and to help others benefit from the intelligence encoded there.

Our search will not be for signals that carry, in time, messages over a distance. The singularity of the wave that each being is attached to means that the encoded information is available instantly, everywhere, all the time.

"Our natural state of being is a relationship—a tango—a constant state of one influencing the other. Just as the subatomic participles that compose us cannot be separated from the space and particles surrounding them, so living things cannot be isolated from each other" (McTaggart, 2002, p. 138). We are a community as much as we are individuals.

Strong "community involvement (is) one of the most important aspects of health" (McTaggart, 2002, p. 139). Also, "those people who live longest are often not only those who believe in a higher spiritual being, but also those who have the strongest sense of belonging to a community" (McTaggart, 2002, p. 195). These are two related reasons why you are encouraged to take a subsequent course, Course Seven: "The Heartwood Path For Groups."

Information-laden waves do not only have person-to-person affects. The electromagnetic waves from all beings have an impact on the rest of the enduring stream, the Zero-Point Field, and the universe. This means, among other things, that we will be needing to look for these effects and the encoded information, not just within our minds but also out in the environment. This is one reason why you are being encouraged to go to an attractive natural being as you begin the activities in this series of courses.

Despite any outer world focus on natural beings, do not fall victim to the illusion that what is outside of your mind and what is inside of your mind are separate. There is no 'out there' because we and the rest of the world are seamlessly and elaborately connected. One's mind extends along the waves that cross the Zero Point Field.

This means that your intention for another being, person or otherwise, affects that being (McTaggart, 2002, p. 132). For such influence to be successful, research has shown that the following conditions are most helpful: "some sort of relaxation technique (such as meditation); reduced sensory input or physical activity; dreams or other internal states and feelings; and a reliance on right-brain functioning" (McTaggart, 2002, p. 134). Apparently, to pick up the coded intelligence, whether it be an intention or some other form of information, a person will need to slow down the "ordinarily chattering brain" (McTaggart, 2002, p. 135). I have found that time with an attractive natural being in its natural environment automatically takes away much of the this chatter.

I sometimes call this series of courses the "Enduring Stream" for several reasons:

1. it is so important to give up past popular notions (such as "the brain is a discrete organ and the home of consciousness," and humankind is "essentially isolated from the world");
2. it is important to adopt the tenets derived from studying the Zero-Point Field (namely that the brain perceives and makes "its own record of the world in pulsating waves;"
3. it is so important to recognize that that everything communicates with everything else,
4. it is so important to know that people are indivisible from their environment, and
5. it is so vitally important to understand that living consciousness "increases order in the rest of the world and has incredible

powers to heal ourselves and to heal the world" (McTaggart, 2002, p. 225). Thanks to the Zero Point Field—what I will here often call the "enduring stream"—we can make the world as we wish it to be.

One experiences the enduring stream in five ways: 1) as the sensations of mindfulness in the Now, 2) through the sensations that occur when there is a lack of words or names, 3) during the sensations one feels when one encounters heartfelt more-than-human intelligence, 4) during the sensations of attraction, 5) during the awareness of the "aliveness" of all beings, and 6) during the sensations of love. Each of these types of sensations will be defined (using the acronym NNIAAL) and described subsequently in words. Read them. Then go outside and experience them, using the techniques described in the activities.

To Experience The Universal Flow Of Information...

HumaNatureConnect Activity

Start-up Protocol

If this is not a day when you prefer to spend time in nature without an agenda, do the Heartwood Path Start-up Protocol found in the Appendix. Then return here to do the remaining portion of this activity:

Experiencing The Enduring Stream

Use the natural sense—the sense of physical place (navigation senses including detailed awareness of land and seascapes, of the positions of the sun, moon and stars)—to experience the Enduring Stream. Maintain in your experience an awareness of the place surrounding your chosen natural being in the present tense. Do not give names to that which your encounter. When you perceive a present aspect of the scene, instead of naming it (such as igneous rock, or sugar maple) call it simply a "connection experience." Look at how each connection experience relates to other connection experiences in intelligent ways. Note your repulsion or attraction to various connection experiences. Note how each connection experience is seemingly drawn to each other. Look for "how the natural universe communicates its multi-sensory intelligence through the Web of Life" . . . how "attraction relationships hold everything from sub-atomic particles to ecosystems to economic systems together" . . . how "The basis of the concept of Love on a Universal scale is that love starts as allurement, which is a form of attraction. This basic binding energy is found everywhere in reality" (Ewolt & Weeks-Ewolt, 2001).

Follow-up Protocol

For best results, write down your impressions of this activity in your journal using the Heartwood Path Follow-up Protocol found in the Appendix. Afterwards, consider sharing your interpretations with others.

Heartwood Path Axioms

Key Assertions From Waypoint 5.2

5.2.1.

Experience the enduring stream.

5.2.2.

Each being is a bundle of energetic charges encoded with information.

5.2.3.

To learn something from the intelligence of natural beings one will need to slow down one's ordinarily chattering mind.

Nocturnal Pilgrimage 5.2

For best results, write down your impressions of each night's dreams in your journal using the Heartwood Path Dreaming Time Protocols found in the Appendix. Afterwards, consider sharing your Dream Tending with others.

The Natural Law Of Divine Wholeness:

Everything you touch and see in the physical realm and
everything you feel and experience in the spiritual realm
are connected and part of the whole.

See your world as an integral part of the whole. Experience the Divinity in everything. Perform random acts of kindness. Refrain from thinking that you are better than anyone else. Overlook anything that can be divisive. Respect the opinions of others. Overcome your fears. Everything you do affects the Oneness of Being.

Pertinent And Instructive Gems From My Dream Tending Journal

Continuing with my previous dream, minutes after the lady with the copies of her niece's wedding left my printshop, a young couple, laughing and smelling a little bit like campfire smoke, came up to my counter and asked if they could use my restroom. I simply nodded in the right direction and silently wondered what made these young campers so giddy.

Lesson Learned: Compared to my dour attitude, formed after weeks of working uninterrupted in the city, the young couple, fresh from a fun time in nature, were happy. Exposure to natures makes one happy, and the positive attitude lasts, sometimes for weeks after the exposure to what is pristine and green. Place yourself in a natural setting and remain there until you notice a lifting of your mood. Only then are you ready for your night's sleep.

Look for dream signs in your dreams. According to LaBerge and Rheingold, dream signs come in four categories. These include:

1. Inner Awareness (as when you "have a peculiar thought, a strong emotion, feel an unusual sensation, or have altered perceptions").
2. Action (as when you, another dream character, or a dream inanimate object or animal "do something unusual or impossible . . .").
3. Form (as when your "shape, the shape of a dream character, or that of a dream object is oddly formed, deformed, or transforms").
4. Context (as when the "place or situation in the dream is strange (or when) objects or characters may be out of place") (LaBarge & Rheingold, 1990, p. 43-45).

With this list and your impressions from the just completed teaching in mind as you prepare for sleep, dream lucidly. As you awaken, tend to your dreams.

Beginning at the next waypoint, we will present key qualities of one's experience of the environment. They will include:

1. one's experience of eternal Namelessness (there are no words to be experienced in nature),
2. one's awareness of eternal Nowness,
3. one awareness of Intelligence,
4. the way one's experience of nature is based on Attraction,

5. the awareness of Aliveness (during this discussion we will put more flesh to the idea of sustainability which, along with happiness, are the two reasons for following the Heartwood Path),

6. the way one's consciousness in nature is pervaded by Love.

These six very important aspects of the awareness of nature—like a Rosetta Stone of the Universe—help Heartwood Path course participants develop appropriate and accurate feelings, thoughts, and spiritual insights about the true essence of nature—an essence I call the "Enduring Stream" and Michael Cohen calls "NNIALL" (Cohen, https://www.ecopsych.com).

When ready to begin to experience the enduring traits of one's appropriate awareness of the essence of nature, move to the next waypoint, entitled "Currently." By the way, before jumping ahead, consider now how "Currently" or "Now" is always the time to do something for others.

Importantly:

**Think more about caring in the present
than you do about acquiring in the future.**

Keep your acts of charity simple, a way to give something back for all that the earth provides.

3

Currently

CONSIDER NOW

"As long as you are unable to access the power of the Now, every emotional pain that you experience leaves behind a residue of pain that lives on in you."

—Eckhart Tolle (Peaceful Rivers Website)

From childhood we are programmed by society, trauma, and excessive television viewing, to be less present in the environment. In these ways we learn to avoid live contact and personal action and to seek instead distractions that are abstract, including images on television sets, movie screens, computer screens, and words in books.

In time, distraction (that leads one away from the felt sense of the real world) and avoidance (not fully experiencing pleasure or pain during the real experience of life itself) become addicting. As this addiction takes hold, one becomes immersed in a superficial world. The feelings of losing the benefits of being alive now on a gloriously beautiful and diverse planet are unpleasant and, to escape from these unpleasant feelings, one tends to become lost in superficial remedies such as drugs, alcohol, unnecessary shopping, mindless television viewing, self-serving political power plays, and promiscuous sex.

To be present in the real world, recover the use of your felt sense to awaken the sensations of being present in your body. As you move through a forest, for example, become aware of its smells, textures, color, and attractive beauty. Using your attention, reflection, and awareness, note how the forest or aspects of the forest are experienced by your body.

Psychologically, take what appears to be the boundary between your body and the forest, for example, and note, as you perceive your attractions in the forest, how that boundary begins to become less and less distinct. You will find what begins to feel like other aspects of your own greater, expanded Self.

Do not let video images and digital photo albums replace your extended sense of self. Instead, awaken your sense of smell in some place like a rose garden.

Do not let movies and TV replace real world current adventure, expansiveness, and friendship. Listen to the natural sounds such as geese flying overhead instead.

Distinguish the image of how you are supposed to feel with how you actually feel. This requires becoming alert to bodily sensations.

Look for ways that you may be going through the postures of caring and replace the resultant feelings of hopelessness with real acts of compassion. Suggestions for how to best be compassionate are mentioned in Book Eight of the Heartwood Path series.

Notice how sadness and anger is a feeling and not a thought. Pay attention to where in your body you feel your various emotions. Notice how paying attention to the physical experience makes it easier to manage a difficult experience or to make a pleasant experience more so.

Be mindful by attending to experience without identifying with it. Bring to your mindfulness a quality of attention that is connected and participatory yet non-judging.

Do not study your experiences like a separate subject. Live in your body in full awareness of it instead.

Think of your experiential sensations as the stage of your awareness. Separate out thoughts as separate things that come and go across your inner world stage. Since thoughts are so fleeting, it is only with our experiential sensations that one can have true intimacy with one's experience.

Even thoughts about one's sensations are fleeting. One cannot, therefore . . .

"rely on any experience whatsoever for lasting happiness. A fleeting experience cannot satisfy us on a basic level, hence on that level, every experience is ultimately unsatisfying. Moreover, we find that an experience has no separate existence; the things that arise are out of our control, and whatever arises cannot be separated from the conditions out of which it arises" (Wilson, 1997).

When one understands with both thinking in the mind and feeling in the heart that the notion of a totally independent self is an illusion and that interconnectedness is reality, then the above-mentioned "superficial remedies," cravings, and holding on to artificial replacements for the real world will naturally fade away and a more true reality will emerge. Experiencing sensations rather than thinking about them or visualizing them helps one meet "reality with full integrity" (Wilson, 1997). The result is a feeling of ease in one's life.

This ease occurs after one begins to separate the sensations of experience (the stage of awareness) from thinking (thoughts on the stage of awareness). When in contact sensually with a natural being in nature, for example, if an unpleasant sensation emerges simply notice it and say or think nothing more than "That is an unpleasant feeling." Better yet, work on being aware of the unpleasant sensation without engaging in conceptual thought. If a thought emerges, which it will, then notice the thought and let it pass.

When contact is made with a natural being in nature that is pleasant say or think nothing more than "This is a pleasing feeling." As with the unpleasant thought, work on being aware of the pleasant sensation without thought.

Better yet, when experiencing either a pleasing or a displeasing feeling simply become aware that you are experiencing a "connection experience." This way you are remaining neutral and judgment-free—a condition that fosters the sense of ease. When one experiences every natural being of consciousness without attachment or aversion one is possessing the important quality of equanimity.

The key to equanimity during mindfulness, by which I mean composure and steadiness of mind, is to remain free of the thoughts beyond the initial recognition of the experience. This initial recognition is not what I mean by thinking. It is rather an awareness of consciousness, limited to the "sensation is pleasant" or "the sensation is unpleasant" or, better yet, the "sensation is a connection experience." Equanimity comes from doing no more than that.

Losing equanimity takes a one-two punch. On the first punch—the awareness of the sensation—composure holds. On the second punch—the thinking beyond the initial awareness—the mind become unsteady and one is no longer experiencing the "now" but is instead contemplating the "what now."

For unpleasant sensations, pay attention to the feelings of the sensation but do not lose your mindfulness by also entertaining thoughts about being resistant or upset. Similarly, beyond paying attention to the sensations that arise from pleasant experiences do not lose your mindfulness by also thinking about how to get more pleasant sensations. It is one thing to experience pain (this is inevitable) and quite another to suffer from the pain (this is avoidable).

When both pleasant (good) and unpleasant (bad) sensations enter into one's conscious awareness as "connection experiences " (neutral) rather than as relationships between a named subject and a named object (Don appreciating a post oak, for example) the springboard used to jump into judgments, into thoughts of avoidance, or into thoughts of clinging is made less dynamic and, so, one can more easily remain mindful. To remain mindful, avoid making judgments, refrain from making decisions, and stop involving yourself in internal commentary.

Be careful not to identify with feelings by considering them your own. To help you avoid feeling like the feelings are your own consider your awareness to be like a signal-receiving television through which feelings—not necessarily from you alone—are made known. Simply maintain a mindful awareness of each moment-to-moment feeling as it presents itself to consciousness.

To live in the now: just feel. Do not do, be. A sense of ease and happiness will follow.

You are not your pleasant and unpleasant feelings and thinking. When this fact becomes fully appreciated, the acts of thinking that lead to clinging and unhappiness—"me," "my," "mine"—will fade away.

Feel your emotions. They are neither good nor bad. They are not the parts that make up a person. The emotions pass but the person remains.

The same is true of states of mind. Bliss, concentration, rapture all pass but the person remains.

All situations in the outer world change. Likewise, states of mind are impermanent. These inevitable occurrences are reasons why living in the now and living in a state of relationship with whatever is happening now are so important. When one remains gentle and compassionate, when one is intimately attentive and fully present with whatever experience arises, when one notices thoughts but lets them pass, when one begins to know the meaning of impermanence, and when one knows that things come and go, then one begins to have insights and one begins to truly live.

You may be wondering if the tones you are making in the activities for this series of books (notes made to entrain with or to represent the resonant tones of natural beings and environments) are the "correct" musical notes for specific natural beings and relationships in nature. This is a typical and valid question.

The ancient Chinese monk Su Ma T'sien writes: "Sounds and music agitate and animate the arteries and the veins. This generates life-giving breath and brings to the heart harmony and rectitude." He claims that the Chinese "kong" musical note "brings saintliness to man," the "kio" note brings "perfect goodness," the "tche" note "the brings harmony of perfect rites," and the "yu" note brings "perfect wisdom." (Bernard, 2004, p. 16). Despite what T'sien says, do not worry yourself needlessly about any preconceived correctness in the notes you are producing. Although the "kong" note may or may not resemble the modern western musical note "C." It is pointless to try to translate ancient Chinese notes into western notes or to try to find the preconceived idealized note for any situation for two reasons: 1) the Chinese and Western scales are inherently different and 2) the western scale has been changed.

In 1953 an international conference "decided that the official value of (the musical note) 'A' (ought to) be raised." As a result, the music we hear around the world twenty-four hours each day is no longer founded on the ancient musical scale that was based on the frequencies created by the position of seven of the known planets in the solar system (Bernard, 2004, p. 121) nor is today's music based on Pythagorus' rigorous observations of the rhythms of nature" (Bernard, 2004, p. 121).

This adjustment in the musical scale is in violation of our the Cardinal Principle "As above, so below." Our human music—the set of songs at the "as below" microcosmic level—was once beautifully and healthfully in synch with the songs at the "as above" macrocosmic level. This means man was a faithful follower of a fantastically intelligent musical blueprint.

That has changed. We now too often vibrate to an artificial prescription and, as a result, our music and indeed our conventions are off. Since the change in 1953, "man is no longer 'in tune' with the laws of the universe. This dangerous error threatens the equilibrium of both macrocosm and microcosm" (Bernard, 2004, p. 121).

We are literally out of step with the song of nature. We can no longer dance very well with the universe. "Bodily frequencies vibrate (or ought to vibrate) in harmony with cosmic frequencies. The physical body vibrates with the galactic body" (Bernard, 2004, p. 122) We need to get back to basing our music and our lives on cosmic vibratory rhythms.

Although there are various guides to which musical notes produce specific effects on the human listener, I cannot with absolute confidence give you the proper notes to engender a specific effect. It is up to you to determine which one feels right for your own situation. According to author and composer Patrick Bernard, "the same musical energies produce different physiological reactions among people, depending upon the individual's emotional state" (2004, p. 107-108).

Sounds used in meditative or spiritual activities are what they are. Having physical, mental, emotional, rational, and spiritual aspects, conditions, and effects, they are too big to be condensed down into a name useful in the realm of reason alone. For this reason, we will not dwell much on the name of specific notes or on the literal translations of mantras. For our purposes here, when a musical note or mantra feels right in your heart, that tone or mantra is the one to use.

Generalized advice: Fly on the wings of sound. Do not give it undue heaviness by condensing it into names and words. Focus on the sounds and feelings that come from the vibrations.

If you are looking for some universal guideline for the establishment of tones and musical scales and know how to convert mathematics into tones the best I can offer is the number 9 or multiples of the number 9. That is the universal frequency: your heart beats an average of 72 beats per minute (6x9), it takes the sun 72 years to travel through one degree in the zodiac, and 72 is the Pythagorean sacred number. I could go on, but do not need to because there is latitude in the appropriateness of tones. Let your own feelings of appropriateness be the best guide.

A rational look at a bumble bee would not lead you to imagine that it could fly, yet it does. Likewise, a rational look at mantras and musical notes, when perceived and decoded with the rational mind alone, will not indicate their total capacity.

It is the sounds and not the names (or words) that trigger the auditory nerves and produce or stimulate physiological and psychological states. The words "Oh thee, jewel in the lotus" may or may not have a significant affect on you, regardless of the philosophical text I could create about its meaning. Instead of using the rational mind to decipher a meaning from that or other mantric phrases, focus on the original, time-tested sounds of the interpreted words.

"Oh thee, jewel in the lotus" is the western translation for a venerable mantra that, when repeated in a low-pitched voice, produces general well being, a relaxed body, peace of mind, and compassion: "Om Mani Padme Hum" (Bernard, 204, p. 108-109). To repeat: as you do the activities of this book, do not worry yourself needlessly over exact translations or the names of musical notes. Focus on feeling with your heart the vibrations created by notes or mantras.

The very act of sliding up and down the musical scale in search of resonant tones from nature is, in itself, a healthy activity. We live too much of our lives indoors and are, therefore, subjected to a relatively small variety of intonations that are no longer in tune with nature. By frequently stepping outside and intoning various notes one is following the advice of Nick Anthony Fiorenza in his article "Planetary Harmonics & Neurobiological Resonances (Fiorenza, 2010). In this piece, Fiorenza says:

> "Although the use of individual frequencies might be used for healing, brain and body coaching etc. the healthy brain and body functions in wide bandwidths of naturally occurring resonances, not as some idealized frequency.

> Remember, living "in a pure and unadulterated environment free of entraining frequencies, attuned to Earth, the lunar rhythms, and to the other natural astronomical cycles of life, is on of the healthiest things a person can do" (Fiorenza, 2010).

For this reason, I encourage you to continue to intone at various resonant vibrations, searching for the one that feels right at any present moment. If, however, you would like to try your hand at using specific tones for specific purposes, do the following activity which calls for making various associations between locations, chakras, colors and tones (Sound Essence Website)

To The Moment...

HumaNatureConnect Activity

Start-up Protocol

If this is not a day when you prefer to spend time in nature without an agenda, do the Heartwood Path Start-up Protocol found in the Appendix. Then return here to do the remaining portion of this activity:

Experiencing The Now

Take your time with this activity. It may take seven or more days to complete. Use your "hearing including resonance, vibrations, sonar and ultrasonic frequencies" (Cohen, website: http://www.ecopsych.com/insight53senses.html) to experience the now of your chosen place and your body's chakra system (and its associations). We shall facilitate this experiencing by helping you to resonate with the musical notes said to be associated with each chakra. We will begin with the First Chakra at the base of your spine and then, chakra by chakra, work up the vertical antenna that is your spine.

First. Witness a sunset and create a psychological link between this sight and your perception of the base of your spine. With your pitch pipe or musical device, listen to and, to the best of your ability, match the tone of the musical note "C" by humming that note. Do not worry about whether you are on key because the key itself has been inappropriately adjusted. In your mind, make this "C" note tone, or your own approximation of the "C" note, a link between the base of your spine and the sunset. Continuing to hum this note consider your fears, your right to be here and your right to have, and any disconnections you have with your body. Humming the "C" note, look for something in nature (most likely the sunset) that is red, and affirm: "I am rooted in life and myself." Continue perceiving red, the sunset, the base of your spine and the "C" note as you consciously work towards vitality, courage, and self-confidence. Focus especially on your foundation.

Second. Witness a moonrise or moonset and create a psychological link between this sight and your perception of your reproductive organs (testicles or ovaries). With the help of a tuning devise, hum the "D" or "C Sharp" note. Mentally, make this note a link between your reproductive organs and the moon. Continue to hum either of these notes; if possible, look for the color orange (in the moon or elsewhere outdoors); and consider any feelings of guilt, any poor social skills, any addiction to or denial of pleasure, your right to fear and have pleasure. As you continue, consciously work on your happiness, confidence, and resourcefulness. Focus especially on movement and connection. Affirm: "I am happy in my connections."

Third. Witness field of wheat or other drying crops and create a psychological link between the crops and your liver located at your solar plexus. Hum an "E" or "E Flat" note. Consciously, make this note into a link between your mid section and the crops. While continuing your resonant intonation, consider any feelings of shame, the need to make positive transformations in your will power, your reliability, your right to act and be an individual, and your sense of self worth. Look for the color yellow and affirm: "I can do whatever I choose to do." Focus especially on wisdom, clarity, and self-esteem.

Fourth. Take a walk in the country and create a psychological link between the countryside and your heart. This time hum the "F" or "F Sharp" note and consciously make this note a linking between the countryside and your heart. Continue to hum either of these notes as you look for the color green in the landscape and consider your need for self-control, sincerity, unity, the easing of loneliness and lack of empathy, and excessive clinging. Affirm: "I open my heart and share it with others." Focus especially on love and balance.

Fifth. Look towards the sky or a body of water and create a psychological link between either of these natural features and your throat. Consciously make the "G" or "G Sharp" notes and/or the color blue, a link between the sky, lake, or river and your lungs. Continue to make this psychological link as you consider expressing your feelings, being shy, being quietly withdrawn, talking too much, having the inability to listen, and your right to speak and hear the truth. Affirm: "I easily and freely hear and effectively express the truth." Focus especially on knowledge, health, and communication.

Sixth. Perceive the stars in the sky and create a psychological link between these heavenly bodies and your forehead. Look for the color Indigo and hum an "A" or "B Flat" note as you consider your intuitive or imaginative abilities, your ability or difficulty "seeing" the future, any feelings of obsession, any delusions, and your right to see. Affirm: "I am perfectly attuned to my vision." Focus especially on intuition, mysticism, and understanding.

Seventh. Perceive the top of a hill, bluff, or mountain. Look for the color violet and hum a "B" note as you make the psychological connection between the precipice and the top of your head. Ponder thoughtfulness and awareness, being open-minded, fear of death, and lack of purpose. Affirm: "I am one with all creation." Focus especially on beauty, creativity, and inspiration.

Follow-up Protocol

For best results, write down your impressions of this activity in your journal using the Heartwood Path Follow-up Protocol found in the Appendix. Afterwards, consider sharing your interpretations with others.

Heartwood Path Axioms

Key Assertions From Waypoint 5.3

5.3.1.

Consider Now.

5.3.2.

From childhood we are programmed by society, trauma, and excessive television viewing, to be less present in the environment.

5.3.3.

To avoid live contact and personal action we seek instead distractions that are abstract, including images on television sets and words in books.

5.3.4.

The key to composure and steadiness of mind, is to remain free of thoughts beyond the initial recognition of the experience.

Nocturnal Pilgrimage 5.3

For best results, write down your impressions of each night's dreams in your journal using the Heartwood Path Dreaming Time Protocols found in the Appendix. Afterwards, consider sharing your Dream Tending with others.

The Natural Law Of Thankfulness:

In order to receive what you want
you have to be thankful for what you have.

Express love and gratitude for the people and natural beings in your life. Show your joy about the blessings you receive. Be sincere in your gratefulness. Release any negative emotions by being forgiving.

Pertinent And Instructive Gems From My Dream Tending Journal

When the couple in my dream returned from the bathrooms, they turned to me and Kim said:

"we have been backpacking for four days, what's been going on?"

I delayed my response for a few seconds as I pondered how to answer their question. They didn't know me, so I assumed that rather than asking about my own auto-accident recovery, they meant what has been foremost on televised news programs. When I told them that President Trump ordered the killing of a top Iranian General their giddiness shifted to alarm and sadness. I thought: "Welcome back to civilization, folks." And I wondered what they would say if I had asked the same question to them. I expected that their responses would be less reactive, more focused and grounded, and more about pleasures than I am accustomed to hearing in my interactions with people isolated from nature.

Lesson Learned: Generally speaking, people are happier when they immerse themselves in the Now in nature. The intrusion of the news about the Iranian General into my urban life—full of demands, worries, planning, and the indoor delight of televised news—is very different from the pleasant benefits people experience when spending time in nature. Campers and hikers often come back to civilization restored, healthier, full of empathy and creativity, and likely to engage—as my dream couple did—with other people and the world.

It will be helpful if you catalogue your dream signs. Here's how:

1. Keep a dream journal.
2. Mark the dream signs in your dream journal. Underline them and list them at the end of each dream description.
3. Next to each dream sign, list the category (inner awareness, action, form, or context).
4. Rank your dream signs by frequency. Use the highest ranking dream sign in the next step.
5. Get in the habit of examining your daily life for events that fit under your highest ranked or most pertinent dream sign category. This will help you prepare to notice when something unusual happens in your dreams, thus helping you fall into lucid dreaming (adapted from LaBarge & Rheingold, 1990, p. 47).

Repeatedly think about these calls to action and your impressions from today's lesson as a way to influence the content of your dreams. Tend to today's dreams before continuing.

When ready, to proceed to the next teaching, go to the next waypoint, entitled "Word-free." The next learning station explains why Dr. Cohen includes a ban on names in his nature-connect activities—sound advice as you pause at the next and all subsequent Heartwood Path waypoints.

4

Word-free

CONSIDER NAMELESSNESS

Until one can learn to set aside a single-pointed focus on words, there will be a pathetic slowing of personal development. Names and words are not as powerful as they were fifty years ago because they convey knowledge that is no longer scarce and, therefore, no longer as powerful. For me, the slickness, blandness, and mass consensus that words promote are boring compared to the authenticity, inventiveness, humor, beauty, uniqueness, playfulness, empathy, and meaningfulness that do not require names and words.

For me, the fun and satisfaction begin when my consciousness shifts out of the verbal function of my mind and into the nonverbal intuitive, creative, and sensory capacity of my mind. It seems that I can process information faster in my non-verbal mind than I can in the thirty-words-per-second capacity of my mind. Given this discrepancy, it is no wonder we all develop faster as children before we use words than we do after we started babbling.

EartHcarts arc about being and arriving more than they are about doing and striving. They live much of their lives in a state of wordlessness. EartHearts do not promote over-using the kinds of technologies that destroy magic (such as keyboards that send you to the word-saturated Internet or e-books that give verbal explanations for things that are mysterious). Consciously living without the domination of words leads eartHearts to bliss, insight, and healing. With all this going for it, you may be wondering how one enters into a state of wordlessness. Life coach and author Martha Beck offers four ways: stillness, torment, delight, and paradox. (Beck, 2012, p. 10-50).

Stillness

Sitting still and meditating fall into Beck's "stillness" route to wordlessness. Beck offers three ways to become wordlessly still, one comes from Eckart Tolle and involves attempting to prove that your hands exist without using the eyes. What you do is close your eyes and silently feel your hands from the inside.

Torment

There is no need for an activity that leads you to torment as a route to the stillness that leads to wordlessness. Without the help of a Heartwood Path activity, you will still be exposed to enough fatigue, hunger, exposure, or illness. The way to make torment a route to wordlessness is, when tormented, quietly surrender all resistance to physical suffering you cannot avoid. I can attest to the wisdom of his path. I have constant pain in my eyes. I always feel like I have painful sand in them and, on occasion, the sensation shifts to the feeling of daggers in my eyes. It is so bad that once, while scraping paint off a ceiling and allowing it to fall directly into my eyes, my mother had to remind me to put on goggles. The extra sensation of paint falling into my eyes was not indistinguishable from the sensation I have all the time as a result of burning my corneas from too close exposure to the dissolving chlorine blocks in the deep-end of a swimming pool when I was a largely unsupervised child. Despite the unpleasantness, constant complaining would only double my torment. I can go long periods of time without noticing my own agony. These periods of wordless and apparent pain-free bliss are occasionally broken when I have to explain, in words, why my eyes make me sometimes look tired or bored. So, except for when I am coerced into offering a verbal explanation, hear now what I have to say about it now and usually: "   ."

Delight

Why do I hear more words from people about discomfort and anxiety than I do from people about comfort and calmness? One can choose any of these feelings no matter the situation. Perhaps if more words were devoted to solutions leading to comfort and kindness, situations would be more apt to resolve themselves for the better.

The doors to delight are opened by several keys: One key to keeping your attention on the positives is to focus on the sensations rather than on the stories. Another key is to "focus not only on your own sensory experience but on the experience of generosity and communion" when you share your delight with someone else. A third key is to connect with nature.

> "Nature exists in a state of continuous Wordlessness. . . . A stroll on the beach or an hour watching the birds in your own backyard may not seem like the answer to your many problems. But by dropping into Wordlessness, you'll arrive at the state of mind that allows all way finders (EartHearts are certainly such way finders) to find the answer they're seeking ... More importantly, the very state of Wordlessness delivers you immediately to your ultimate goal: peace of mind and body, gratitude of the present moment, joy in living" (Beck, 2012, p. 21).

Living without words throughout a day can make life exquisite. As we will see in the following activity, the key to making your days delightful is to open your focus, to open what Beck calls "the aperture of your nonverbal mind to more and more aspects of enjoyment" (Beck, 2012, p. 18). Two good ways to go down the pathway of delight to a state of wordlessness—1) finding sweetness and 2) drenching your senses—are included in the next activity.

Paradox

Paradox—by which I mean inconsistency, incongruity, and anomaly —helps everyone get out of their mindset of verbal preconceptions and into the wordless realm of pure perception, observation, and open-mindedness. Just as the finger that points to the moon is not the moon, and just as the map is not the territory, words—even those that are well-written and accurate—lead us *toward* the experience of the truth. Heading there and being there are not the same thing.

Words, mine or anyones, are not the truth. Words are necessary occasionally but meaningless in the non-dualistic Everywhen. Truth is not read, it is lived. No words could ever adequately describe honey, or love-making. When finding yourself believing a statement, seek a way for the opposite to be true and you will be on your way to a state of Wordlessness. Without the falsehood of words, it is easy and fun to fall into the paradoxical insight that, for example, you are an individual unique gift to the world but also that you and the tree outside of your window are one entity. Words can be made to say anything.

I have combined Beck's four ways to wordlessness into the following activity (leaving out torment just to be merciful):

To The Lack Of Speech Through Calmness, Elation, and Incongruity...

HumaNatureConnect Activity

Start-up Protocol

If this is not a day when you prefer to spend time in nature without an agenda, do the Heartwood Path Start-up Protocol found in the Appendix. Then return here to do the remaining portion of this activity:

Entering Into Wordlessness

This activity may take seven or more days to complete. Take your time.

Wordlessness Through Stillness

Use your natural sense of "hearing including resonance, vibrations, sonar and ultrasonic frequencies" as you enter into wordlessness through stillness (Cohen, website: http://www.ecopsych.com/insight53senses.html). To do so, determine that your hands exist without using your eyes. This is done by closing your eyes, holding both hand up so that they touch nothing, focusing your attention on the inside of the hands. Once you can feel the blood pulsing inside your hands without talking about it, you are entering into wordless stillness. Next, use any of the yoga postures recommended for when you visit your natural being (standing, sitting, or lying down). Focus your attention on your chosen attractive natural being. "Without moving your eyes, broaden your attention until it registers everything in your field of vision, including the original object of focus (your chosen being) . . . Now, still without moving your eyes at all, make the object the foreground of your attention, and everything else the background . . . Next, make the object the background, everything else the foreground (Beck, 2012, p. 10-11) . . . Focus on everything in the area, including your being, at once while repeating the mantra: "Ground to sky, east to west, north to south, all things equal." When you feel you have said this mantra sufficiently, silently imagine the space between your eyes. Doing so will put you into a deeply relaxed, alpha, wordless state.

Wordlessness Through Delight

Use several of your natural senses as you enter into wordlessness through delight (Cohen, website: http://www.ecopsych.com/insight53senses.html). To do so, focus on the delightfulness of your chosen natural attractive being.

"Put your full attention on it . . .Without moving your eyes, listen to the sounds around you, and then listen to something deeper: the silence in which the sounds are taking place . . . Find a spot on your body that feels comfortable. It may be just one toe. While still watching beauty and listening to silence, fully feel the comfort in that toe . . . Breathe in slowly, feeling the sensation of your lungs filling with air and nourishing your bloodstream. If you can smell anything fragrant or delicious, focus on that scent . . .Practice focusing your attention on all these pleasurable things at once. Feel the calm that arises as this process drops you out of language" (Beck, 2012, p. 18).

Next, drench your senses according to the following method presented by Beck:

"Start by imagining the taste of your favorite food or beverage . . . Add a memory of a favorite scent that unrelated to the taste . . . Without dropping the memory of the state or the small, add a delicious tactile sensation (I'll leave this one to your own imagination) . . .While still holding the taste, small, and tactile memories, add the memory of sounds you love . . .Throw in a specific remembered sights . . . As you hold all these sense memories, you'll have too much activity in your brain to continue thinking verbally. Try to vividly experience all these sensory experiences at once. You'll have to stop reading to do this. In fact, you'll have to stop thinking. And that's a very good thing" (Beck, 2012, p. 19).

Wordlessness Through Paradox

Use your natural sense of mental and spiritual stress (Cohen, website: http://www.ecopsych.com/insight53senses.html) to find a way to use paradox to enter into a state of wordlessness through paradox. Here's how Beck says to do it:

Make "a list of five thoughts that hang around your brain, bothering you. It works best if these thought cause you great worry, anger, or sadness . . . Now comes the hard part: think of a way the opposite of each though could also be true. Your verbal mind will reject the very possibility that this could happen. Your job . . . is to pick apart your own words until you can find a way it could . . . The embrace of verbal paradox eventually shows us that all fixation on words-as-truth is "just plain nonsense . . . Truth is never any statement. It's an experience, one that can come only from full presence in the infinite variety of the Wordless Web" (Beck, 2013, p. 41-42). Another way she recommends is to repeat any one word for forty-nine seconds as a way to dissociate the sound from its original meaning, making it instead a meaningless noise. Doing so can help you remove the sting of painful internal dialogue (Beck, 2013, p. 41-42). A third way Beck recommends is to involve yourself in koans, which are paradoxical questions or statements such as "the direct path seems long" or "the path into the light seems dark, or the path ahead seems to go back" (Beck, 2013, p. 45) The point is it become so befuddled that you lose your patience with words themselves.

Follow-up Protocol

For best results, write down your impressions of this activity in your journal using the Heartwood Path Follow-up Protocol found in the Appendix. Afterwards, consider sharing your interpretations with others.

Heartwood Path Axioms

Key Assertions From Waypoint 5.4

5.4.1.

Consider Namelessness.

5.4.2.

Wordlessness comes by sitting still and meditating; by accepting rather than explaining your pain; by silently focusing on positives, generosity, and communion with nature; and by thinking of opposites.

5.4.3.

Without words or names, the enduring stream reveals itself within the manifest world through polyrhythmic pulses—a form of speech embedded in the ebbs and flows of nature.

5.4.4.

The world swims in unwritten, invisible, and inaudible communication and much of it has to do with love, healing, and understanding.

Nocturnal Pilgrimage 5.4

For best results, write down your impressions of each night's dreams in your journal using the Heartwood Path Dreaming Time Protocols found in the Appendix. Afterwards, consider sharing your Dream Tending with others.

The Natural Law Of Affection:

Love started with the Creator's affection for what was created
and it is that same divine fondness that enables you to reach the highest levels of growth and awareness.

Be true to your spiritual essence. Be a beacon of love. Let your loving actions speak for you. Without conditions or expectations, treat those you love with honor, dignity, and respect. Share your affection with all of the natural beings of the world.

Pertinent And Instructive Gems From My Dream Tending Journal

As the couple in my dream talked to me in my printshop, I felt envy. I had my fried chicken, but they saw birds flying, uncooked. I too wanted to not know about deadly drone strikes. I wished that I too could be immersed in the kinds of outdoor experiences that would make me happier and the best person I can be. I thought, "I had been just adding change to my pocket while these backpackers were adding to their well-being sufficiently to add quality time to their lifespans."

Lesson Learned: Continue with the development of your mind, an organ that turns out to be more bio-centric than we have previously known. You do not have to go to the wilderness all the time to affect your nature-loving brain, although the wilder the better. A good boost to your well-being and longevity will occur as you make (as you do in our activities) your inner and outer world journeys from the land of buildings with electrical sockets to to the nearby land with natural qualities.

At the end of your day, sleep and dream. The next morning, tend to your dreams before you do much movement in bed.

As an inducement for actually doing the next activity in nature, know that research shows that a walk in a park has been shown to help children's attention and functioning as much as a medication for ADHD. Additionally,

1. driving on roads with vegetation has been shown to reduce agitation;

2. scenes with vegetation lower anger levels;
3. scenes of nature from apartment windows has been shown to lower impulsivity;
4. vegetation viewed through window helped girls favor long-term rewards over short-term rewards; and
5. walking in a forest (compared to walking the same length of time in an urban setting) is associated with exposure to significant levels of the naturally-occurring neurosteroid DHEA, which improves cognitive performance in adults.

With such findings, doesn't it make sense to continue to begin each Heartwood Path Activity with an outdoor session communing with nature?

When ready, move to the next waypoint, entitled "Biognosis." You are to be commended for making it this far down the Heartwood Path. Keep going. You are more than half way to Gladandgreen Junction.

5

Biognosis

UNDERSTAND THE EXCHANGE
BETWEEN HUMANS AND NATURE

"Remember that creativity expresses itself in many ways and
each person has his or her own unique way . . . Passing on
to others what we have received and learned is an important
part of completing that process at each level of our healing
and growth. We have not fully integrated anything until we
have manifested it in our experience in a way that impacts
others in some transformational way."

—Shakti Gawain (Gawain, 2000, p. 224-225)

The enduring stream—the essence of nature—does not reveal itself
through words or names. Except for on trailhead signs and discarded
waste, there are no words in nature. Nature does not speak in words.
Limit, therefore, your use of words during this course, as much as
possible, to the reading of this text and to the writing of words in your
journal or related online communications.

Personal, social, and environmental problems occur because there
is a schism between the way the world is and the way we think, read,
learn, speak, and act. This schism occurs because we mostly do these

things in a linear fashion, which makes us out of kilter with the way nature works, which is in a nonlinear fashion.

This linear way of thinking and acting is "a process or development" that "changes or progresses straight from one stage to another, and has a starting point and an ending point" (Reverso Online dictionary). Comparatively, nonlinear systems such as nature do "not progress or develop smoothly from one stage to the next in a logical way. Instead, it makes sudden changes, or seems to develop in different directions at the same time" (Reverso Online Dictionary). This means that our common pattern of applying linear thinking and communicating to nature results in, at best, approximations of the way nature really functions—which is too complex for our typical linear ways of thinking, writing, speaking, and acting. As Walt Whitman says: "...there are divine things more beautiful than words can tell" (Buhner, 2004, p. 132).

Though too imprecise to allow for adequate learning, precise describing, or appropriate responding to nature's chaotic, expansive, non-mechanical, and nonlinear structure and behavior, we . . .

"in the West have been immersed in a particular mode of cognition the past hundred years, a mode defined by its linearity, its tendency to reductionism, and its insistence on the mechanical nature of Nature... But it is increasingly obvious that there are inherent problems with this mode of cognition..." (Buhner, 2004, p. 1).

I believe Buhner is correct. Fortunately, there is a largely unknown alternative way of communicating and thinking. I am referring of the way nature communicates to our animal bodies and how we speak though our actions. This gathering and sharing of knowledge directly from "the wildness of the world" is called . . .

"biognosis—meaning 'knowledge from life'—and, because it is an aspect of our humanness inherent in our physical bodies, it is something that everyone has the capacity to develop (Buhner, 2004, p. 3).

Some of the best ways to gather and share knowledge directly from the wildness of the world (the process of biognosis) is enumerated by Stephanie Kaza and summarized subsequently. Before we can get to biognosis more fully more needs to be said about human failings and the environmental dilemma.

Failing to note that "nature is not linear and (failing to note) that the heart is an organ of perception" (Buhner, 2004, p. 4) are two of the key ways humans have brought so much calamity to the earth. As Goethe says: "The phenomena (has to) be freed once and for all from their grim torture chamber of empiricism, mechanism, and dogmatism" (Buhner, 2004, p. 25). All of these conceptual shortcomings are also why we fail to see both the extent of our troubles and the solutions to them.

"We are blinded to these subtle (eco-cataclysm warning) signs because we have been taught that matter is dead and inert. Considering nature to be inanimate makes it available for exploitation as a resource (Lakota Sioux). Lame Deer insists that "the earth, the rocks, the minerals, all of which you call 'dead,' are very much alive." He implores us to "talk to the rivers, to the oaks, to the winds as to our relatives" (Erdoes and Lame Deer, 2009, p. xv). For those who are skeptical of the possibility and worthiness of such conversations, let us be very clear about the nature of the interchange.

Stephanie Kaza helps us put more flesh on the idea of talking to non-human natural beings in her book **The Alternative Heart: Conversations with Trees** (1993). Just as I did with Martha Beck's "stillness," "torment," "delight," and "paradox" I shall now do with the eight elements of the human/natural being interchange, quoting from Kaza's book, beginning with the "Just Sitting" section that follows and ending with the "Shared Impermanence" section.

1. Shikantaza – Just Sitting

"I spent time in silence, close to trees, doing my best to be simply present with the tree as Other, aware of my thoughts, moods, and projections . . . I did not go to the trees with an agenda or story in mind, but chose rather to see what would unfold by being completely present in the specific place and moment" (Kaza, 1993, p. 5).

2. Meeting the Natural Being in Context

"I need to meet these trees in sycamore context, investigating the wholeness of their lives. Can I be bold enough to step aside from what I know in order to be available to what I don't know?" (Kaza, 1993, p. 22).

3. Interchange Through Shared Natural Senses

Such as Rhythm, Touch, and Awareness of the Light of the Sun

"I meet this tree from my own experience of sunlight and stillness . . . The tree itself is a manifestation of rhythm, of the way the light works. . . . This is what my hands recognize—the movement of the sun, earth, and water. At some fundamental level this tree and I are made of the same rhythms. We share a common understanding, available in the meeting place of touch" (Kaza, 1993, p. 29).

4. The Desire to Merge

"I have been propelled into the company of maples, irresistibly pulled by the desire to meet. Now, in the actual presence of the tree, I soften with the tenderness of the dance between two beings" (Kaza, 1993, p. 51).

5. The Sharing of Vastness, Time, and Fire

Referring to a Manzanita tree:

"I sense the core of your being that has been still for hundreds of years. This is how I know you; perhaps this is how you know me. You are a stillness container; so am I (Kaza, 1993, p. 67).

6. Sharing of Burdens Age, Relationship, and Whatever Comes

"Now I see what drew me back here–the need to remember what it is to just survive, to exist, to go through the bare experience of living through whatever comes. . . (Kaza, 1993, p. 76).

7. The Sharing of Chaos Versus Control

"The mind of chaos is the mind of wilderness–pure expression of uncontrolled and untamable life force. The mind of control is the mind of plantation–in which trees from a strange land are slaves . . ." (Kaza, 1993, p. 84).

8. Shared Impermanence

"The voice of impermanence is the only one signing into the black night, with little to offer the listener. In the poignancy of this melody it is hard to leave the light" (Kaza, 1993, p. 90).

Intelligent And Communicative

Being in touch with living non-human aspects of nature only makes sense if they are intelligent and can communicate; which, indeed, they are and do. "Self-organized systems are living identities that engage in communication, both internal and external. They are not isolated, static units that can be understood in isolation. To examine them in isolation kills the living entity itself, and paying attention to the thing and not its communications—its balance-initiated information exchange—reveals very little about the true nature of what is being studied" (Buhner, 2004, p. 41). Buhner seems to agree with Lame Deer and tells us that not only are our fellow earth "relatives" alive, but they are also intelligent: "All self-organized systems are, in fact, intelligent. They have to be. For they (have to) continually monitor their environments, internal and external; detect perturbations; decide on the basis of those perturbations what the likely effect will be; and respond to them in order to maintain-self organization" (Buhner, 2004, p. 45).

"To the Lakota people, the cosmos is one family. To live well within the cosmos, one (has to) assume responsibility for everything with which one shares the universe. There are familial obligations toward water, plants, minerals. Any harm done to the slightest of these relatives has devastating consequences for the whole ecosystem" (Erdoes and Lame Deer, 2009, p. xiv).

When we do use linear thinking and words we are not communicating to nature. We are not thinking about or conveying anything close to a natural being, an ecosystem, or a planet in its entirety. "The harder the linear mind tries to grasp reality, the more slippery it becomes. A self-organized system is a living thing, ever changing identity that comes into being of its own accord in a gesture of acquiescence and cooperation that is never static" (Buhner, 2004, p. 39). Words, having narrow and precise meanings, can really only describe a part of nature. They usually leave out something that connects the parts. Considering and communicating in a linear fashion typically robs the parts of their total context and the richness of their meaning.

Word-smithing and naming is an unnatural act. Often done by writers on the paper leaves of books, the human tendency to focus on symbols programs us to disregard the messages embedded in the chattering leaves of oaks and hackberries. Naming anything "is a wonderful yet perilous act" (Buhner, 2004, p. 31).

This may be one reason why we no longer view the earthly world as merely fallen, sinful, and demonic, for such leanings tend to come from minds of people living in the world's pervasive religious-based cultures that were still substantially focused on the natural body. Now, when we focus more on machines than we do on bodies, the earth is spoken of in the pervasive secular cultures as being mostly mechanical, determinate, and inert—too unnatural to be seen as sinful or fallen.

Writing conveys to other humans mere signs of the real thing. Writing, therefore, leaves the bulk of the actual messages blowing in the wind.

No wonder, with the mind being filled with the widespread and frequent use of signs for nature rather than the direct experience of the real thing, that we destroy the natural world. Relying on signs for nature rather than relying on the real thing is also making dysfunctional an important organ in our bodies.

The hippocampus, a horseshoe shaped sheet of neurons located within the temporal lobes and next to the amygdala, helps one retain memories and . . .

"We are made to be in the wild nonlinearity of the world, and this immersion is needed for the hippocampus and our central nervous systems, to be healthy" (Buhner, 2004, p. 65-66).

Given this information about the impact of nature on the hippocampus, the remedy for memory loss and Alzheimer's disease and our sense of a lack of meaning is perhaps the opening of "ourselves to whatever pulse rides within each thing we meet" (Abram, 2010, p. 299). In this way, the direct experience of nature serves to help with the recall of data, the recollection of memories, and the formation of meaning. Thus, if one wants to recall information, remember in the latter years of life the names of one's children and the location of the bathroom, or find the meaning of events in one's life, go outside a lot and commune with nature, including the enduring stream.

The way the enduring stream swells within the manifest world is revealed not through printed words, such as those found on pages or computer screens, but through polyrhythmic pulses—a type of message or a form of speech embedded in the ebbs and flows of nature—that "stirs a new humility in relation to other earthborn beings" (Abram, 2010, p. 3). In this way, as Pope Benedict XVI states: "The earth speaks to us, and we (have to) listen if we want to survive" (Maathai, 2010, p. 166).

"Many prophets from various religious traditions were inspired by nature or withdrew into it to tap its wisdom. In addition, we humans often don't have the vocabulary to express our thoughts and ideas about the numinous, so we use symbols, many of which we find in the natural world, such the tree, river, sun, moon, and animals" (Maathai, 2010, p. 18).

We spend almost all of our time indoors, separate from nature, and we have done so for generations. Says Thoreau:

"The creature of institutions, bigoted and a conservatist, can say nothing hearty, He cannot meet life with life, but only with words" (Buhner, 2004, p. 70). "If you would make acquaintance with the ferns you (have to) forget your botany...you (have to) approach the object totally unprejudiced...Your greatest success will be simply to perceive things as they are" (Buhner, 2004, p. 136). "A man has not seen a thing who has not felt it" (Buhner, 2004, p. 147).

I do not believe Thoreau is speaking here of touch with fingers, "but the touch of the heart. This kind of touch has another dimension, deeper than that possessed by fingers" (Buhner, 2004, p. 148).

As a result of our excessive time spent indoors, our long training in specialized institutions, and our over-reliance on words, we have forgotten how the land is alive and animate. We no longer generally believe that humans and the earth are capable of participating mutually in the process of communicative give and take.

Thus, we . . .

"cannot help but interpret what we hear of such participatory beliefs according to our own stunted capacity for emphatic engagement with the sensed surroundings—a capability that was stifled in us before it could blossom, and which therefore remains immobilized in us, frozen in its most immature form" (Abram, 2010, p. 43).

By encouraging those who follow the Heartwood Path to move away from their books and computers and go outside and experience nature, those seeking to communicate with nature are no longer torn out of nature and reading mere representations of it. They are, if they fail to enter into the depths of the real world, stepping "back from the world's presence into a purely human sphere of reflections" (Abram, 2010, p. 4). Indoors, we feel supported in contending that the earth is inanimate and non-communicative. There, we a lulled into thinking that it is childlike ignorance to say that the earth is anything but inert. To say that the earth speaks is called by those living in the realm of dusty books and glimmering computer screens, a derogatory word which means giving beings in nature human characteristics: "anthropomorphic." While a few people believe in the talk-to-the-animals power of Dr. Doolittle, to contend that a person can receive a message from any aspect in nature is widely considered "a credulous projection of humanlike feelings on to mountains and rivers, which surely amounts to madness for any adult soul" (Abram, 2010, p. 43). Why is this so?

Our life indoors –where we walk on the soles of shoes and sleep in beds rather than touch the ground—is soothing because that is where we are "buttressed with abstractions" and, due to this distraction, feel sheltered "from the harrowing vulnerability of bodied existence (Abram, 2010, p. 7). The technology of our housing—which is a synthetic "haven in which to hide from the distressing ambiguity of the real" (Abram, 2010, p. 8)—gives us a "way to avoid direct encounter" (Abram, 2010, p. 9).

The use of words and written stories allows us to hide behind an imagined protective shield "etched with lines of code and cryptic jargon" (Abram, 2010, p. 7-8). Blinded by this shield we have "lost our ear for the music of language—the rhythmic, melodic layer of speech by which earthly things hear us?" (Abram, 2010, p. 175). More than that, many of us have come to accept a narrowed artificial answer to the question: "What do I want?" To find the best answer: "Put down the book. Go outside... Pet the bark of trees. Smell the soil. Listen to a river. Ask them what they want, Ask your heart what you want...Then figure out how you're going to get it" (Jensen, 2006, p. 534). "It is important to not switch into the verbal/intellectual/analytical...for you will kill this living process with the word" (Buhner, 2004, p.216).

Written stories and names give us simple definitions and cheap explanations. The ideas they produce "isolate our intelligence from the intimacy of creaturely encounter with the strangeness of things" (Abram, 2010, p. 8). Relying on words rather than experiences encourages us to continue talking as the world burns. This would not be the case if we would, instead of relying so much on words, delve into a deeper, more heartfelt, give and take with nature. "The flow of life to life and back again binds you into the web of life from which you have come and in which you belong. There is an ecstasy in the process, a coming alive again" (Buhner, 2004, p. 159).

Buhner is speaking of a way that is better than the worded path, a way that begins by answering an important question. When pondering the relative merit of words compared to the embedded messages in the rhythms of nature, we are left like David Abram with the question: "Can we find fresh ways to elucidate these earthly phenomena, forms of articulation that free the things from their conceptual straitjackets, enabling them to stretch their limbs and begin to breath?" (Abram, 2010, p. 9). If one can, and we will see that indeed one can, one will trade the lifelessness of pages and computer screens for the an appreciation of the earth as described by Thoreau: "I am attuned to the universe, I am fitted to hear, my being moves in a sphere of melody, my fancy and imagination are excited to an inconceivable degree. This is no longer the dull earth on which I stood" (Buhner, 2004, p. 159).

Coming "more directly into felt relation with the wider, more-than-human community of beings that surrounds and sustains the human hub-bub"(Abram, 2010, p. 9) is a mode of discourse that becomes a reenactment of the kind of give and take that occurred regularly in a previous time when a mysterious universe spoke to people in a plethora of idioms. The result can be finding out what is worth knowing. More worthy than the bulk of meanings on pages and computer screens, the messages from the world of river otters, box elder trees, and granite alter the drumming of a perceptive beating heart in ways that are helpful.

This conversion of feeling informs us. It tells us that "our own sentience" is "part and parcel of the sensuous landscape" (Abram, 2010, p. 47). The heart entrained to a sentient planet awakens us to citizenship in a "broader commonwealth" (Abram, 2010, p. 9) It arouses a sense of "place-based community," a sense of "planetary solidarity," a "commitment to justice and the often exasperating work of politics" (Abram, 2010, p. 9).

Doing the practices allayed along the Heartwood Path helps us humans receive messages from and speak directly to the wild world. Those that have direct experiences with communicative attractions in nature unfold "a nuanced respect for the manifold life of the world, a steady pleasure in the profusion of bodily forms and the innumerable styles of sentience that compose the earthly cosmos" (Abram, 2010, p. 40). Attractions grab our attention and, once we learn to become more sensitive to all of our senses—including the fifty-four natural senses— we become aware that our moroseness and our ecstasy, our anguish and our pleasure—to name but a few emotions—are not solely the result of independent internal moods but are actually also passions conveyed to us by our awareness of the erratic yet communicative terrain. These "senses do not deceive, judgment deceives" (Buhner, 2004, p. 233).

Really, the experience of communicating with nature is well beyond the realm of a fanciful pastime. Jensen (2000) says, "The violence of civilization provides us with two options. We can distance ourselves from the world of experience, sense and emotion, or we can die" (p. 122). As we shall see, following the Heartwood Path infused with Dr. Cohen's methodologies, provides a much needed third option. This option, in its fullest measure, has to answer the "central question of our time: what are sane and appropriate responses to insanely destructive behavior?" (Jensen, 2000, p. 188) And so, continuing on our path to this third option, one that is based more on "What can I give back?" than on "What can I get out of this?" and, therefore, one that I trust will help future generations judge us in a more positive light, we continue with our description of the second main component of the enduring stream —its more-than-human form of language which, when you remove the human component, presents us with a refreshing void of words and, therefore, names.

Language—the ability to communicate, the power to convey information "across the thickness of space and time" . . . "the means whereby beings at some distance from one another...manage to apprise each other of their current feelings or thoughts" is not the sole possession of humans (Abram, 2010, p. 166). "Human speech is simply our part of a much broader conversation" (Abram, 2010, p. 172). Language is a characteristic of the animate earth—a place that "is alive" with a "vibrant play of relationships in which our own lives are participant (Abram, 2010, p. 42).

> "Only in the wake of the alphabet does language come to be experienced as an exclusive human power. The experiential shift can be attributed, in large part, to the way a phonetic script focuses our attention upon the specific sounds made by the human mouth. The written letters of an alphabet are no longer associated, by their stylized forms, with various entities and events in the surrounding earth. There is no indirect reference by the written characters to the sensuous world..." (Abram, 2010, p. 176).

Instead of being like "windows through which one might glimpse the wider landscape, the letters of an alphabet function more like mirrors reflecting the human back upon itself" (Abram, 2010, p. 177). With help, modern humans can participate in the human to nonhuman communicative exchange. Despite the cultural conditioning that typically makes one feel like the earth/human communication is figment of one's imagination, as Abrams (2010) says: "Something other than the human mind is at play here" (p. 12).

Generalists capable of interpreting human and nonhuman language may be the first to come into touch with the non-human aspect of the communicative exchange that goes on in the wild. Specialists, steeped in the jargon of various human academic specialties may, at first, have a hard time being able to see "a whole topic involving all the earth, including humans, living organisms, the ocean, atmosphere and surface rocks" (Lovelock, 2010, p. 48). Academic divisions and an inability to interpret the Earth's more-than-human language means that most scientists cannot see "the Earth as a dynamic interactive system, or as . . . (Lovelock, the initiator of the Gaia theory) . . . would put it, somehow alive . . . It would not be so bad were there more general practitioners to interpret between them" (Lovelock, 2010, p. 49).

Part of the reason I can experience the communications of non-humans and see, not just the parts, but the interrelationships that form the bigger picture when I do Heartwood Path activities may be because, in my early years in college, I specialized in being a generalist. Doing so may have kept me from being immersed too much in narrow, specialized human communication. I kept an interdisciplinary generalist view during much of my education specifically because I believed that somebody has to be available to make important observations and generalizations about interdisciplinary matters.

Chandler Brooks agrees, saying: "It is becoming obvious that channeled vision is not good enough. There (has to) be a return from overspecialization to the generalist who can see totalities" (Buhner, 2004, p. 16). Taking this point from mere seeing to how one speaks, Henry David Thoreau says: "See not with the eye of science, which is barren, nor of youthful poetry, which is impotent....As you see, so at length you will say" (Buhner, 2004, p. 18) and I will add "as you see and say, so will you do."

What is true for scientists is also true for human and non-human communicators: there is a need for more people trained in how to be both cross-scientific and cross-species interpreters of language. Let us now look at the cross-species form of communication—using how plants and people communicate as an example of cross-species interpretation.

"The true matrix of human life is the greensward covering mother earth," writes Thompkins and Bird (1973, p. viii). "Instinctively aware of the aesthetic vibrations of plants, which are spiritually satisfying, human beings are happiest and most comfortable when living with flora . . ." (Thompkins and Bird, 1973, p. ix). Why would this be if plants were insensitive, unresponsive, and soulless? There is growing evidence that plants, like animals and humans, are sentient. If we would watch them patiently, we would discover how they move their bodies. "If a plant is growing between obstructions and cannot see a potential support it will unerringly grow toward a hidden support, avoiding the area where none exists" (Thompkins and Bird, 1973, p. xi). Two other examples of the sentience of plants: "The sundew plant will grasp a fly with infallible accuracy" and some "parasitical plants can recognize all obstacles that crawl in its direction" (Thompkins and Bird, 1973, p. xi). After hooking up plants to lie-detector machines, Cleve Backster discovered in the 1960s what had been known and forgotten: "plants appear to be sentient" but instead of shouting to the world "Plants can think!" He quietly worked to determine how plants were reacting to his thoughts" (Thompkins and Bird, 1973, p. 5). After years of "meticulous investigation" here are some of his findings:

1. plants show evidence of seeing without eyes, better than humans do with them" (Thompkins and Bird, 1973, p. 6);
2. faced with "'overwhelming danger or damage' plants pass out or go into a deep faint" (Thompkins and Bird, 1973, p. 7);
3. plants may wish to be eaten, but "only in a sort of loving ritual" instead of the "usual heartless carnage" (Thompkins and Bird, 1973, p. 8);
4. "plants may be able to remember" (Thompkins and Bird, 1973, p. 9);
5. plants react to stimuli over a great distance, showing evidence of awareness of slight emotional adventures from across town" (Thompkins and Bird, 1973, p. 10);

6. the existence of pulsations in fetal animals (specifically eggs) without any circulatory system—a "sort of force field not conventionally understood" (Thompkins and Bird, 1973, p. 15); and, significantly:

7. "all sorts of things which have been conventionally considered to be inanimate may have to be re-evaluated" (Thompkins and Bird, 1973, p. 12).

Given the sentience now known to exist in plants and other beings, two questions arise: "How can we communicate with our fellow non-human earthlings?" And, "How can we humans and the earth benefit from inter-species communication?" A little more background is required to answer these important questions.

There is some skepticism about any form of nonhuman to human communication because usually no sounds are heard and no communication-proving sights are seen. "Just as the most important interactions between people are invisible (for example, the love and caring that flows between people who deeply care for each other) so too are the most important interactions in the living system of the earth invisible" (Montgomery, 2008, p. xi). Similarly, while there may be audible and visible expressions of love and care, much of the loving and caring goes on in the invisible, silent, and private inner world of the lover and caregiver and is, therefore, unseen and unheard. Although much of what is communicated is unseen and unheard, there is still invisible and inaudible communication going on and much of it has to do with love, healing, and understanding. This is as it ought to be. Mostly silently and quietly we "relate to our internal and external surroundings" (Montgomery, 2008, p. 9). "We are meant to love, to heal and to understand, and to live according to our own true nature" (Montgomery, 2008, p. 3).

To Indescribable Potential...

HumaNatureConnect Activity

Start-up Protocol

If this is not a day when you prefer to spend time in nature without an agenda, do the Heartwood Path Start-up Protocol found in the Appendix. Then return here to do the remaining portion of this activity:

Experiencing Namelessness

Use the natural sense of weather changes to experience namelessness. Instead of calling a natural being a "willow tree" which distinguishes it from "sandstone" boulder or a "zebra," call the aspect of nature you are experiencing by how it will, like you, be experiencing a change of weather. Before a rain, each aspect is a "soon-to-be wet-connection-experience," or, when in your area the blue sky the North indicates the end of a storm or a "soon-to-be dry" or "soon-to-be warm" "connection-experience." When conditions warrant, call aspects in nature "soon-to-be-covered-in-snow-connection experience" or "soon-to-be-hidden-by-fog connection experience." Aren't such names just as useful as "Lily of the Valley" or "box elder?" To heighten your sense of weather change, look for signs in nature that predict the weather. Smoke from a fire rises straight steady when the weather is going to be immediately clear and dry but swirling and descending when lower air pressure brings in clouds and precipitation. White, high and small clouds predict dry weather while low, black and large clouds predict precipitation. Insect eating birds fly low to the ground before storms. Bees and butterflies disappear before a downpour. (Wilderness Survival Skills Website). No matter what the weather, refrain from naming it "good" or "bad." It all serves a purpose.

Follow-up Protocol

For best results, write down your impressions of this activity in your journal using the Heartwood Path Follow-up Protocol found in the Appendix. Afterwards, consider sharing your interpretations with others.

Heartwood Path Axioms

Key Assertions From Waypoint 5.5

5.5.1.

Understand the exchange between humans and nature.

5.5.2.

Walt Whitman says: "there are divine things more beautiful than words can tell."

5.5.3.

It is possible to gather knowledge directly from "the wildness of the world."

5.5.4.

The direct experience of nature serves to help with the recall of data, the recollection of memories, and the formation of meaning.

Nocturnal Pilgrimage 5.5

For best results, write down your impressions of each night's dreams in your journal using the Heartwood Path Dreaming Time Protocols found in the Appendix. Afterwards, consider sharing your Dream Tending with others.

The Natural Law Of Vibration:

Pure energy undergirds existence
and this energy vibrates
at its own unique frequency.

Embrace your lightness of being by surrounding yourself in goodness and positivity. Align your physical, emotional, mental, and spiritual vibratory frequencies by being truthful and pure in your intentions. Since what you send out to the universe will be reflected back to you, anything is possible as long as you are in vibrational alignment.

Pertinent And Instructive Gems From My Dream Tending Journal

Every time the woman wanted to say something, usually about her feelings of joy about their outdoor adventures, her boyfriend would intervene with some unsolicited information, like he was doing now (about the technical aspects of vibrations) when no one was listening or cared.

Lesson Learned: Let positive reminiscences be expressed and heard, even if they are excessively sentimental. Too many negative "ruminescences" spoil a good bonfire chat session and, perhaps, even a good relationship.

Setting goals helps with lucid dreaming. Establish a goal of remembering one dream per week or one dream every night. Whatever goal you choose, set a goal to improve upon it. Set difficult but realistic goals. Record and evaluate your progress.

Block out mindless mental chatter by putting these suggestions and your impressions from the latest lesson foremost in your mind as you drift off to sleep. Upon waking, immediately tend to your dreams.

When you are game, move to the next waypoint, entitled "Igno-rance-free." Consider doing the next activity near a small stream or a big river. Water flowing in nature consistently and rapidly captures one's attention. Note how, if at all, you feel charmed by the movement of the water.

6

Ignorance-free

CONSIDER NATURE'S
INTELLIGENCE

"None of us is really complete, really whole, really enlightened until we have to some extent walked all of the six spiritual paths—until we have . . . known how to love deeply and without selfishness, known how to understand, found something we can create, served our fellows, and know the servant leadership that serves God."

—Danah Zohar and Dr. Ian Marshall

We will never know the kind of completeness, wholeness, and enlightenment that Zohar are Marshall are speaking of until we know that the earth and its attractions are intelligent. "If intelligence is the capacity to acquire and apply knowledge, then absolutely plants are intelligent," says University of Utah biologist Leslie Sieberth (Montgomery, 2008, p. 24). Even plant cells are said to be "thoughtful," according to Nobel prize-winning geneticist Barbara McClintock (Montgomery, 2008, p. 24).

While plants and other nonhuman life forms can be considered intelligent in some ways, humans can be considered unintelligent in some ways (Abram, 2010, p. 80). Although we see the earth as an object, it . . .

"is, the very body of wonder—a shuddering field of intelligence in whose round life we participate. And if, today, this dreaming land has been forgotten behind the clutch of glowing screens that intercept the fascination of our focused eyes...then it is time to listen, under-neath all these words, for the animal stirrings that move within our limbs and swelling torsos" (Abram, 2010, p. 80).

Such listening will make us humans more intelligent as we will be able to apply our knowledge in ways that support the whole community of life on earth. "If human consciousness can be rejoined not only with the human body but with the body of earth," writes Laura Sewall,

"what seems incipient in the reunion is the recovery of meaning within existence that will infuse every kind of meeting between self and the universe, even in the most daily acts, with an Eros, a palpable love, that is also sacred" (1999, p. 191).

Listening and Eros does not only occur along a pathway that involves primarily sound waves traveling from the ears to the brain. The heart also plays a huge part in inter-species communication. It does much more than simply pump blood.

According to Buhner (2004):

"The heart not only transmits field pulses of electromagnetic energy, it also receive them, like a radio in a car. And like a radio, it is able to decode the information embedded within the electromagnetic fields it senses. It is, in fact, an organ of perception" (2004, p. 88).

Of the four ways the heart communicates with the brain—1) neurologically (the transmission of nerve impulses), 2) biochemically, (hormones and neurotransmitters), 3) biophysically (pressure waves), and 4) energetically (electromagnetic field interactions)—the energetic way is by far the most powerful (Montgomery, 2008, p. 42).

What I am about to state in the pages that follow is critical to understanding the importance of both the silent and invisible form of interspecies communication that involves the human heart and a way for humans to alleviate the silent killer of stress and our destructiveness towards the environment. The way for these corrections begins with the heart.

The heart's field both permeates every cell in the body and radiates outside of us. Disharmony "in our heart rhythms lead to inefficiency and increased stress on the heart and other organs while harmonious rhythms are more efficient and less stressful to the body's system" (Montgomery, 2008, p. 44).

Positive heart-based feelings of appreciation, love, compassion, and care...

"generate the smooth and harmonious HRV (heart rate variability) rhythms that are considered to be indicators of cardiovascular efficiency and nervous system balance... Showing appreciation elicits an immediate response in your body that lessens the stress response, causes entrainment with the brain, and affects the electromagnetic field around you with ordered coherence. It is easy to come into coherence while in a state of gratitude, because your heart responds immediately to any appreciation you can elicit...This causes your nervous system to naturally come into balance, lessens the burden of stress, and frees up energy to be available for creative outlet" (Montgomery, 2008, p. 45-46).

It also makes you more receptive to interspecies communication. When one is freed up to be receptive in this way, one moves "beyond ego" and begins "to experience something greater than ourselves; we come to understand that the world is larger than we anticipated, encompassing an entire unified field of interconnected relations" (Montgomery, 2008, p. 144). We begin to "derive meaning from the world around us by translating what we receive through vibration, light, and position (the inclusion of all the components that make up the picture that tells a complete story)" (Montgomery, 2008, p. 145). Compared to reading a book or watching a televised documentary, this means of learning and communication may seem like a significant amount of work. I suppose it is. As Luther Burbank says:

"Nature is an exacting mistress and a jealous teacher; she does not revel herself wholly to the amateur or the dabbler, and she will not cooperate fully and generously with the man who takes her lesson or her work lightly" (Buhner, 2004, p.249).

Without the use of words Mother Nature tells a story. In the **Idea of Wildernesses** Max Oelschlager (1991) writes:

"All nature will fable (which means, speak as if it is true), Thoreau tells us, if we will but let it speak. We have to forget our conventional wisdom, for this is a positive ignorance, and return to nature. We have been weaned early from her breast, and we are not as wise as the day we were born. But our Mother will speak to us, if we will listen. Her words yet have earth clinging to their roots; her statements are grounded in granite. Such fables are revealed, however, only to a person of Indigen (meaning indigenous or native) wisdom, who seeks no more than a sympathy with intelligence..." (p. 351).

To elaborate, here's what Thoreau also said regarding nature "fabling:"

"He is richest who has the most use for nature as raw material of tropes (which means a figure of speech, a rhetorical device that produces a shift in the meanings of words) and symbols with which to describe his life. If these gates of golden willows affect me, they correspond to the beauty and promise of some experience on which I am entering. If I am overflowing with life, am rich in experience for which I lack expression, then nature will be my language full of poetry—all nature will fable, and every natural phenomenon be a myth. The man of science, who is not seeking for expression but for a fact to be expressed merely, studies nature as a dead language. I pray for such inward experience as will make nature significant" (Thoreau, Journal).

Oelschlager and Thoreau are speaking of scientists. Notice that they are not using the word "fable" as a noun, as in Aesop's Fables nor as a verb without and object as in "to fable about what happened" (which means to tell a lie about what happened). Both writers are using the word "fable" as I will, as a verb with an object as in Thoreau's statement "all nature will fable." When fable is used as an action word with an object it means to describe as if so. Since Aesop's noun "Fable" is a tale with animals that offers a moral lesson, the use of the word as a verb with an object often likewise has the following mental association: to illustrate a moral point by describing as if so. Later in this section of this book I will describe how I have received fables from nature regarding creating valued personality traits and other moral or ethical topics.

Along with Oelschlager and Thoreau, others also laud the richness of nature's expressiveness. There seems to be some disagreement about the singularity or plurality of the sender of nature's messages. As we shall see, some contend the cosmos is one family; which, if it is a family like mine, has many points of view. Others contend that nature, being one organism, or acting like one organism, is able to speak from its own singularity. These are important distinctions, one's that determine whether when we pick up messages from nature we are communicating with an organism with a singular voice, from a community having a designated "speaker," or from some other type of entity having many potentially conflicting voices.

"To the Lakota people, the cosmos is one family. To live well within the cosmos, one has to assume responsibility for everything with which one shares the universe. There are familial obligations toward water, plants, minerals. Any harm done to the slights of these relatives has devastating consequences for the whole ecosystem" (Erdoes and Lame Deer, 2009, p. xiv).

Note here that the Lakota considered the cosmos to be a family. This is an apt metaphor, one that may also be pertinent when thinking of the earth.

"In his old age, Goethe conceived the earth to be an organism animated by the same rhythm of inspiration and evaporation as a plant or an animal. He considered the earth to 'be a great living being perpetually inhaling and exhaling'" (Thompkins and Bird, 1973, p. 11).

Dr. Cohen, the originator of the Natural Systems Thinking Process used in each activity in this series of courses, considers the earth and its human parts to be one organism. He contends that that organism is richly expressive.

James Lovelock is an inventor and the originator of the Gaia Theory. He considers the earth to indeed act as if it is one organism.

"All of life is one," says Alex McInnes, a man known to be sensitive to the radiation of plants. (Thompkins and Bird,1973, p. 316). In response to McInness' statement one might ask: One what? One organism? Or, one community?

These questions arise because there is some debate over whether humans ought to be considered a part of one earth organism or if it would be more appropriate and accurate to state that humans are members of the earth's one community. Esbjorn-Hargans and Zimmerman (2009) offer reasons why considering humans to be a part of the earth organism may not be accurate:

"There is an important difference between being a part of something (and thus subject to its will and domination) and being a member of it (retaining autonomy while connecting and contribution). An organ is a part of an organism, but an organism is a constitutive member, a partner—not a part—of its ecosystem . . . Analysis of the logic of wholes and parts demonstrates that humans' noospheric dimension is not a 'part' of the web of life." If humans were just parts, then individuals would be willing to sacrifice their ambitions, property, and lives for the good of the web of life. All too often environmentalists assign intrinsic value solely to the web of life, thereby concluding that the parts of the web (individual life forms) either lack value of their own or at best have equal value. Such an approach provides no criteria for making difficult moral decisions. Moreover, this approach indicates that if individual humans or classes of humans are harming the web of life, then other humans (who shall they be?) (ought to) prevent such behavior at whatever cost" (p. 480-481).

Here is what Buhner says about what is revealed when one trades the linearity of words and thus sees mostly the parts for the nonlinearity of feelings which allows one to better grasp the whole:

"For Universe is not a place but an event, not a collection of solids but an interaction of frequencies. Not a noun but a verb.

Though the linear mind can examine parts of Universe through ever greater magnification, the living fabric of truth can be experienced only with an open heart" (Buhner, 2004, p. 260).

When communing and communicating with nature a strong, multi-part message has come through to me, one that I do not believe I would have come up with on my own. Here I will share this message, and, for those who appreciated corroboration, I will offer what some other humans say about such matters:

1. All inhabitants have to live within the carrying capacity of the earth. As Charles Wohlforth (2010) says: "Earth is finite in size, not large enough if all its inhabitants strive to be their own gods of power and wealth" (p. 83).
2. Do not bother children with our grim reality. "Each children remembers on the abundance of its own youth, not the life that is already gone. Our children don't yet know this loss. They think they are born into plenty, too" (Wohlforth, 2010, p. 109).

3. It's not all about competition. There is also substantial cooperation. People "also cooperate, even when they are not compelled, when reputation isn't on the line, when they are beyond the reach of a contract to reciprocate" (Wohlforth, 2010, p. 132).

4. Good, new ideas come from a small group but they spread to the whole. "Ideas, led by a vanguard, spread invisibility, until one day society is simply different" (Wohlforth, 2010, p. 141).

5. People can borrow from nature but they have to leave what they are using undamaged. George Perkins Marsh called man's proper way to use the earth's commodities "usufruct" which means "a loan for use only, with the obligation to leave the borrowed item as it was found" (Wohlforth, 2010, p. 143).

6. Make choices right where you live.

7. Develop social norms for "enough-ness. We "cannot create social norms for sufficiency. For that we need wise people with control over their own actions and environment" (Wohlforth, 2010, p. 254). Social movements and cultural change typically precede legislation and institutionalized reform. Buoyed by a sense of community spirit, activists at the periphery of a culture lift the center. They, like others in a culture, are "built with a sense, in some form, that nature is worth saving regardless of its material benefit to humanity" (Wohlforth, 2010, p. 264).

8. The "hedonic treadmill" is the "process of always wanting more but receiving no satisfaction from receiving it" (Wohlforth, 2010, p. 352). "Those with high incomes are not happier than those who make half as much, and the wealthy are more likely to feel angry and tense" (Wohlforth, 2010, p. 352-533). Since 1950 we in the United States have doubled the size of the average single-family house, built enough storage units to enclose "every person in the country," and consumed land at twice the rate of population growth yet "we're no happier than we were when we started" (Wohlforth, 2010, p. 353). This begs the question: "Is the wealthy tycoon sleeping alone in his mansion happier than the penniless lovers sleeping under the stars?"

9. We can do something better than to grow our property lists and bank accounts. We can, for example, favor community over competition and caring over acquiring. We can "allow the many gardens of community to grow" (Wohlforth, 2010, p. 359).

10. Sufficiency need not arise from Puritanical self-denial. Sufficiency or the sense of "enoughness" can instead be based on altruism and cooperation, and the elevation "of our loves instead of our drives" (Wohlforth, 2010, p. 358).

11. Regarding the environment, put less bad stuff in and take less good stuff out. "We need to be gentler, to listen, and to adjust our actions as we see their results. To do these things, we need to restore our sense of touch, moving closer enough to nature to appreciate its scale and our role there . . . Government bureaucrats running computer models can't do this for us. The change has to come first in our hearts, then in our relationships, and finally in our politics" (Wohlforth, 2010, p. 315).

12. Follow the heart of a place. "The human heart, sensing the meaning in this place and sensing its spirits, whatever their names— it survived the maze of history, the wounds of oppression, the numbness of wealth" (Wohlforth, 2010, p. 325).

13. Teach the young ones. "...schools affect change faster than traditional environmental activism" (Wohlforth, 2010, p. 342).

14. Stop over-consuming. "If everyone needs things without limit, we will surely fill our ecological niche, leaving no undomesticated space for other species...we may be programmed for selfishness . . . but ample evidence exists of other ways of relating to each other and the environment" (Wohlforth, 2010, p. 352).

15. Nature lifts the spirit. "We need nature, and particularly its wilderness strong-holds. It is the alien world that gave rise to our species, and the home to which we can safely return. It offers choices our spirit was designed to enjoy" (Wilson, 2002, p. 148).

16. Save enough nature for our non-human relatives. How much? "Half of the world for humanity, half for the rest of life, to

create a planet both self-sustaining and pleasant" (Wilson, 2002, p. 162).

17. Establish ecological values, for they are priceless and define our humanity. For Nobel Prize winner and leader of the Green Belt Movement Wangari Maathai, these include: loving the environment, showing gratitude and respect for the Earth's resources, self-empowerment and self-betterment, voluntarism, and the spirit of service (Maathai, 2010, p. 14-15)—especially a form of service that does "not create victims of predatory leadership that exploits the vulnerability of its followers" (Maathai, 2010, p. 158).

18. Where the values of loving the environment, showing gratitude, respecting the earth's resources and service "are ignored, they are replaced by vices such as selfishness, corruption, greed and exploitation, and can even lead to death" (Maathai, 2010, p. 16). "The same values we employ in the service of the earth's replenishment work for us, too... We can love ourselves by loving the earth; feel grateful for who we are, even as we use that self-empowerment to improve the earth; offer service to ourselves, even as we practice volunteerism for the earth" (Maathai, 2010, p. 17).

19. In such acts of voluntarism it has to be pointed out that, for the service to be most beneficial to the activist, it is not a matter of winning, not a matter of passing the legislation, and not even a matter of saving the natural area. The "primary satisfaction has to come from the fact that you tried—from the service" (Maathai, 2010, p. 184).

20. Service is usually taxing, both emotionally and spiritually. When fighting greed and entrenched powers, one can often become very drained, very overwhelmed, and prone to burnout. This bad effect is magnified if one tries to solve problems beyond those that are immediately present and if one becomes attached to the outcome (Marathas, 2010).

21. The current political setting in the United States is not suitable for preserving the planet by perfecting people. "The time is ripe for the Democratic Party to embrace a new story about America, one focused more on aspiration than complaint, on assets than deficits, and on possibility than limits" (Nordhaus and Shellenberger, 2010, p. 13). "It is time for us to draw a new fault line through American political life, one that divides those dedicated to a politics of resentment, limits, and victimization from those dedicated to a politics of gratitude, possibility, and overcoming" (Nordhaus and Shellenberger, 2010, p. 189).

22. Environmentalists only have it half right and so have only taken the world halfway to a solution to global environmental problems, problems Jensen (2000) calls "the dance of world destruction" (p. 2). Public awareness has been expanded and a fairly good legislative safety net is in place. But, according to Nordhaus and Shellenberger (2010), what environmentalists have attached to these successes—"environmentalist cautionary tales"—have had "the opposite of their intended effect" (p. 131). Doomsday scenarios have provoked "fatalism, conservatism, and survivalism among readers and the lay public, not the rational embrace of environmental policies" (p. 131). To get solutions fully right, environmentalists and other scientists and policy makers will need to reach a comprehensive understanding of how the world works, both the inner world of intensions and ethics and the outer world of behaviors and nested physical systems. "We cannot understand our complex interiors through natural or social scientific methods, nor can we understand the natural world solely through our interior experience. We need both" (Esbjorn-Hargens and Zimmerman, 2009, p. 6).

23. Fight the things that harm nature. This revelation reminds me what Henry David Thoreau (1965) said in 1859: "Let your life be a friction against the machine" (p. 259). In reading this one might ask, "A friction that does what?" To which I join with Jensen

(2006, p. 16) who says: "The task ahead of us is awesome, to meet human needs without imperiling life on the plant" (p. 16).

24. It is possible to be too successful for your own good. "Any fully matured science of ecology will have to grapple with the fact that from the ecological point of view, man is one of those animals which is in danger from its too successful participation in the struggle for existence" (Krutch, 1955, p. 104).

25. When I am glad or sad, I am not sure if nature is glad or sad along with me. "Are we so separate from nature that our states are actually discontinuous with it? Is there nothing outside ourselves which is somehow glad or sad? Is it really a fallacy when we attribute to nature feelings analogous to our own?" (Krutch, 1955, p. 114).

26. While I feel a great kinship to all of my natural relatives in nature, I do feel as a human a unique capacity for concepts and destructiveness. "On the elaborate organization is based the much superior intelligence of man as compared to other mammals, and his ability to modify the external environment in extraordinary ways" (Cannon, 1963, p. 248).

27. To know nature is to know truth. In reference to departed Native American Ishi: "And so, stoic and unafraid, departed the last wild Indian in America...He knew nature, which is always true. His were the qualities of character that last forever. He was kind; he had courage and self-restraint, and though all had been taken from him, there was no bitterness in his heart. His soul was that of a child, his mind that of a philosopher" (Krober, 1961, p. 237-238).

28. Discernment does not occur only in the human brain. It can happen even with the tiniest of cells. "A white cell that can distinguish between invading bacteria and harmless pollen is making an intelligent decision, even though it floats in the bloodstream apart from the brain" (Chopra, 2004, p. 7).

29. The parts of nature do not seem to need us, but the whole does. "Through us the universe gets to play. Play at what? At giving

someone else the controls to what he or she comes up with. The one thing the universe can't experience is getting away from itself. So, in a sense, we are its vacation" (Chopra, 2004, p. 190). To take on this role well may seem frightening to some because it requires a diminishment of the sense of the individual self. Do not worry: "It's not that you destroy who you are. You just expand the sense of "I" from your little ego to the cosmic ego. That's a big proposition, but what I liked about this version is that nothing gets excluded" (Chopra, 2004, p. 222).

30. The sentiment that leads to saving nature has to be on an equal par with the sentiment for self-survival. "Failing this," said Aldo Leopold in a 1924 essay entitled "The River of the Mother of God," 'it seems to me we fail in the ultimate test of our vaunted superiority—the self-control of environment. We fall back into the biological category of the potato bug which exterminated the potato, and thereby exterminated itself" (Leopold, 1924, p. 123).

31. The living thing I perceive and my perceptions of it are inextricably intertwined. Fritjof Capra (1996) says:

> "...the organizing activity of living systems, at all levels of life, is mental activity. The interactions of a living organism— plant, animal, or human—with its environment are cognitive, or mental interactions. Thus life and cognition become inseparably connected. Mind—or, more accurately, mental process —is immanent in matter at all levels of life" (p. 172).

Pertinent to discussions about the intelligence of natural attractions and nature, according "to the Santiago theory, the brain is not necessary for mind to exist" (Capra, 1996, p. 174). The "process of knowing, is thus much broader than that of thinking. It involves perception, emotion, and action—the entire process of life" (Capra, 1996, p. 175).

To The Mother Of All Perception...

HumaNatureConnect Activity

Start-up Protocol

If this is not a day when you prefer to spend time in nature without an agenda, do the Heartwood Path Start-up Protocol found in the Appendix. Then return here to do the remaining portion of this activity:

Experiencing Nature's Intelligence

Use the sense of emotional place, of community, belonging, support, trust, and thankfulness to experience nature's intelligence. Also, use your natural sense of "hearing including resonance, vibrations, sonar and ultrasonic frequencies" (Cohen, website: http://www.ecopsych.com/insight53senses.html) to hum a tone that resonates with how you, your chosen natural being, and the surrounding environment belong together, create and require mutual support, trust one another, and justify a spirit of thankfulness. In what ways are the relationships between yourself, your attractive natural being, and the surrounding environment intelligent? In what ways are your sentiments about such relationships intelligent?

Follow-up Protocol

For best results, write down your impressions of this activity in your journal using the Heartwood Path Follow-up Protocol found in the Appendix. Afterwards, consider sharing your interpretations with others.

Heartwood Path Axioms

Key Assertions From Waypoint 5.6

5.6.1.

Consider nature's intelligence.

5.6.2.

To say that "all nature will fable" means that nature—a rich storehouse of myth and symbolism—describes as if so.

5.6.3.

The brain is not necessary for the mind to exist, for the process of knowing—much broader than that of thinking—involves perception, emotion, action, and the entire process of life.

5.6.4.

Eco-psychology is not all about the brain, for mental processes are immanent in matter at all levels and the heart plays a huge part in inter-species communication.

Nocturnal Pilgrimage 5.6

For best results, write down your impressions of each night's dreams in your journal using the Heartwood Path Dreaming Time Protocols found in the Appendix. Afterwards, consider sharing your Dream Tending with others.

The Natural Law Of Determination:

It takes honorable, clear, and focused intentions
to speed up receiving what you want in life.

Trade wanting and wishing for intending and allowing. Keep your ego out of your intentions by thinking about what you give rather than by thinking about what you will receive. Your determination will become deeper and purer if you concentrate on being forgiving, loving, virtuous, reverent, sincere, kind, supportive, and aware of universal truths. Give and be happy with what you have. Live in your truth. Attachments and expectations block positive results. Expect nothing from your service and you will be rewarded.

Pertinent And Instructive Gems From My Dream Tending Journal

Before the backpackers in my dream left my printshop, wanting some of what they had, I asked them where they have been.

Together, they said with some glee:

"the Healing Forest."

Don:

"How does it heal?"

The Female Customer:

"It's like VapoRub, but not as greasy" laughing at the image she was putting into my mind.

Male Customer:

"More like a rub that you put on meat for a bar-be-cue. The impact of the invigorating foresty rub goes right down to your cells."

As I watched them go, body and soil, I wondered if their rub could be
bottled, or if it requires visiting a forest like you do a resort, or a retreat, or
a spa. Looking at them, I could tell the healthy elixir was not added to any
bath oil. Then, I started to worry about what, in my my own urban
comings and goings, I had been absorbing, especially indoors at work. The
smell of printers' ink cannot be as healthy as the scent of decaying leaves,
pollen, or ocean breezes.

Lesson Learned: Maybe the elixir of nature is something like the smell of pine sap on Ozark trails. Or, maybe nature's tonic is something like the turpentine-like aromas of cypress trees in Southern Illinois. However it does it, being in a natural setting stimulates my respiration and helps me to relax. Whenever I spend extended time in nature, I feel stress lifting, as if the cortisol in my blood, intolerant of nature's peace, leaves me with my perspiration.

In numerous ways, Nature rubs me the right way. In her presence, I feel happier, more relaxed, less anxious, and more optimistic. I don't eat much of nature as I move through her. I do know, however, that being with natural beings in natural landscapes is good for me. Like eating from a healthy food group, I consider nature experiences my vegetable.

To increase your chances of remembering dreams or having lucid dreams, focus on the last two hours of sleep. Write LaBerge and Rheingold: "the probability of your having a lucid dream during these last two hours of sleep is more than twice as great as the probability of your having a lucid dream in the previous six hours . . . (If) you normally get only six hours of sleep, you could double your chances of lucid dreaming by extending your sleep by two hours" (1990, p. 50).

With these statements and your impressions from today's lesson foremost in your mind, drift off to sleep. Dream and then tend to your dreams upon waking. When ready, move to the next waypoint, entitled "Pull," to begin the next teaching on the topic of attraction.

7

Pull

CONSIDER ATTRACTION

The real voyage of discovery

consists not in seeking new landscapes,

but in having new eyes."

—Marcel Proust (Garon, 2006, p. 5)

Without looking for attractions in nature and doing the methodologies associated with the Natural System Thinking Process (NSTP) one will omit nature's essentials and thus not get all that is possible from its guidance. When this happens, as it does essentially everyday for most people in modern society, the way we conduct our thinking produces . . .

"the destructive, hidden ruts that create our disorders, ruts that deepen each time we travel them. Without using natural system fundamentals our best efforts to increase inner and outer peace and personal and environmental health seldom succeed" (Cohen, 1987, p. ii).

This is one reason why it is so important to pay attention to your natural attractions in nature, one of the key steps to bonding with and supporting nature within you, in others, and in the land around you. "That's when things improve," writes the founder of Project NatureConnect (Cohen, 1987, p. ii).

"Our excessive disconnection from nature's attractive and intelligent perfection underlies the insanity of our suffering, greed and destructiveness. Unadulterated natural systems seldom suffer them" (Cohen, 1987, p. vi).

When we occupy our time with careers, television, academic study, reading, and most non-sensual indoor pursuits, we become psychologically closed-off and inattentive to the real-world experience of the attractions from and in nature. Cohen (1987) calls this malady NADS (Natural Attraction Desensitization Syndrome) (p. 10). Over time, most of us humans in modern cultures become accustomed to the linear thinking that occurs as a result of our indoor lifestyle.

"We seldom register this way of thinking as a desensitizing, intellectual, emotional and spiritual amputation. Earth suffers from the impact of our emotional pain, insensitivity and ignorance" (Cohen, 1987, p. 11).

A big problem occurs when we psychologically separate ourselves from nature by not paying attention to potential natural attractions. "We seldom realize that in order to escape or tranquilize the pain our separation causes," writes Cohen (1987), "we often insensitively trespass or invade the integrity of natural systems within and around us. This produces many of our seemingly unsolvable problems" (p. 11).

"Without seeing, sensing or respecting the strings in nature and our inner nature, we break, injure and ignore them. Their disappearance in our consciousness produces an organic void, an uncomfortable psychological emptiness in our thoughts and lives that we constantly try to fill. We want, emotionally and materially, and when we want, there is never enough. We become greedy, stressed, and reckless as we try to gain webstring fulfillment. This places the Earth, others, and ourselves at risk . . .

NSTP's nature–reconnecting activities enable us to bring webstrings —natural sensory attraction relationships—back into our lives. Their presence in our thinking helps reinstate balanced personal and environmental relationships" (Cohen, 1987, p. 43).

To Magnetism...

HumaNatureConnect Activity

Start-up Protocol

If this is not a day when you prefer to spend time in nature without an agenda, do the Heartwood Path Start-up Protocol found in the Appendix. Then return here to do the remaining portion of this activity:

Experiencing Attraction

Use the sense of self including friendship, companionship, and power to experience and communicate about attraction to answer the following questions: How does friendship determine what you are attracted to? How does your attractions affect your friendships? Does your sense of power affect your attractions or does your attraction influence your sense of power? Are you attracted to power? Are you attracted to your community? What aspects in your community are attractive and unattractive to you? Hum a tone that resonates with your attractions to your companions and hum a tone that resonates with those who you share no companionship. What is different about the tones, and why?

Follow-up Protocol

For best results, write down your impressions of this activity in your journal using the Heartwood Path Follow-up Protocol found in the Appendix. Afterwards, consider sharing your interpretations with others.

Heartwood Path Axioms

Key Assertions From Waypoint 5.7

5.7.1.

Consider Attraction.

5.7.2.

When we occupy our time with careers, television, academic study, reading, and most non-sensual indoor pursuits, we become psychologically closed-off and inattentive to the real-world experience of the attractiveness of nature.

5.7.3.

As we escape the pain caused by our separation from nature we tend to disrespect the natural systems within and around us.

5.7.4.

Separation from nature produces many problems.

Nocturnal Pilgrimage 5.7

For best results, write down your impressions of each night's dreams in your journal using the Heartwood Path Dreaming Time Protocols found in the Appendix. Afterwards, consider sharing your Dream Tending with others.

The Natural Law Of Desirability:

What you put out to the universe
will come back to you.

Since like attracts like, you will attract things that have the same vibrational frequency as your spiritual self. Say "I am" rather than "I wish" to attract more. You have to be 100% truthful and completely convinced or the power of desire will not work. Creative visualization and surrounding yourself with like-minded people are two good ways to manifest your desires. With absolute truthfulness, you cannot have fair and positive desires that are too large, so you might as well go big with your intentions. Appreciate everything you receive.

Pertinent And Instructive Gems From My Dream Tending Journal

For some reason, in my dream, I did not want the nature wayfarers to leave me alone in my sterile and smelly printshop. So I asked them an inane question, just to get them to linger with me for a little while longer.

Don:

"How's the traffic out there?"

Female Customer, whose name is Kim:

"Busy."

The man, apparently always wanting to have the last correct word, had something to add.

Male Customer:

"It really seems true, I read someplace that since I started driving in 1970, the number of vehicles on the roads have tripled."

Don:

"It makes driving scary and frustrating."

Kim:

"And loud!"

I began to wonder if she was always this pleasant in her brevity. Not to be outdone, the man continued.

Male Customer:

"According to the National Forest Service, about 80 percent of the land in the Lower 48 is close enough to hear vehicle noise."

I was beginning to think that I was hearing enough about it.

Lesson Learned: You can be efficient with things, but never with people. Give them time to lapse away from efficiency. Be efficient with tasks, but be effective with people by being a good listener.

Dreams help you interpret the vibratory communications you may be receiving, consciously and unconsciously, from nature. You can increase your chance of having a lucid dream—the most informative type of dreams—by rearranging your sleep time. This can be accomplished by setting your alarm to awaken you two to three hours earlier than usual, get out of bed when the alarm goes off, think about what you want to dream about for the half hour before returning to bed. Use the half-hour before returning to bed to incubate a dream. Give yourself at least another two more hours of sleep to dream.

With these points and your impressions from the present lesson utmost in your mind, drift off to sleep. Dream purposefully. Begin tending to your dreams before you move in bed after waking.

When ready head to the waypoint that puts more flesh on one of the two main purposes for heading down the Heartwood Path: namely, the goal of creating a sustainable environment. Proceed to the next waypoint, entitled "Flourishing Continuously," to reach another key milestone in your journey to "GladandGreen Junction."

8

Flourishing Continuously

CONSIDER ALIVENESS

Flourishing, which we will define as *thriving*, is part of our definition of sustainability, along with *aliveness.* The avoidance of mass deaths due to human folly is certainly a big reason to work towards sustainability.

The avoidance of greed-caused extinction or the avoidance of the continuance of life in a merely withered and declined way, as commendable as these goals may be, is not the end of following the Heartwood Path. We eartHearts want everyone to both survive and thrive; to live, but to live in a gratified and dignified way that allows everyone to be developed, impassioned, and self-actualized. The world of the past gave us the opportunity to prosper. For those of the future, without considerable effort, this gift may not be forthcoming.

We live in a world that is alive but imbalanced. The imbalances include having so much man-made carbon in the atmosphere that we are causing changes in the world's climate, having not enough safe drinking water, having too many people living in poverty, losing too much topsoil, and producing and ingesting too much unhealthy food. These imbalances make sustainability a big challenge.

We may not be thinking of these problems with any frequency; but, being a species with a propensity for empathy and compassion, such imbalances have an insidious affect on our subconscious minds, our conscious minds, our feelings, and our emotional well-being. We eartHearts want our fellows—human and otherwise—to not only survive; but to flourish, by which I mean to continue to live a good life, good in the sense that it is healthy and, for fellow humans, a life based on the precepts of time-tested sages and philosophers.

Our conscious minds may be thinking about all sorts of consumptions and divisiveness. Still, we feel a yearning for a sustainable ecosystem—one that creates a high level of vitality and health. We feel a need for ecological resilience, an adaptability that allows human and nonhuman beings to live and evolve.

Such feelings are part of our deepest nature, far more so than contemporary yearnings, including what has become a societal sickness: the mindless desire for more and the divisiveness we believe is necessary for us to bury our heirlooms in throwaway commodities. When we dig within ourselves, past the mental commotions caused by our attention to modern media and advertising, we begin to hear the deep cry of the heart that is a plea from the future to include its fellows into our deliberations. Those in the future will need us to stop creating, using, and disposing of products that do not last beyond six months. It is as if future beings can see how the current paradigm—wherein there is human mastery over nature, divisiveness, and widespread waste of resources—and, seeing these, they are crying: "will there be any part of the good life left for us?" Concern for the beings of the future is a form of empathy, one that is both painful and illustrative of our deep and admirable capacity for care beyond ourselves and our nearby folks.

After the following activity, which asks you to ponder how you attempt to meet your own unsatisfied needs through either the misguided consumption of commodities or the attainment of authentic modes of satisfaction, and the following waypoint on the topic of "love," which is said to be "all you need," there will be more waypoints on "sustainability"—one on a clearer idea of what it is, and another on ways to achieve it.

When ready, turn your attention to the next waypoint, entitled "Indifference-free." For the next activity, consider taking a loved one with you. Perhaps go to the closest tumbling river, beach, or waterfall. If you do not know where to go, ask around or do an internet search. It won't just be the mesmerizing allure of the water tumbling and spraying that will make you glad you came. If you sit close-by, the two of you can benefit from the health-producing negative ions in the watery spray, air that makes you feel psychologically uplifted.

To A Demarcation Of What Is Really Sustaining For You...

HumaNatureConnect Activity

Start-up Protocol

If this is not a day when you prefer to spend time in nature without an agenda, do the Heartwood Path Start-up Protocol found in the Appendix. Then return here to do the remaining portion of this activity:

Truly Meeting Unsatisfied Needs

Think about the best ways to meet your unsatisfied needs. You may be buying items to satisfy emotional needs when a better strategy would be to work directly of satisfying the emotional need that is causing the misguided buying. In the chart below, list items you have bought that you now regret, or that you really did not need. List those items on the left column. On the right column, list your conscious needs, your emotional wants, and your deep unmet yearnings. You can keep the two lists separate or you can determine if a certain misguided purchases was caused caused by a certain heart-felt need (your Soul's desire). If you can make a link between a Soul Desire and a misguided purchase, place the two side by side in the chart. Think about what you can do to avoid make further misguided acquisitions.

My Misguided Purchases	The Desires Of My Soul

List What You Are Doing To Merely Survive	List How You Could Make Each Mere Survival Action Into An Action That Meets Your Soul's Desire

List What You Are Already Doing To Meet Your Soul's Desire	List What You Would Like To Do In The Near Future To Meet Your Soul's Desire	List An Action Step You Can Take To Meet Your Soul's Desire

Follow-up Protocol

For best results, write down your impressions of this activity in your journal using the Heartwood Path Follow-up Protocol found in the Appendix. Afterwards, consider sharing your interpretations with others.

Heartwood Path Axioms

Key Assertions From Waypoint 5.8

5.8.1.

Consider Aliveness.

5.8.2.

We eartHearts want everyone to both survive and thrive; to live in a gratified and dignified way that allows everyone to be developed, impassioned, and self-actualized.

5.8.3.

We live in a world that is alive but imbalanced in ways that have an insidious affect on our subconscious minds, our conscious minds, our feelings, and our emotional well-being.

5.8.4.

Our felt need for ecological resilience is part of our deepest nature, far more so than contemporary yearnings, including our mindless desire for more.

Nocturnal Pilgrimage 5.8

For best results, write down your impressions of each night's dreams in your journal using the Heartwood Path Dreaming Time Protocols found in the Appendix. Afterwards, consider sharing your Dream Tending with others.

The Natural Law Of Bountifulness:

Everything flows abundantly towards you.
All you have to do is receive it.
But the world of earthly things is finite.
So do not ask for more than your fair share.

Remove anything that thwarts the abundant flow of positive ideas, knowledge, and emotions. As for things, you can have it all; but you ought not deprive others of needed material possessions. If you doubt the finitude of things on earth, wait until the oil runs out and then you will see that the Natural Law of Bountifulness refers to things from the universe, like sunshine, and not to things from the earth, like coal. Still, to get your fair share by using this law, invite things into your life.

Pertinent And Instructive Gems From My Dream Tending Journal

After the woman's boyfriend went outside to rearrange their Toyota Cruiser, the woman in my dream, after holding the stainless steel and glass door open for him, used her hip to gently close the door while cupping her ears with her hands.

Kim, turning to me,

shuttered as she said, almost whispering:

"It's so loud."

Not letting her get off two sentences without his interjections, the boyfriend came back inside and asked me what was wrong with her.

After I told him, he resumed his know-it-all persona and, now almost comically.

Male Customer:

"We just got back from one of twelves places in the United States where you cannot hear human-made noise for at least 15 minutes at dawn. It takes her a while to adjust back to living where human noise increases background noise by an average of"...(airplane noise drowns him out).

Don:

"I'm sorry, by how much?"

Male Customer:

"It's called the anthrophone—the human-made soundscape that is 30 decibels—yelling now—"louder than nature's relative silence."

Lesson Learned: My first thought after this dream: where can I get that list of quiet places? Then, I thought about that proverbial question: If a tree falls in the forest and no one is there to hear it, does it make a sound? If there is no person, bird, fish, or other organism capable of hearing it, then the answer is no. Assuming that is true, what about the answer to this question: if no being is there to perceive it, does any being—attractive or not—even exist? My answer to that question: the matter that makes the being may be there as an incoherent mass, but the being itself only takes its form and behavior pattern after it is perceived. It is not even an object until it is interpreted in some way. You invoke your attractive natural beings by your perception and interpretation of them. As far as we know, no being exists or is named unless it is perceived, interpreted, and labeled by a human. So, let's all make interpretations that lead to human happiness and a beautiful and sustainable environment. Make them your own, but make them good for all.

Keep going. Be like a postage stamp that sticks to the mailed envelope until it gets there. Don't be just a bundle of beginnings. The tide turns for the worse the moment one gives up. Your defeats are temporary until giving up makes them permanent. Remember, even the smallest snail reached the ark. If your mind is saying, "I can't keep going," listen to what your heart says. Giving up is the greatest weakness. Unless you are sleeping for recovery or to foster dreaming, turn up your sleeves or don't turn up at all. Be smart and keep your honor bright. Consider your continuance on the Heartwood Path as exercise for your perseverance. Don't turn this into one long race. Make it many short ones. Falling often is what allows the rain to put a hole in the rock. Those who succeed in life owe their success to their perseverance —the foundation of all actions. If you are afraid that going down the Heartwood Path is using up too much time, consider how the time will pass anyway so you might as well find happiness and sustainability as it does. There is no rush. Nature gets everything done in its own time. Let your will lead you on your way. Unless you work nothing else will.

Sleep well tonight. Upon waking, before you move in your bed, begin tending your dreams, as previously instructed. When ready, move to the next waypoint, entitled "Indifference-free."

9

Indifference-free

CONSIDER LOVE

"We cannot live for ourselves alone. Our lives are connected by a thousand invisible threads and along these sympathetic fibers our actions run as causes and return to us as results."

—Herman Melville (Cohen, 1987, p. 43).

"Nurture your felt love or respect for nature" writes Dr. Cohen. "Never deny it. That love is nature's voice . . . It is the root source of our deeper hopes and ideals" (Cohen, 1987, p. vii). It is also the solution to our biggest personal, social, and environmental problems. But only if you know how to love nature truly. This involves being: 1) lovingly grateful for natural beings in a specific way that leads to something called "coherence" and 2) sensing and feeling nature's webstrings through the Natural Systems Thinking Process—the two related key tasks for those who want to lovingly communicate with nature in the most significant way.

For those advancing down the Heartwood Path (I could also say "flowing with the enduring stream") the goal at this point in this writing is to help the reader become (or remember to become) earnestly grateful to The Absolute's creation. By this I mean being thankful in body, mind, and spirit for the wholeness of Earth's natural systems, including met natural beings which are all perceptive in some way. The two related means to foster this enriched and enriching heartfelt sense of gratitude come from Rollin McCraty's group effort on "coherence" (the main topic of Waypoint 5.15, still to come) and Michael Cohen's "Natural Systems Thinking Process" (the basis of the Start-up Protocol to the HumaNatureConnect Activities). This more-than-casual sense of gratefulness is the key two-method step, often overlooked, in the development of valued traits, especially those that have spiritual, ecological, and organizational significance.

To Deep Affection Toward The Natural World...

HumaNatureConnect Activity

Start-up Protocol

If this is not a day when you prefer to spend time in nature without an agenda, do the Heartwood Path Start-up Protocol found in the Appendix. Then return here to do the remaining portion of this activity:

Experiencing The Love Of Nature

Try all or some of Dr. J. Mark Dangerfield's tips for how to love nature when you live in the city:

1. "Locate some soil, the real dirt that plants grow in, and take a pinch of it between your fingers.
2. Find a plant, any plant will do, and put your nose right up to it. Not just close, but onto a leaf, as near as your eyes will allow without losing focus. Keep your nose there for at least a minute and see what happens.
3. Find a spot outside where you can sit. Take your earphones out of your ears and listen. Scan the world of sounds with your ears

until you identify a natural noise. It could be a bird or insect calling, the rustle of leaves or just the sound of the wind. Focus on that noise until it is all you can hear.

4. Next time you are out in some weather stop for a moment and just feel it. Let the wind rush past your cheeks and chill your ears.

5. Watch what happens to the rain; see it bounce, or disappear or splash. Follow a drop until it falls onto a plant, your coat, the pavement, anything.

6. In winter put the thermostat on the air-con down by a degree, wait a week then put it down again, leave it there for a month then put it down again. By spring you will have become quite comfortable in a lower room temperature, learnt about acclimation, saved on your heating bill and lowered your carbon footprint.

7. When you next see a great wildlife documentary, view it without the sound. Look at the images for what they are without the emotive music and dramatization of the narrative. See what emotions come up for you without the added triggers.

8. Watch a cat.

9. Take up gardening and sometimes do the weeding without gloves.

10. If you are still young enough to participate in a sport played on grass, go do it. Only make sure you put your hand on the soil at some point in the game." (Dangerfield Website)

Follow-up Protocol

For best results, write down your impressions of this activity in your journal using the Heartwood Path Follow-up Protocol found in the Appendix. Afterwards, consider sharing your interpretations with others.

Heartwood Path Axioms

Key Assertions From Waypoint 5.9

5.9.1.

Consider Love.

5.9.2.

Being grateful for your experiences with natural beings, the development of coherence, and the Natural Systems Thinking Process are keys to the creation of valued traits.

5.9.3.

Sleeping twice each night, the second time being at least two hours, promotes the lucid dreams that are the nocturnal source of so much good guidance.

5.9.4.

Love is the voice of nature that tells us how to solve our deepest personal, social, and environmental problems.

Nocturnal Pilgrimage 5.9

For best results, write down your impressions of each night's dreams in your journal using the Heartwood Path Dreaming Time Protocols found in the Appendix. Afterwards, consider sharing your Dream Tending with others.

The Natural Law Of Radiance:

Empowerment, knowledge, and connection
are lit by an inner glow
that can be shown to others
in one's good works.

By radiance I mean the glowing inner light of goodness. This beam, seen in the mind's eye only, is generated by the divine empowerment that puts you on the right side of causes. It reveals the truth, transforms self-consciousness into self-acceptance, guides others to positivity, and gives glowing creativity to your visualizations. It feels like high vibrations of inner warmth.

Your own goodness will radiate invisibly to others who may then glow in their joy, hope, and deep affection. With an ability to heal the wounds of fear, anxiety, and misgivings, radiance responds to both requests and gratitude. Use it responsibly.

The Natural Law Of Appropriateness:

We are appropriate
when we make our own decisions,
do what is right,
act independently
add to organic wholeness,
help all beings flourish,
are accountable for our actions,
and do not blame others.

Take care of yourself, but watch over others as well. We grow as we respond to the needs of others, especially those without an adequate voice in their own affairs. Do not assume other people's burdens. Those help them grow. Be careful not to dim their radiance.

Pertinent And Instructive Gems From My Dream Tending Journal

Still cupping her ears, the woman in my dream said,

"They need to establish more quiet zones."

The man said:

"Noise is a pollutant."

Don:

"Where would we establish your quiet zones?"

Her boyfriend, now becoming annoying, answered:

"In many forests, public transportation vehicles, and public buildings."

Lesson Learned: In my dream the man was informative but not nearly as motivating as his emotive and briefly-speaking girlfriend. Her visceral responses to being recently bathed in silence motivated me to experience what she experienced. His comments were helpful, but distracting. She had me the moment she cupped her ears.

"Redistributing sleep can be a remarkably powerful way to facilitate lucid dreaming," writes LaBerge and Rheingold (1990, p. 51). To get you started, set your alarm clock so it awakens you two to three hours earlier than usual, go to sleep at your normal time, get out of bed when the alarm goes off, stay awake for two or three hours, go about your business until about a half hour before going back to sleep. During this half hour, think about what you want to accomplish in your lucid dream and incubate a dream about a particular topic. Make sure your place of sleep is quiet enough to sleep soundly for the next two hours. Go back to sleep for two hours. During this time, you are likely to fall into one or two long REM (Rapid Eye Movement) periods and have a lucid dream or two (LaBerge and Rheingold, 1990, p. 51 & 52).

With these helpful points and your impressions from the previous lesson most prominent in your mind as you drift off to sleep, get a good night's rest. Dream and then tend to your dreams upon waking.

When ready, turn your attention to the next waypoint, entitled "Sustainability Clarified." For the next activity, perhaps go back to the waterfall, beach, or rapids. Note how being close to natural spraying water makes you feel relaxed or even sleepy. If this happens to you, indulge yourself: find a safe and isolated spot to sleep outdoors. You will awaken refreshed and ready for the next activity.

10

Sustainability Clarified

KNOW HOW SUSTAINABILITY IS A VESSEL FOR THE HIGHEST HUMAN ASPIRATIONS AND VALUES

Beyond the continuance of biological aliveness, which is the prerequisite for sustainability and one Dr. Cohen's six components of NNI-AAL (his "Rosetta Stone" for how to best be aware of nature) are its other important characteristics: dignity, flourishing, justness, fairness, equity, the preservation of wildness, the avoidance of major ecological disturbances, and the achievement of authentic lives for all. In this list, note the lack of big bank accounts or a growing Gross National Product. One reason for this omission has to do with the fact that the wealthiest countries do not have the happiest people (Ehrenfeld, 2008, p. 62).

We who dwell in the so-called wealthy nations may not be as happy as expected because we spend too much time indoors watching the television or social media. This powerful pusher of consumption keeps the viewer perpetually unsatisfied, as one commercial after another, as one image of wealth after another, causes feelings of lack, feelings of desire, all amounting to a pervasive and long-lasting addiction to consumption. When one's attention is dominated by images of others who have more, one rarely has a chance to be satisfied. One tends to work long hours for little pay, making the stuff depicted on television commercials and programs. What little time and money one has after working all day (and often well into the night), one spends on the stuff depicted on television commercials and sponsored ads. In so doing, one tends to gradually lose his or her humanity, giving up a chance to be vulnerable, unpredictable, and excitingly colorful humans for the security, predictiveness, and blandness of being a mere cog in the economic engine of Modernity. There is more to life than watching flickering images, working, and spending. Pura Vida—long live the good life. How to do so is the topic of the next waypoint.

To A Clarification Of Sustainability...

HumaNatureConnect Activity

Start-up Protocol

If this is not a day when you prefer to spend time in nature without an agenda, do the Heartwood Path Start-up Protocol found in the Appendix. Then return here to do the remaining portion of this activity:

Clarifying Your Vision Of Sustainability

Fill out the chart that follows. For each of the components of sustainability, describe in the first column how this quality is currently sustained in your life, if at all, in the second column and describe your vision (mental picture) of how you would like to sustain each component of sustainability if you had little or no constraints soon. Space if provided for your own additional reflections.

Components Of Sustainability	How This Component Is Currently Sustained In Your Life	Your Vision Of How You Would Like To Sustain Each Component
Continuance of Aliveness		
Flourishing		
Justness		
Fairness		
Equity		
Avoidance of Ecological Disasters		
The Preservation of Wildness		
The Achievement of an Authentic Life		

Follow-up Protocol

For best results, write down your impressions of this activity in your journal using the Heartwood Path Follow-up Protocol found in the Appendix. Afterwards, consider sharing your interpretations with others.

Heartwood Path Axioms

Key Assertions From Waypoint 5.10

5.10.1.

Know how sustainability is a vessel for the highest human aspirations and values.

5.10.2.

Biological aliveness, dignity, flourishing, justness, fairness, equity, the preservation of wildness, the avoidance of major ecological disturbances, and the achievement of authentic lives for all are all prerequisites for sustainability.

5.10.3.

We who dwell in the so-called wealthy nations may not be as happy as expected because we spend too much time indoors watching the television or social media.

5.10.4.

Watching too much television indoors gradually causes us to trade the chance to be vulnerable, to be unpredictable, and to be excitingly colorful members of the human race for the security, predictiveness, and blandness of being a mere cog in the economic engine of Modernity.

Nocturnal Pilgrimage 5.10

For best results, write down your impressions of each night's dreams in your journal using the Heartwood Path Dreaming Time

Protocols found in the Appendix. Afterwards, consider sharing your Dream Tending with others.

The Natural Law Of Mercy:

Releasing
anger, hatred, bitterness, and resentment
allows love to overcome
negative emotions.

Forgiveness is not about accepting someone's bad behavior. It is rather about releasing negative feelings in yourself, for your own benefit. Dispensing negative feelings helps you move on, heal, forget, and showcase the unity of the one Absolute Being.

The Natural Law Of Congruity:

All so-called parts
work together
as fragments
of the one spiritual being.

We all share the same Divine energy. It takes the recognition of this interconnectedness to, in an appropriate way, sustain helpfulness, remove fear, moderate the effects of the Ego, and deal with anger. Unblock your lack of congruity by working through any feelings of jealousy, envy, and bitterness. Once you have heightened your sense of unity, indiscretions can be more easily forgiven.

Pertinent And Instructive Gems From My Dream Tending Journal

Assuming that his girlfriend was done talking with me, the man strutted back out to his vehicle on my asphalt parking lot.

As soon as she noticed that he was out of range, and not able to interrupt so fast,

The female customer said:

"I just love the windy silence of the desert in the Kelso wilderness in Southern California, even more than the drip-drip silence at the Hoh wilderness in Washington. We're on a mission to seek the quietest places in America. The next place is in Minnesota, I believe."

Just when I thought she was beginning to brag by dropping wilderness place names, she became endearing again by asking me what are my favorite sounds. Caught off guard with that one,

I asked,

"Do you mean any sounds?"

Female Customer:

"Sure!," she said, as if tantalized by the opportunity to get to know me.

I said the sound of the voices of my children and grandchildren. Then, I watched to see if my answer was off-putting.

Female Customer:

"And?"

She was letting me know she wanted more.

After noticing that her boyfriend was coming back in, I replied, sugges-
tively, and with a nod toward the front door.

Don:

"I'll have to get back with you. I'll have to sleep on it first."

Peeking his head in, the Male Customer asked:

"Ready."

Knowing she was sending two different messages to each of us with one
word.

Female Customer:

"Ready."

Lesson Learned: In addition to the voices of my offspring, I like the happy sound of birds, the rhythmic sound of drums, any music that inspires creativity (such as Bach, Brahms, Beethoven, the Beatles) and the soothing sound of moving water. Unlike many, the looming sound of strong wind often makes me feel anxious. But that's me, an emigrant from tornado alley in the Midwest, someone who chooses to face wildfires, tsunamis, earthquakes, and mud slides rather than an approaching Twister. What about you? What sounds do you like or not like? As I just did, turning the attention around to your conversation partner is a good way to demonstrate that you are a person with valued traits; in this case, the trait of being empathetic towards others

During the day, as you struggle, as you inevitably will, to keep up the motivation to stop your busy day and head for an attractive natural being in the wild, remember that it is acceptable and even wise to take the time to rest, recover, and renew yourself. Sometimes I too feel conflicted about stopping my active routines to sit for a while with a natural attraction. To overcome this internal conflict, I become motivated by what Jesus said to His apostles as they returned to him weary and exhausted: "Come with me by yourselves to a quiet place and get some rest" (Mark 6: 31). Go to a natural attraction in a quiet place and get some rest. Let nature do its work on you. Engage in the HumaNatureConnect activity. As an alternative, think and do nothing. Either way, you will be renewed.

During the evening, continue practicing your dream techniques and tending to your dreams. When ready, move to the next waypoint, entitled "The Road To Sustainability."

11

The Road To Sustainability

HELP NATURE AND THE GOOD LIFE LAST

A main cause of unhappiness and environmental destruction is the pervasive but largely unconscious addiction that causes harmful patterns of indoor living, sedentariness, and TV-promoted consumption. Fortunately, it is possible to break the pattern. To do so requires new habits for yourself and a new dominant social paradigm for the culture.

In the new pervasive view, matter will not be seen as leading to mind. Instead, mind and matter will be seen to co-arise or, if one is thinking more purposefully, mind will be seen to lead to matter.

We have to imagine a new world as one emerges or, more purposefully, we have to imagine a new world before the one we want can emerge.

Discounted by educators who seem to have either sniffed too many chemicals in laboratories or breathed too much mildew in stuffy libraries, the kind of experiential learning presented in this series of books is vitally important to the development of an eco-centric paradigm. Beware the professor who discounts the importance of getting out into nature. Nature is the best model for sustainability. Do not just dissect natural beings in a lab or read about them in a library. Explore the outer reaches of your own Greater Self. Go outside. Find examples of sustainability in nature. Use these examples as you help to design a wonderful world that works for all sentient beings.

The answers we need for a sustainable world lie not in artificial commodities but in natural communities, in natural sources of inspiration, sources that cannot be seen through observational lens molded by reading words, by viewing specimens under microscopes, or by the incessant use of televisions or computers. There is more to the world than meets the indoor eye.

Do not focus much on what you have or what you need. Get out into nature, instead. Begin to see and feel. Feel what caring feels like.

"For the first time in history," writes Erich Fromm, "the physical survival of the human race depends on a radical change in the human heart" (Ehrenfeld, 2008, p. 108). Having and needing leads to unhealthy consumption and, ultimately, to war, as one nation covets what another nation has. To do what you can to minimize the impetus of war, replace the structure of having (a mindset dominated by thoughts of acquiring) with the structure of being (a mindset dominated by thoughts of living and caring for others in the present).

You will never have enough as long as you always feel you need more. The objects you acquire build the structure of having. Love and happiness builds your structure of being. Even the buying of a service is part of the structure of having if all you are trying to do is use the service to get, maintain, or replace material objects. Buying your girlfriend a pizza, for example, is a nice gesture but it does not replace the love that is, in the end, all that really matters. In this instance, the focus ought to not be on the physical pizza, good as it may be. You can convert this act from a building block of the structure of having to a building block of the structure of being by focusing on, not the pizza, but of your love for your loved one. If your action is an attempt to meet a *need-for-something*, you are providing a thing and, therefore, you are building the structure of having. If your action is based on your a *need-to-do-something*, you are showing your care and, therefore, you are building the structure of being.

To continue to build the structure of being, in whatever you are doing or, additionally, in whatever you are planning to do, ask two questions: "What am I doing this for?" and "Ethically, is there something better I could be doing?" Asking such questions before the actions are better than correcting any problems that occur because you were not diligently promoting being over having. As Goethe says: "Precaution is better than cure" (Ehrenfeld, 2008, p. 188).

Expanding the relevance of Goethe's prudent statement outward to include caring for the whole world (which is complex and unpredictable) leads one to another needed question: "In areas of great complexity, isn't it better to listen to those who know that an action will result in a bad outcome than it is to hope that nothing substantially bad will occur?" Seems to me that in matters such as the impact of man-made carbon dioxide on the Earth's climate the prudent thing to do is to minimize the chances of feeling regret over not acting sooner or stronger by cutting emission rates now and a lot.

This example leads to an important ethical axiom:

The broader the impact,
the broader the participation needs to be
in solving the problem.

We cannot leave matters that affect the many to a few partisan politicians, to a few zealots, or to a few activists.

Like fairness and liberty, sustainability can become a part of humanity's ethical foundation. We can change our paradigms, our stories, and our words. We can create new visions for a better future.

Here's how:

1. Go to nature to learn how to dismantle the structure of having. Think less about acquiring.

2. Using nature's example, build the structure of being. Think more about caring.

3. Trade in your preoccupations with having stuff with frequent notions about caring.

4. Study war no more.

5. Engross yourself in the care of another person, in the care of a few people, or in the care of a natural being or two, as suggested in the next two waypoints.

To The Structure Of Being...

HumaNatureConnect Activity

Start-up Protocol

If this is not a day when you prefer to spend time in nature without an agenda, do the Heartwood Path Start-up Protocol found in the Appendix. Then return here to do the remaining portion of this activity:

Overcoming The Structure Of Having

Consider how you can think more about caring than you do about acquiring.

Follow-up Protocol

For best results, write down your impressions of this activity in your journal using the Heartwood Path Follow-up Protocol found in the Appendix. Afterwards, consider sharing your interpretations with others.

Heartwood Path Axioms

Key Assertions From Waypoint 5.11

5.11.1.

Help nature and the good life last.

5.11.2.

Nature is the best model for sustainability which, like fairness and liberty, ought to be part of humanity's ethical foundation.

5.11.3.

To minimize the impetus of the depletion of natural beings, replace the structure of having (a mindset dominated by thoughts of acquiring) with the structure of being (a mindset dominated by thoughts of living and caring for others in the present).

Nocturnal Pilgrimage 5.11

For best results, write down your impressions of each night's dreams in your journal using the Heartwood Path Dreaming Time Protocols found in the Appendix. Afterwards, consider sharing your Dream Tending with others.

The Natural Law Of Impelling Force:

> All beings
> have a purpose and
> are able to fulfill
> that purpose.

Your purpose is programmed into your energy as part of your core spiritual essence. Your specific aptitudes help you express your core purpose, which is to be authentically awakened to your spiritual being—the reason for your existence. You know you have found your core purpose when you are most happy as you help the world. It is the radiant joy of compassion that highlights one's core purpose. All things come to you when you are in this glow.

Light your inner fire by making a list of your passions, situations that excited you in your past, and what gives you joy today. Take some quiet time examining your desires, your values, and your innermost thoughts. Examine any fears you may have that are keeping you off-purpose. Make plans to live your purpose. Give yourself permission to experience novelty. Recognize that secondary purposes can lead you to your core purpose. Keep looking until you find your spiritual essence.

Pertinent And Instructive Gems From My Dream Tending Journal

Dreaming lucidly now (meaning that I was aware that I was dreaming and could, more-or-less, control my dream) I decided that I did not want this dream, or should I say this "Dream Girl," to end. So I lured them back to my desk with a question that I knew would engage Dr. Know-It-All and, thus, keep his lovely girlfriend in my dream.

Don:

"What do you think about those young people who seem to be listening to nothing but the music emitting from their EarBuds?"

He sat down, as if pondering my question. She stood behind him, rubbing his shoulders.

Male Customer:

"They live within their own personal soundscapes,

They will eventually become deaf to nature. And they are avoiding something in the real world."

Female Customer:

"I use Earbuds, sometimes,"

secretly pointing to her boyfriend and mouthing silently: "For the same reason—avoidance."

He turned around briefly, to see why she was giggling. I remained stoic.

Lesson Learned: When we forget to listen to nature, we lose a chance to be restored.

To help foster sustainability become a caregiver. Be a part of the continual embodiment of the fringe of Jesus's cloak. Let those who touch you be healed by your touch. Do so quietly, to not draw attention to yourself. Helping others only to bring glory to yourself is hypocritical. If you love The Absolute and your neighbor—both humans and nonhumans—as yourself, you will not violate the Ten Commandments handed down to Moses. To keep your life on the right track, commune with nature by day, as described throughout these Heartwood Path books, and at night dream dreams that help you understand the guidance that comes your way. After tending to your next dream, as previously directed, move to the next waypoint, "Caregiver Praise."

12

Caregiver Praise

BE AN INSPIRED AND INSPIRING CAREGIVER

One way or another you will be affected by caregiving. You may have already been a caregiver, you may be a caregiver now, you will likely be a caregiver in the future, or you will someday need caregiving. In any event, among life's greatest values is one person caring for another person.

Caregivers light the world like stars light the night. They have possibly the hardest job in the world. They are often highly trained, and indeed sometimes it takes an educated eye to see what needs to be done. Still, much of what caregivers do is not the result of specialized learning. Sometimes all it takes is a hand held. Being exceptional people, caregivers know that just being there for someone can bring hope when all seems hopeless. Nurturing, along with being trained observers, are the two pillars for the compassion caregiver offer to the world.

Caregivers—those who raise hope as assuredly as the rising sun—manage at least two lives—the supported individual and their own. They do best when they balance both lives, receive adequate training, and wear comfortable shoes.

We are all entrusted by the Absolute Spirit to care for the flock, not because of what we get out of it, which is plenty, but because it is a way to be supportive. The rewards, often hard to see in the urgency of daily care, are, without question, a source of the greatest happiness possible. One's capacity to offer care gives priceless meaning and significance to life.

Caregivers—the roses among us—often trouble themselves for those who have made possible the life we all enjoy. They may care for those who have little or no voice. They also often give of themselves to the point of losing themselves in the process. They, who make the world beautiful one supported individual at a time, give to others and, at times, need someone to be there for them. So seek out a caregiver and offer your support.

Caregivers—before they go to their special place in Heaven—often do what no one else will do. When the supported individual is weak, the caregiver gives strength. When there is frustration, the caregiver is patient. When there is a lack of wisdom, the caregiver knows how to handle daily cares. When there is pain, the caregiver provides comfort. The caregiver helps the supported individual make it through each night and day, often like no one else can.

In my years of caregiving, both personally and professionally, many people have asked me how I have the patience for it. I tell them that the secret is to look at the job as you would trying to herd a group of wild cats into the back seat of a car.

You can see this task as horribly frustrating. Alternatively, you can find the humor in it. I recommend the latter perspective: laughter during caregiving may not add years to your life, but it will at least add life to your years.

Everyone knows that if the individual you support swallows your pile of quarters, there won't be any change for quite some time. Be patient. Never trade a mistake for a mistake, or an evil for an evil. There is no tolerance for revenge. You won't look good in prison stripes. I often wear mechanics' one-piece coveralls because they go well with other people's bodily fluids. You know you are a caregiver when going to the grocery store alone feels like a mini-vacation. If you run into another person at the store you know they are not a caregiver if they say they are calm and well-rested. If, however, they say they are agitated, they are becoming critical of others, they are having difficulty having fun, they are avoiding others, they are feeling depressed, they are feeling trapped in their responsibilities, they are feeling manipulated, they a feel guilty when they take time for themselves, and you think "Chuck Norris Approved" when they say they are a CNA, you can be pretty sure they are a caregiver. You are never too old to be a caregiver, unless people start saying they like your alligator shoes when you are barefoot, or when the sight of a pretty girl makes your pacemaker open your garage door, or when going bra-less pulls the wrinkles off your face, or when "getting a little action" means you ate enough fiber, or when getting lucky means you found your car in the parking lot, or when an "all-nighter" means you did not have to get up to go to the bathroom. Most caregivers are women. I often wonder what would have happened if instead of the Three Wisemen there were Three Wisewomen. I have pictures in my mind of them asking for directions, not knowing which way was West, finding Mary and Joseph somehow, telling Joseph to go boil some water, delivering the baby, and cleaning the stable—much more helpful than the Three Wisemen, who, after delivering some cool stuff, seem to do nothing but pose in their fancy robes.

To Offer Gratitude To One Of The Roses Among Us...

HumaNatureConnect Activity

Start-up Protocol

If this is not a day when you prefer to spend time in nature without an agenda, do the Heartwood Path Start-up Protocol found in the Appendix. Then return here to do the remaining portion of this activity:

Giving Praise To A Caregiver

Think about what you can do for a caregiver. Consider thanking them out loud at thanksgiving dinner, giving them a day off, sending something to them as a gift, burying the hatchet, sending flowers to them at work, offering a bonus, making a donation in their name, and saying thank you in person.

Follow-up Protocol

For best results, write down your impressions of this activity in your journal using the Heartwood Path Follow-up Protocol found in the Appendix. Afterwards, consider sharing your interpretations with others.

Heartwood Path Axioms

Key Assertions From Waypoint 5.12

5.12.1.

Be an inspired and inspiring caregiver.

5.12.2.

Caregivers raise hope as assuredly as the rising sun and do best when they manage at least two lives—the supported individual and their own.

5.12.3.

One's capacity to offer care gives priceless meaning and significance to life.

Nocturnal Pilgrimage 5.12

For best results, write down your impressions of each night's dreams in your journal using the Heartwood Path Dreaming Time Protocols found in the Appendix. Afterwards, consider sharing your Dream Tending with others.

The Natural Law Of Activity:

To get a reaction,
one has to go into action.

Achieving something requires doing something. Fulfill your dreams, goals, and desires by going into action. You have to act to receive.

Since we learn from our mistakes, any action is better than no action. Positive thoughts, making a To Do list, and creative visualization help to manifest what you want. Procrastination and not staying focused doesn't. Move the desire from your mind to the physical world by taking action. But not constantly.

Periodically, it is prudent to be inactive and to simply accept the status quo. Sometimes the best answer is no response. There has to be a balance between activity and inactivity. If you are too aggressive, become passive. Turn down the volume, if necessary. Don't be rigid or hurtfully domineering. If you are too passive, become active. Mind your speech so as not to offend. By allowing others to participate in decision-making processes, you will gains helpers, supporters, and friends. Greatness comes by balancing your own self-respect with being respectful of others. Feel free to say "no" when you do not want to do something for another person. Feel free to change your mind or your opinion. Express yourself. You will explode if you hold too much inside. Do not let others take advantage of your good nature.

Pertinent And Instructive Gems From My Dream Tending Journal

Continuing with my lucid dream, I asked the couple why they are seeking to visit quiet natural places.

Male Customer:

"They bring us peace and harmony."

Don:

"Do you just go there and listen with your ears or do you also use your eyes, noses, hands, and other sensing body parts?"

Male Customer:

"We use all of our senses, but it seems that we get the best rewards from the quiet places."

When the woman added the question "Did you know that there are more than six senses, that actually we share 49 more senses with all of nature?" I said, happy that she was participating in the conversation.

Don:

"No, tell me more!"

Female Customer:

"Well, here's some examples, the turtles and I share the sense of thirst, the plants and I can tell where the sun is without looking, and you and the bunnies have the procreative sense."

Don:

"Don't I ever!"

I was happy with where this dream was going.

Lesson Learned: when looking over the list of 54 natural senses, it becomes obvious that there is a sturdy and powerful position of alliance between each of the senses and their surroundings. This alignment is strapping, robust in its togetherness in a way that only happens when two entities or powers co-evolve. Given this match-up between a being's neurons and the outside stimulus being sensed—or, being more specific, between an eartHeart appreciating a flower—it is no wonder Beethoven said:

"How happy I am to be able to walk among the shrubs, the trees, the woods, the grass and the rocks! For the woods, the trees and the rocks give man the resonance he needs" (Williams, 2017, p. 117).

Jesus's recognition of the needs of his apostles (when they returned to Him exhausted, for example), his willingness to serve everyone (including the common people of Gennesaret, for example), and his call to rest (to his apostles just before the miracle of feeding the gathering crowd) tell me several important things that are useful to eartHearts:

1. It's important to be a keen observer of the needs of others.
2. It's OK to take a break and recover.
3. It is noble to serve all, tirelessly and without distinction.

4. Spending time alone in a quiet place is justified by the guidance, information, and healing that can be found under such circumstances.

Use these lessons as you do the job of an eartHeart by day and set yourself up for lucid dreaming at night. Both natural beings and lucid dreams are sources of inspiration, guidance, insight, and healing.

When ready, continue on your pilgrimage down the Heartwood Path by proceeding to the next waypoint, entitled "Good Care." Your progress continues both day and night. This will be even more true if you turn off your hand-held brain enhancer game and, instead of spending more time in front of another electronic screen, head outside and commune with nature for a better way to temper any cognitive decline caused by living mostly indoors in an urban area.

13

Good Care

CARE FOR YOURSELF AS A CAREGIVER, OR CARE FOR A CAREGIVER

A good caregiver will need to recognize the signs of stress. He or she will need to work to overcome being exhausted and worn out. He or she will need to work to overcome being resentful, stressed, and bitter. He or she will need to work to overcome feeling used and unappreciated. And he or she will need to work to overcome being financially overwhelmed and depleted.

To be a good caregiver, one will need to manage one's stress level, be realistic, give oneself credit, overcome occasional bouts of guilt, take breaks, accept that all situations change, and seek continued self-improvements through training and reflection. In addition to doing these things, one's ability to withstand being a caregiver is all a matter of perspective.

If you have a poopy view about life as a caregiver, think of the Heartwood Path as an "optorectomy" (a procedure that cuts the cord that has developed between your eyes and your rectum). In any event, don't be "Fed Up." That can only happen when Federal Express merges with UPS. Despite all that you will have to go through as a caregiver, do what nobody else will do. And do it in a way that nobody else can do. There is no time for burnout. The world needs your talents, full time and for a long time. Persevere. And be ethical.

The theme of this Heartwood Path book is ethics and certainly rules about how people ought to think and behave are important when giving good care to others. We will discuss nine ways caregivers ought to apply ethics in their work with others. We will also discuss many other tools caregivers ought to use: such as observation, communication, decision-making, and documentation. Along with these tools, the caregiver has the responsibility to respect the rights of the supported individual (as specified subsequently) and to understand and respond effectively to challenging behaviors, if any.

The topic here is how to do a better job giving care to supported individuals and how to better help others achieve a good quality of life—wherein the supported individual can make choices in their lives; have close relationships; live in a home where their is security, safety, and care; participate in recreational activities; and generally be satisfied with their lives.

To help others, the caregiver will need to be a partner, a teacher, an ambassador, an advocate, a supporter, but not a boss. Do not just follow the Golden Rule (treating others the way you want to be treated). Follow the Platinum Rule (treating others the way they want to be treated).

Caregiver or not, I encourage you to always check your balance. I am not speaking of your checking account. If you are a typical professional caregiver, you can count on that being low. I am referring to finding a balance between work and rest or recovery.

You have to take care of yourself or you cannot take care of others.

That statement was highlighted because it is the philosophical underpinning for the entire Heartwood Path course of study.

There is too much to say about caregiving for this book. We at Great Work! associates offer tutorials on caregiver ethics, the importance of communication and observation, and the rights of the supported individual. And Heartwood Path Publishing has a caregiver's manual that covers topics such as health issues, challenging behaviors, and reducing risk. Contact Don@heartwoodpath.com for help with caregiving.

To Prepare Yourself To Become A Caregiver ...

HumaNatureConnect Activity

Start-up Protocol

If this is not a day when you prefer to spend time in nature without an agenda, do the Heartwood Path Start-up Protocol found in the Appendix. Then return here to do the remaining portion of this activity:

Preparing To Become A Caregiver

Think about the suggestions listed previously about becoming a good caregiver. Determine who might need such assistance. Offer your help, when ready.

Follow-up Protocol

For best results, write down your impressions of this activity in your journal using the Heartwood Path Follow-up Protocol found in the Appendix. Afterwards, consider sharing your interpretations with others.

Heartwood Path Axioms

Key Assertions From Waypoint 5.13

5.13.1.

Care for yourself as a caregiver, or care for a caregiver.

5.13.2.

A good caregiver will need to manage one's stress level, be realistic, give oneself credit, overcome occasional bouts of guilt, take breaks, accept that all situations change, and seek continued self-improvements.

5.13.3.

You have to take care of yourself or you cannot take care of others.

5.13.4.

The supported individual has the same rights as everyone else.

Nocturnal Pilgrimage 5.13

For best results, write down your impressions of each night's dreams in your journal using the Heartwood Path Dreaming Time Protocols found in the Appendix. Afterwards, consider sharing your Dream Tending with others.

The Natural Law Of Consonance:

When something is out of kilter
occurrences restore
balance and harmony
to the situation.

Every experience is an opportunity to learn, and grow. Fear is a way of knowing that something is out of balance. It tells you that it is time to reflect. In doing so, you will likely realize that whatever you give to others is created for yourself, as well. When you share negativity, you receive negativity. Be sure to share positivity instead. That means to feel the love within yourself, share it with others unconditionally. Treat everyone with respect. Honor others with your tolerance, friendliness, and kindness. And focus on calmness rather than drama.

Pertinent And Instructive Gems From My Dream Tending Journal

Don:

"So it's not that you are going all over to treat your ears only to nature's silence,"

Female Customer:

"Nope, it's a treat to all of the senses."

Don:

"And not just the regular six."

Female Customer:

"That's right, why use such a small part of your capability?"

Lesson Learned: we all live under the same sky. We all benefit from the earth's offerings. There is an extra benefit when we remember our universality, when we reflect expansively, and when we participate, not only with our individuality, but also with our shared Humanity, our complete humaNature. We have revered traits because the universe has revered traits. Open all 54 doors of perception by using all of your senses daily. Doing so will let in the causes of happiness, the shareable traits, and the revered characteristics those who are open to nature use to prevail and persevere.

The Bible reports that people came to Jesus to be healed by touching his clothing. You can be a part of the continual living embodiment of the fringe on Jesus's cloak. Allow people to come to you to be healed through your growing knowledge of nature's healing powers. As you help people, be sure to stay humble. Do not lengthen the fringe on your clothes or otherwise make yourself appear special in any way. Helping others only to boost your own standing is hypocritical.

At the next waypoint, entitled "The Plunge," the topic switches from human care giving to environmental activism. While caregivers focus most on helping individual selves, environmental activist focus most on the collective self, the more-than-individual realm of the "Greater Self," often called "nature," the "environment" or the "universe."

14

The Plunge

BECOME AN ACTIVIST ON BEHALF OF THE GREATER SELF

Environmental activists see a need and do something about that need on behalf of people and the environment. Driven by passion and a vision of a better tomorrow, environmental activists tend to work on behalf of the many, including those still to come. Here is how to become an environmental activist:

1. Figure out what stirs your passions.
2. Educate yourself about the issue of concern.
3. Determine what you really want from your activism.
4. Find out if there are existing efforts to work on your cause.
5. Determine what you can do to help your new-found allies.
6. Find out who is responsible for the problem.
7. Learn from more experienced activists.
8. Stick to your guns.
9. Pick good issues, ones that capture the public's imagination. My mentor David Brower, for example, always worked on monumental issues and was successful because the public rallied behind his causes.

10. Always tell the truth.
11. In order to get the vote, you will have to do the work.
12. Do not expect or allow the government to take the lead. It is in the business of finding compromises or protecting the financial elites.
13. Make sure meetings are productive (see Heartwood Path Book: "Collectivos" for suggestions).
14. Educate yourself about how to work with the media, how to influence legislation, and how to monitor or influence administrative bodies, such as the U.S. Forest Service.
15. Determine your favorite method of activism, considering, for example whether you want to work by yourself or with a group.
16. Be prepared to volunteer. Most environmental activism is done by citizen amateurs.
17. Speak up about your opinions, being unhesitatingly bold yet patient.
18. Pass out fliers.
19. Set up information tables.
20. Practice armchair activism, using your computer, Facebook, Twitter, and the phone.
21. Sponsor an environmental speaker in your community.
22. Expect to encounter dissent. I thought when I became an environmentalist that everyone will love me for it. I was wrong.
23. Organize like-minded people through Facebook and by holding meetings.
24. Create subcommittees to divide up the work. The optimal size for leadership groups is between 8 and 15 people.
25. Have an affirmative vision and express it in ways the allay people's fear about change and job loss.
26. Keep an eye toward the future by thinking about what to do even after you complete your immediate campaign.
27. Pace yourself.
28. Raise money.

29. Convert being against something into being for something instead.
30. Live and act in synchrony with your conservation message or program.
31. Resolve conflicts and bridge differences.
32. Know your facts.
33. Mind your English.
34. Care.
35. Find like-minded people.
36. Create broad coalitions.
37. Use social media.
38. Remember that more people will follow a leader than will follow a cause.
39. As an activist, be a loving person; by which I mean be a person who has desire, believes in all possibilities, is realistic about what you yourself can do, is positive, experiments, is a keen observer, accepts responsibility, is interested in others, seeks positive companions, is present and enjoys life, stays active, lives a life that is their own to live and is not based on the expectations of others, keeps a journal, meditates, embraces change, allows themselves to be wrong, says "thank you," and avoids being phony.
40. Be creative.
41. Have fun with your activism.
42. Take on leadership roles.
43. When working with Congress on your issue, send emails to your member of Congress, make phone calls, generate letters, get to know the congressional aide, speak up at town hall meetings or candidates forums, meet face-to-face with your member of Congress, establish regular video meetings or conference calls, take your member of Congress to pertinent sites, get to know your member of Congress and top aides.
44. When working with the media, write a letter to the editor, generate an op-ed, meet face-to-face with the editorial board,

generate an editorial or an article in your local paper, organize a press conference, conduct a statewide media call, and work with TV producers to get the message out to the public.

45. To work with your community, organize a letter-writing party, speak to local groups, train a local community group in advocacy, hold good outreach meetings, organize a community action network, organize public site visits, raise money, build a coalition, and hold a community forum.

46. Persevere, the main topic of Heartwood Path Book: **Remeos**.

To Prepare Yourself To Be An Environmental Activist...

HumaNatureConnect Activity

Start-up Protocol

If this is not a day when you prefer to spend time in nature without an agenda, do the Heartwood Path Start-up Protocol found in the Appendix. Then return here to do the remaining portion of this activity:

Preparing To Be An Environmentalist

Fill out the chart below:

Questions To Ask Yourself Regarding Preparations For Environmental Activism	Your Answers To Preparatory Questions
What issue or issues stir your passion?	

What do you need to learn about your issue(s) of concern?

What do you want to get back from your activism (i.e: saving a place, fame, a paycheck, self-pride, companionship, a sense of accomplishment . . .)?

Who else is working on your issue(s)?

What can you do to help existing allies?

Who is responsible for causing the issue of concern?

Who are the experts in the topic(s) of your concern and what do you need to learn from them? Can you get them involved, if not already?

How will you know if you are "sticking to your guns?"

How, if at all, does the issue of concern capture the public's attention or imagination? If it does not, do you want to pick a new issue or can you reframe your issue to generate a stronger outcry amongst the public?

What are the five most significant
true facts about your issue of concern?

What work is needed to be accomplished before there is a resolution
of your issue? What part of this
work can you perform? Who can
you get to do the rest?

What will be the governments role
in the resolution of this issue?
Think in terms of regulators (from
agencies to police departments),
legislators, and the courts.

How often should you meet with
allies, who should attend meetings,
and how can you make the meetings both enjoyable and productive?

What do you need to learn that will
help you accomplish your environmental protection goals?

What is your favorite mode of
activism? Do you want to work
alone or with others? Do you want
to lead or follow?

How can you support yourself
while doing amateur activism? Are
you prepared to make some financial sacrifices?

How would you state your issue of concern in the boldest possible way? Or in the clearest possible way? Or in a way that garners the most support?

What would your best handout look like? Do you have the words, illustrations, photos, and design in mind? If not, work on a model of it now.

Where could you set up an information table? What do you need for that table? Who can help you?

How can you use social networking such as Facebook, Instagram, and Twitter?

Who could you bring to your community as a speaker on your issue of concern? Where would he or she speak? If you were to organize a conference on your issue of concern what would be its agenda and who would participate?

Who will be your likely dissenters? What are they apt to say? What will be your responses?

What is the contact information for twenty of your best supporters?

From your total list of supporters, how would you divide up the work? Who would you like to see in each of your subcommittees (which ought to have at least 8 and no more than 15 active partici- pants)? If you have 16 or more participants consider breaking the committee into two groups.

How would you respond to peoples' fears about job loss or other mat- ters?

How is your issue likely to play out over time? What will you do after the issue is resolved?

What pace of work suits you best?

What is your plan for raising money?

How can you frame your issue so that instead of being against some- thing you are for something?

What changes will you have to make so that you are living and acting in harmony with your issue of concern? How can you be the change you seek?

What will you likely have to do to build bridges and resolve conflict?

What are your ten best documented facts about your issue of concern? Make a list with references.

If not you, who is the best spokesperson for your issue of concern?

Who cares about your issue as much as you do?

To broaden your support base, who would be the members of your coalition or task force? What issues are you likely to encounter as you broaden the membership in your group?

If not you, who will be your leader that most people will want to follow?

How can you display your love and creativity during your activism?

What fun can you bring to the activism?

If not chairperson, what other leadership role would you like to have? What other roles are needed?

What skills do you need in order to best work with legislators, agencies, the media, and the public?

Other questions of your own?

Follow-up Protocol

For best results, write down your impressions of this activity in your journal using the Heartwood Path Follow-up Protocol found in the Appendix. Afterwards, consider sharing your interpretations with others.

Heartwood Path Axioms

Key Assertions From Waypoint 5.14

5.14.1.

Become an activist on behalf of the Greater Self.

5.14.2.

Driven by passion and a vision of a better tomorrow, environmental activists tend to work on behalf of the many, include those still to come.

5.14.3.

Figure out what stirs your passions.

Nocturnal Pilgrimage 5.14

For best results, write down your impressions of each night's dreams in your journal using the Heartwood Path Dreaming Time Protocols found in the Appendix. Afterwards, consider sharing your Dream Tending with others.

The Natural Law Of Explicitness:

Desires are obtained
only after
one's intentions
are clear.

Be focused and know what you want. Zero in on a goal and make it happen by giving it your undivided attention. Take small steps, if need be. To clear up confusion about what you want, make a pro/con list, set goals and deadlines, do something everyday to reach your goal, and disengage from distractions. Be specific and detailed.

Pertinent And Instructive Gems From My Dream Tending Journal

Male Customer:

"When all of the 54 doors of perception are open the cumulative impact is considerable."

Female Customer, shaking her head in amazement:

"It's magical! I feel pleased with a new-found sense of purpose. I feel like I'm on track. I have new and improved skills that I can use to bring beauty and

sustainability to the world. It has nothing to do with having and every-
thing to do with doing, tempered by simply being, so I won't burnout."

Don:

"Sounds good to me. But I imagine that there must be more to it than
simply visiting attractive natural areas. And what about the likelihood that
if your travel hobby catches on, there will not be enough wild places for
everyone to visit without destroying the amenities found there?"

Lesson Learned: Even if the acreage of suitable public land is substantially increased—a prospect that is far from assured—there would
still be a need for the right-to-roam on private lands (like they have
in United Kingdom, Sweden, Finland, and Norway) if we are going
to have access to enough appealing natural areas to accommodate the
quietly meditative visitors, especially those who want to take short
nature walks daily near their homes. With the right-to-roam freely
on private property—that is, with the right to walk, to camp, and
to build campfires on someone else's private land—visitors would be
able to do Heartwood Path-type activities on private land while being
prohibited from cutting timber or hunting game. Besides providing for
more space for HumanNatureConnect activities, the benefits of both
increasing suitable public lands and being allowed to roam on private
lands would include lower health-care costs, improved mental health,
and the promotion of fitness.

Generally, there is essentially no right to roam in the United
States. Landowners here are protected by the Constitution from any
"taking" without being compensated. With this background information, eartHearts are encouraged to look into possibilities of establishing
right-to-roam locations and legislation in their local areas. Also, urge
America's leading walking organization to work to establish the right
to roam, nationally or wherever possible: americawalks.org. Perhaps
landowners could be compensated for granting the right to roam by
receiving tax breaks, in the same way that landowners are compensated

for giving up their development rights for their important wildlife habitat. Don't laugh, it could happen.

We all know that humor is reason gone mad and comedy is a funny way of being serious. To those who do not like the interjection of humor along this path, don't worry you won't be subjected to any good one-liners here. I say: "he who laughs last thinks slowest."

Those who are traversing the Heartwood Path do so to improve themselves—to gather up more revered traits—so that they can play a bigger role in improving the world. Yes, things are bad; but don't be historical. It's not a thing of the past to worry about the future. The longer one waits, the bigger the job will be to make things right. I, for one, do not want to be around when Jesus comes back and reacts to the mess we have made.

Join the ranks of those working to make things better. To do so, uncork your imagination and bottle your reason. As you proceed along the path, don't do or drink to the extent that makes you look like the wrath of grapes.

Despite your trepidations about the depth or the length of the Heartwood Path, laugh at your foibles along the way. At least that way you will always be amused.

Seriously now, sleep well, dream, and tend to your dreams upon waking. When ready, move to the next point of discovery, a waypoint entitled "Positive Emotion."

15

Positive Emotion

BENEFIT FROM PASSING THROUGH THE GATEWAY TO THE STATE OF COHERENCE

Imagine that you are standing in front of a gate that blocks your headway along the Heartwood Path. Imagine that the key to open this gate is gratitude. Also imagine that there is a sign over this virtual gateway that says:

Coherence "is a psycho-physiological state characterized by increased emotional stability and by increased synchronization and harmony in the functioning of physiological systems" (McCarty, 1006, p. 2).

It is unlikely that one can pass through the gateway to coherence, or any gateway to valued traits, or any gateway to a magnificent future when one's feelings or emotions are felt as being "bad;" by which I mean, out of balance, negative, painful, and stress-producing. To move easily through this and the other gateways one needs "good" feelings and emotions—those that "reflect body states in which the regulation of life processes becomes efficient, or even optimal, free-flowing and easy" (McCarty, 1006, p. 3). What we are after along this portion of the Heartwood Path is a state of optimal functioning.

To pass through this gateway to optimal functioning requires a metaphorical "key" that, in reality, for us is the following information in this and the next paragraph. Like any good modern house key, our key has what locksmiths call "bittings"—those series of bumps on a typical key's blade. As you shall see, ours has three teeth. Each of the following three metaphorical teeth are actually summarized statements and quotes from the Heartmath Institute (McCarty, 2006) that together provide the necessary background information needed to understand "coherence:"

Three aspects of "coherence" are important for eartHearts to keep in mind:

1. Coherence is a distinctive organization of parts that relate to form an emergent whole—one that is "sustained and maintained over time," more than the sum of its parts and qualitatively different from the parts themselves. Certain conditions are necessary to achieve a coherent flow of behavior—conditions described in the next concept (McCarty, 2006, p. 5).

2. Coherence is a uniform pattern of cyclical behavior—an ordered distribution of energy in a waveform such as a sine wave ... The more stable the frequency, amplitude, and shape of the wave-form, the higher the degree of coherence. Coherence occurs when different oscillatory systems interact and there is "increased harmony in the rhythmic pattern of their interaction"—the topic of the next concept (McCarty, 2006, p. 5).

3. Coherence can occur as a result of the synchronized interactions among multiple systems, as when two or more waves are locked together in their interaction (examples include when a musical chord that is composed of notes of different frequencies resonate as a harmonious sound or when "two or more of the body's oscil-latory systems, such as respiration and heart rhythms, become entrained and oscillate at the same frequency" (McCarty, 2006, p. 5). Entrainment—the synchronization of one frequency to another—becomes more likely when "coherence is increased in a

single system" and this contagious synchrony of frequencies can "cause cross-coherence in the activity of other related systems" (McCarty, 2006, p. 5).

Throughout one's body, "information is encoded in waveforms of energy as patterns of physiological activity. Neural, chemical, electromagnetic, and oscillatory pressure wave patterns are among those used to encode and communicate biologically relevant information" (McCarty, 2006. p. 5). Changes in the patterns of input to the brain "cause significant changes in physiological function, perception, cognition, emotion, and intentional behavior" (McCarty, 2006, p. 5).

Different emotions are "associated with distinct patterns of physiological activity" (McCarty, 2006, p. 5) "This is the result of a two-way process by which, in one direction, emotions trigger changes in the autonomic nervous system and hormonal system, and in the other direction, specific changes in the physiological substratum are involved in the generation of emotional experience" (McCarty, 2006, p. 5).

More than the main pump for blood through one's body, the heart plays a central role in the generation and transmission of system-wide information essential to the body's functioning as a coherent whole. It is important for eartHearts to understand that:

1. the heart is the most consistent and dynamic generator of rhythmic information patterns in the body;
2. the heart has an intrinsic nervous system that is a sophisticated information encoding and processing center that operates independently of the brain;
3. the heart functions in multiple body systems and is thus uniquely positioned to integrate and communicate information across systems and throughout the body; and
4. the heart possesses by far the most extensive communication network with the brain. Input from the heart not only "affects the homeostatic regulatory centers in the brain, but also affects the activity of higher brain centers involved in perceptual,

cognitive, and emotional processing, thus in turn affecting many and diverse aspects of our experience and behavior" (McCarty, 2006, p. 6).

The rhythmic pattern of heart activity is directly associated with the subjective activation of distinct emotional states. Heart rhythm patterns reflect changes in emotional states, in that it co-varies with emotions in real time. There are "strong differences between quite distinct rhythmic beating patterns that (are) readily apparent in the heart rhythm trace and that directly (match) the subjective experience of different emotions" (McCarty, 2006, p. 6). The pattern of the heart's activity is "a valid physiological indicator of emotional experience and . . . this indicator (is) reliable when repeated at different times and in different populations" (McCarty, 2006, p. 6)

Researchers at the Heartmath Institute have shown that "the natural fluctuations in heart rate, known as heart rate variability (HRV) is a product of the dynamic interplay of many of the body's systems. These same researchers "found that it is the pattern of the heart's rhythm that is primarily reflective of the emotional state. Furthermore, the Heartmath Team found that it is the rhythm, rather than the rate, that is most directly related to emotional and physiological dynamics (McCarty, 2006, p. 6).

Researchers have documented a wide array of effects of positive emotions on cognitive processing, behavior, health and well-being. Positive emotions have been found to broaden the scope of perception, cognition, and behavior, thus enhancing faculties such as creativity and intuition. While reason is sure to be improved by greater cognition, notice that reason is not singled out as a benefit of positive emotions. My former mentor, the late and great conservationist David Brower, believes that reason "is probably incredibly junior to intuition, but few people yet think so. It would help if everyone would look hard at the progress reason has wrought" (Sewall, 1999, p. 251).

Sustained positive emotions such as appreciation, care, compassion, and love show up as a smooth, sine-wave-like pattern in the heart's rhythm. This smooth graphic illustration of one's heart rhythm depicts increased order in the nervous system. This positive state is transmitted externally where it interacts with other energy fields in the environment. Over the eons of living mostly outdoors, our evolution has made us humans well-adapted to picking up these beneficial transmissions as they beam through the natural environment. This is one reason most people tend to feel best when they are outdoors and stressed when they are indoors.

Two common indoor preoccupations—the television and the Internet—create and amplify stress waves, causing a background feeling of unease. Failing to cope with this uneasiness causes unrest in society (Institute of HeartMath).

"This increased stress is causing an increasing number of people to look to their hearts for guidance to adjust to the pace of change, manage the stress, and make more peaceful adjustments. The Global Coherence Initiative, described in detail below, is a scientifically-based initiative to facilitate heart rhythm coherence and heart-based living." According to the Institute of HeartMath,

"Many people recognize that their meditations, prayers, affirmations and intentions can and do affect the world. Researchers suggest that these activities can have even more transformative and lasting impact by adding heart coherence to the process" (Institute of HeartMath).

Launched by the nonprofit Institute of HeartMath, the Global Coherence Initiative is designed to help individuals and groups work together, synchronistically and strategically to increase the impact of their efforts to create positive global change. Its purpose is also to increase individual coherence, shift the planetary consciousness baseline from self-centeredness to earth-centered (Institute of HeartMath).

Heartmath's Global Coherence Monitoring System (GCMS) will utilize more than a dozen sensors located around the world. These sensors will enable a new level of scientific inquiry into the relationship between the earth's magnetic field, collective human emotions and behaviors, and planetary changes (Institute of HeartMath).

Author Jack Canfield, founder of the Transformational Leadership Council, calls the Global Coherence Initiative "perhaps the greatest experiment in the history of the world" (Institute of HeartMath). Here's why:

The research of Dr. Elizabeth Rauscher and Dr. William Van Bise has led to some significant findings. For example, two or three weeks prior to earthquakes or volcanic eruptions, the earth's magnetic field changes, suggesting that a multi-station monitoring system could predict earthquakes and volcanic eruptions. Not only did Drs. Rauscher and Van Bise predict the cataclysmic eruption of Mount St. Helens in Washington, in the year and a half following the eruption, they predicted 84 percent of the seismic activity occurring within a 100 square mile area around a single detector. This finding alone would justify the development of a global monitoring system, but there are even more important reasons for doing so.

"The scientific community," according the the Institute of Heart-Math, " is just beginning to appreciate how the fields generated by living systems and the ionosphere interact with one another. For instance:

1. "the earth and the ionosphere generate a symphony of frequencies ranging from 0.01 hertz to 300 hertz, and some of the large resonances occurring in the earth's fields are in the same frequency range as those of the human heart and brain" (Institute of HeartMath);

2. "changes in the earth's magnetic field are associated with changes in brain and nervous system activity" (Institute of HeartMath);

3. "changes in geomagnetic conditions affect the rhythms of the heart more strongly than all the physiological functions studied so far" (Institute of HeartMath);

4. "people's brainwaves can synchronize with the rhythm of the electromagnetic waves generated in the earth's ionosphere" (Institute of HeartMath);

5. "emotions not only create coherence or incoherence in our bodies, but, like radio waves, also radiate outward and are detected by the nervous systems of others in our environment" (Institute of HeartMath);
6. "human consciousness and emotionality create or interact with a global field, which affect the randomness of these electronic devices" (Institute of HeartMath); and
7. "two National Oceanic and Atmospheric Administration (NOAA) space weather satellites monitoring the earth's geomagnetic field also displayed a significant spike at the time of the September 11th attack and for several days thereafter, indicating the stress wave possibly caused by mass human emotion created modulations in the geomagnetic field" (Institute of Heartmath).

Researchers theorize that when large numbers of humans respond to a global event with a common emotional feeling, the collective response can affect the activity in the earth's field. Providing the evidence that collective coherent intentions have an impact is a purpose of the Global Coherence Initiative. If this is proven to be the case then those involved with the Global Coherence Initiative will be called upon to "send coherent heart care to the people" in adversely affected areas "for a specified amount of time to help reduce the suffering and negativity" (Institute of HeartMath).

The Global Coherence Initiative may prove to be vitally important to the health and future of our planet. The Initiative will help senders and receivers of emotional vibrations get more out of the rhythmic reception and bring more to the heart-felt transmission because senders and receivers will have a methodology for participating more fully in the whole earth's communication field.

The work of the Institute of Heartmath demonstrates the link between individual happiness and the vibrational state of the world. We simply have to become coherent so that we can be suitably prepared to help make a better world. We shall now present specific ways to do so.

To A Smooth Emotional Sine Wave...

HumaNatureConnect Activity

Start-up Protocol

If this is not a day when you prefer to spend time in nature without an agenda, do the Heartwood Path Start-up Protocol found in the Appendix. Then return here to do the remaining portion of this activity:

Experiencing Coherence

Balance your autonomic nervous system, inhibit your stress response, enhance your cognitive performance, normalize your blood pressure, stabilize your mood, reduce anger, put a check on any depression or anger, and balance your adrenal glad hormone levels by taking the following three steps from Steven Templin of Inner Balance Consulting:

"Step One: HEART FOCUS

Focus your attention very gently around your heart in the center of your chest. You may want to gently rest your hand over your heart to help you to maintain focus. While noticing sensations and feelings around your heart make no attempt to analyze, change or fix anything. Simply be aware. If your mind drifts simply return to noticing around your heart with an attitude of patient, respectful attention.

Step Two: HEART BREATHING

As you continue to focus on the area around your heart, sense your breath flowing in and out of that area. Allow your breath to be soft, smooth and rhythmical. Find a natural inner rhythm that feels good to you. Again, if your attention drifts, that's o.k., simply return to the awareness of your heart and breath.

Step Three: HEART FEELING

Continue to breathe with an awareness of your heart. As you do, allow yourself to appreciate any good or pleasant feelings. You can allow yourself to appreciate any sense of ease, relaxation, or calm that is available to you. You may also focus on a feeling of appreciation, care, or gratitude that's connected to a person, pet, (we will add "natural being") or place that touches your heart in a positive way. Again, if your attention from this feeling experience drifts away, simply return calmly and patiently" (Templin Website).

There are more Heartmath Coherence Activities yet to come.

Follow-up Protocol

For best results, write down your impressions of this activity in your journal using the Heartwood Path Follow-up Protocol found in the Appendix. Afterwards, consider sharing your interpretations with others.

Heartwood Path Axioms

Key Assertions From Waypoint 5.15

5.15.1.

Benefit from passing through the gateway to the state of coherence—a beneficial and uniform pattern of cyclical behavior.

5.15.2.

It is unlikely that one can pass through the gateway to a magnificent future when one's feelings or emotions are out of balance, negative, painful, and stress-producing.

5.15.3.

Positive emotions have been found to broaden the scope of perception, cognition, and behavior, thus enhancing faculties such as creativity and intuition.

5.15.4.

More than the main pump for blood through one's body, the heart plays a central role in the generation and transmission of system-wide information essential to the body's functioning as a coherent whole.

Nocturnal Pilgrimage 5.15

For best results, write down your impressions of each night's dreams in your journal using the Heartwood Path Dreaming Time Protocols found in the Appendix. Afterwards, consider sharing your Dream Tending with others.

The Natural Law Of Accomplishment:

One has to
decide what success means
in order to achieve it.

While one's chief purpose in life is to reconnect with the core spiritual being, a main secondary goal is required for a satisfactory life. It usually requires the releasing of control to reach one's main secondary purpose. Without force or constant struggle, work to align your everyday vibration with your higher secondary purpose enough so that your frequency is pulled upward and falls into synchrony with the universal rhythm. This universal entrainment results in astonishing joy, growth, and fulfillment.

You have reached Gladandgreen Junction when your purposes are in synchrony with the universal vibration and you feel love, peacefulness, joy, gratitude, the helpers high, a desire to fight injustice, and a measure of clairvoyance. You are now a prophet, a secular saint, driven persistently and easily to stand up and take others with you to your vision. You are now a worthy manifestation of "the promised land." Expect this arrival, and it will be so. It may require pivots. Take them in stride. Make way for a new existence. You will have to work hard, be strong, and never give up. You can do it.

Pertinent And Instructive Gems From My Dream Tending Journal

Apparently, I was wanting to dream about being in nature so I lucidly directed the dream to have the couple leave my printshop, get in an argument, break up, and have the woman accompany me on, as I have often done in real life, a long canoe trip down the Missouri portion of the Missouri River.

As we were about to embark the woman—whom I now know as "Kim," with some trepidation, asked:

Kim:

"Are those whirlpools I see?"

Don:

"Nope, I replied, those are called 'boils.' They are just the river water bouncing off a submerged rock or something. Totally harmless."

Kim:

"Where will we camp?"

Don:

"On sand bars, giant sandy beaches."

Kim:

"How will we cook our food."

Don:

"Using some of the tons of firewood on the beaches, we will build nice bonfires."

Kim:

"What about the barges? Are they a worry?"

Don:

"There are not many of them. They are loud and cannot sneak up on you. And the river is huge. There is plenty of room for both big commercial vessels and little canoes."

Kim:

"You're not gonna lecture about the benefits of silence, are you? Just kidding."

Don:

"You're safe with me."

Lesson Learned: Facts inform. Emotions motivate.

"If lucid dreams do not come to you rapidly, perhaps you need to work more on putting yourself into "a state of attentive relaxation, with alert mind and deeply related body . . . Lucid dreaming requires concentration, which is nearly impossible to achieve with a distracted mind and a tense body" (LaBerge and Rheingold, 1990. p. 53). To do so, LaBerge and Rheingold suggest that you lie down on a firm surface, deepen and pay attention to your breathing, progressively tense one muscle after another (each for five to ten seconds), relax all the muscle groups of your body, and let go of all tension (LaBerge and Rheingold, 1990, p. 53-54). A more elaborate relaxation technique is provided in the next Nocturnal Pilgrimage section.

With these suggestions and your impressions from the previous lessons recanted in your mind as you drift off to sleep, dream and then, upon waking, tend to your dreams. When ready, turn to "Role Models," the next waypoint. Here's some good advice for your next connection-experience outings.

Invest a bit more in your trips to the natural places by perhaps walking the extra mile so that you can find yourself far away from picnickers, campers, partiers and any unwanted noise that would distract you from your upcoming connection experience. Your best results—which may be optimal functioning, healing, or specific insights—will mostly likely arise where there is both solitude and ecological diversity.

16

Role Models

FIND MODELS IN NATURE WITH VALUED PERSONALITY TRAITS

The Natural Systems Thinking Process does not directly create valued personality traits. But it does lead to optimal functioning. In this state, one is better prepared to adopt and utilize valued personality traits. Soon I will provide some examples of ways nature experiences have given me an opportunity to listen to my own heart regarding how animals, plants, and rocks provide models of valued personality traits. Look over the two sections that follow—"**Find Paragons in Nature**" and "**Learn Lessons About Valued Personality Traits From Nature.**" From the information you glean from these sections, pick the traits you would like to have prior to going into action as an individual—a topic covered in Heartwood Path Book Six. The more valued traits you adopt for yourself, the greater will be your chances of success in whatever you do in your life. Valued traits may also direct you to make choices in your actions that lead to:

1. personal happiness,
2. an expansion of perspective that includes compassion for all sentient beings, and

3. a protected environment—each being purposes of the Heart-wood Path.

Find Paragons In Nature

I will begin with a detailed description of few of my favorite animal-inspired lessons about personality traits and then continue with a summary description of a wide array of animal-inspired lessons. To obtain lessons from my descriptions is a linear exercise—a teaching that forms a direct line from my written interpretations of animal lessons to your learning about nature-inspired lessons regarding the development of valued personality traits. This linearity is fine, but it only represents an extremely narrow aspect of the total communication that nature can provide to those who know how to listen—a skill described in this series of books.

I strongly urge the reader to learn from my linear descriptions—which Cohen would call five-legged teachings (as in a book writer calling a wolf's tail his fifth leg) but to also open up your heart-felt receptivity to nature so that you can become attuned to the whole message which would be both my so-called "five-legged" descriptions (found immediately below) and your own NSTP-influenced observations in nature which you are encouraged to trust (Cohen calls these NSTP-influenced observations "four-legged" descriptions). The goal here is not to teach you that the dogs tail is not its fifth leg. The goal is to get you in the habit of making nine-legged descriptions which utilize both five-legged linear learnings (as from scientific textbooks) and four-legged non linear learning's (from your own experiences made more heart-felt by the Natural Systems Thinking Process).

What you are about to read may be instructive (and helpful for the specific purpose of using nature to inspire valued personality traits) but remember it is a vastly narrowed bit of the whole chorus of voices nature presents to those who know how to listen. The wider conversation is nature *fabling*—speaking as if it were so. Through her highly symbolic and metaphorical presentation, Nature presents an endless variety of messages that can be interpreted in endless ways.

If one engages in open-hearted communication with Nature, her poly-rhythmic message-embedded communications lead to optimal functioning. In this state of coherence one is made refined enough to become more competent, to glean more information, and to act more appropriately during one's next experience or set of subsequent experiences.

I will now present some five-legged linear lessons and later in this book I will present a way for you to obtain more of, as the famous radio announcer Paul Harvey repeatedly says, "the rest of the story"—the four-legged non-liner part that is far too non-verbal for the radio or print media. In this way, you will have a holistic nature-inspired nine-legged linear and nonlinear methodology that can be used to bring forth for yourself and others a more magnificent future.

Learn Lessons About Valued Personality Traits From Nature

Humans have the capacity to exhibit many valuable personality traits. In this section I will take the lesson from Romans 1:20, which states:

"For since the creation of the World God's invisible qualities— the eternal power and divine nature—have been clearly seen, being understood from what has been made, so that men are without excuse."

I will also discuss the way certain animals can provide important lessons about personality traits. Then, at the end of this section, I will present an activity wherein the participant can look for examples of other personality traits not mentioned in the next subsections.

Ants And Grasshoppers

In the Fall of 2010 I gained (as noticed by my continued attraction to the ant colony) the little critters' permission to "go to the ants" and consider its ways so I could, as promised in the Bible, "be wise" (Proverbs 6:6-8). Watching the tiny black ants carrying food in and wastes out of their underground home, it was difficult to not psychologically overlay on top of my physical sensations both this directive from the Bible and Aesop's fable "The Ant and the Grasshopper." Given the time of the year it was predictable that, as I watched the tiny ants, grasshoppers would be flying about in my grass.

Reading my words here about what I learned while watching these frenetic workers is a five-leg linear lesson: the ants work hard and survive the winter while the grasshopper dies soon after securing the continuation of its genetic heritage by laying eggs. The obvious moral: it is best to prepare for the days of necessity. While watching the scurrying of these tiny ants I could not detect any grumbling. Each ant, with no commander in sight, seemed to portray itself as a "servant leader." Watching them I could not help but feel that they feel proud of themselves and work with no regrets. This is a predictable linear lesson, one that I may or may not have generated without also reading the Bible and Aesop's Fables. Watching the ants was a simple, predictable, linear lesson that seemed to be generated from watching the scurrying of the ants and processing the visual signals through my brain: a direct flow from the watching of working ants to the creation of a simple human concept: prepare for times of need.

As I sat with my ant neighbors for about half an hour I noted (but detached myself from my thinking) and focused almost exclusively on the sensations in my body from the feelings being generated by the arrival of subtle emotions: a flushness in my face that indicates apprehensiveness and a heat in my chest and arms that typically manifests itself when I feel scorn. These were surprising, nonlinear, unpredicted, emotional feelings. They were based on a multiple-meaning symbol (the scurrying of ants and grasshoppers) that triggered one of my natural senses—rational thinking—which, in turn, narrowed down the vast array of symbolic meanings into a single sign: the ants told me that I scorn myself for not working more with a swarm of others. As I continued to watch I felt my limbs grow heavy as I shamed myself into not being more ant-like. I continued this self-abuse until I felt that out-of-breath sensation that, for me, goes with exasperation.

Had I limited myself to linear learning, the ants would have conveyed the long-established lesson about preparing for times of need and such thoughts may have left me feeling uneasy. But, by also paying attention to my feelings I learned that I would feel better about myself if I too would work with a swarm of hard workers. For sixteen years I worked with a highly-functional team and, after leaving this post to pursue my writing interests, I have worked largely alone. I did not realize until I encountered those ants that, well beyond the obvious mental extrapolation about working hard to prepare for times of need, I was also feeling the body sensations that accompany self-scorn and even shame. These sensations, however, were not debilitating as they came mixed with feelings of sentimentality, caring, and a bit of zeal as I began to feel the joys that might be had when I do begin again to work with an ant-like swarm of eco-psychologists we have been calling "eartHearts." Instead of leaving me feeling tormented, disgusted, guilty, or anxious, the feeling-full nature lesson left me with a host of sensations that seemed to leave me in a better state of mental, physical, emotional, and social functioning, characterized by:

1. expansiveness in the lungs, indicating elation;
2. a sense of thickness between my ears, indicating amazement;
3. and a nervous energy that made me want to walk around, indicating eagerness, optimism, and hope.

Being happy about the results that came from gaining consent from the natural attraction (in this case, the ants), I thought, as a way to make a comparison, I would attempt to see what would happen if I lingered with an unattractive aspect of nature and, therefore, did not have consent for the nature-to person connection experience.

Hornets

There was once a spot in my grass that if I was not careful I would, when cutting the grass, be stung by hornets. This happened repeatedly and it is a very unattractive situation. There is nothing warm and fuzzy about a hornet. They look mean. They chase you and sting you. It hurts a lot. But I live with their presence, thinking that they have to have some valid purpose in nature. Despite my otherwise humanitarian leanings, I cannot sit close to that hornet's nest without breaking out in a sweat (an indication of fear) and a rapid heart beat (an indication of anger). That is about it. Not much linear learning and certainly very little in the way of a symbolic "Ah-Ha" moment. Without attraction, the payback for spending time in nature was greatly diminished, if not eliminated. To overcome such feelings of diminishment, I am frequently driven to spend time with one of my all-time favorite natural attractions: the otters near Greer Spring Branch in the Ozarks of Southern Missouri.

River Otters

Few actions in nature recharge my batteries better than spending time with river otters while swimming in or canoeing on a clear free-flowing stream. No child at recess has ever experienced more fun than otters apparently have most of the time. In the winter I see them body-sliding down river banks. In the summer, I have seen them following my canoe apparently just for the thrill of experiencing something novel. They never seem wanting for food or shelter. They appear to be care-free. They seem largely locked in a playful attitude. As a former aquatic athlete, I am always impressed with their comfort in the water, their skill at swimming, and their ability to move objects from otter-to-otter in what seems like their own makeshift version of water polo. From this description, it is not a surprising stretch of the imagination that the vivid linear lesson from otters is typically the importance of having fun. That is what enters my mind, at least. But what happens when you become mindful and, instead of attaching yourself to thoughts about otters, you put thinking aside and focus on feeling?

Feelings that arise when I am with otters have to do with the release of tears that occurs from sheer joy, a nice feeling of warmth that overtakes you when feeling love, and a shakiness of legs that comes from utter empathy. Sometimes I feel like I have become the otter. I feel its movements, the chill of the water, the crackle of leaves as it runs along shore, the touch of its partner's fur. These are all positive sensations, occasionally broken by a very harsh imposition on my feelings.

When I occasionally see a steel-jaw trap in an intermittent stream near the river—trapping of otters is legal in Missouri—I get a lump in my throat, my breathing quickens and deepens, and I clinch my teeth while I steal the trap and hide it deeply in the trash bag I carry to remove trash from the riverway. When my positive feelings about the otters are mixed with my angry feelings a swirl of emotions arises which is confusing, distracting, and altogether unproductive. Until these sensations settle into a feeling of quiet resolve, indicated by the narrowing of my eyes, a furrowing of the brow, and a stiffness in my neck, I am prone to throwing equipment around in the canoe, slapping the water with my canoe blade, and engaging other ridiculous behaviors that do not impress people or otters alike.

Prior to taking additional anti-otter trapping actions (both obedient and disobedient) I now decide to unleash my best optimal functioning by seeking consent to have a connection experience with my otter friends. On one occasion, I sat in my canoe at the base of a huge root mass from a Sycamore tree, just feeling my sensations as the otters peaked out from the roots and occasionally swam under my canoe, apparently just to get a look at me from all angles. Soon the conflicting feelings—of love for the otter and hatred of the trapper—became reconciled as I got this relaxing feeling that my sense of reason interpreted to mean I am convinced that the otters can take care of themselves, that I am not solely responsible for their welfare, and that from a wider perspective that includes the trapper and the whole river scene life goes on with or without my involvement. Given the arousal of the embracing feeling of calmness, as a result of the NSTP nature connection experiences I have with otters, I continue to feel kindly towards the otters, I mentally view the trappers with less contempt—they are, after all, simply trying to protect their commercial fishing businesses—and, instead of stealing more traps I simply spring them with a stick and leave a rather polite, apologetic and explanatory note. Thus, I achieve a more optimum state of functioning—I am less angry, I am less distracted, I become a good model for the cause of non-violent civil disobedience, I achieve a greater sense of self-worth, and I am even more resolved to help in ways that help both otters and trappers alike, ways that do not compromise my ethics (such as writing letters to the state legislators about allowing some limited trapping but limiting it in streams heavily used for nature-oriented recreation) and, as a possible small consolation, one of my beloved otters—perhaps even the one that was barking at me playfully from under the root mass at river's edge— is spared being caught in a trap, at least for another day.

Had I not had my NSTP connection experience, I would have likely either done nothing about the traps—and felt impotent in doing so little—or stole the traps—and felt a sense of guilt. The nonlinear experience that occurred as a result of me focusing on my feelings— the narrowing of the eyes which I have learned indicates an awareness of a solution and the willingness to carry it out—enabled me to arrive at a more complex, more unanticipated, more ethical, more attractive, and more expansive solution. Doing so, not only enabled me to model better behavior it also simply felt good (as indicated by the ease of my breathing) and it felt right (as indicated by my upright posture). I became better prepared for whatever was to be my next experience. To make sure that the resultant better functioning as a result of NSTP nature experiences with the otters is not a fluke, I previously frequently opened up my feeling to . . .

Horses

Having been a barn manager for my family's horse breeding business (we had, among other horses, the two-time Paso Fino Grand National Pleasure Stallion) I am familiar and empathetic towards horses. While paying a visit to a local equine therapy center, where I once did an internship for a graduate degree, I decided to linger with a few horses out in the pasture and engaged in an NSTP activity.

My related linear message, like most linear messages, is simple and direct: horse love to run and, seeing that, people can become more motivated to spend more time exercising. Exercise makes the horses feel better both physically and emotionally and typically active physical activity does the same for humans. My experience as a barn manager tells me that horses also like to work. They seem eager to be trained, rode, and exercised. So what can be gained from the non-linear part of the "conversation" that occurs between people and horses? That question requires an attunement to one's feelings in the presence of a horse like I did one day at the equine therapy center.

For over an hour I stood, as I am prone to do, in the large pasture with a herd of horses. When I moved closer they moved away. When I stood still, a few of them approached me. There was no verbal communication between us. I chose not to use my words, some of which they may or may not have been trained to understand. I watched their movements as they did mine. Then, once I felt safe in focusing on my feelings rather than my thoughts of being trampled or of being thought of as crazy for standing out in a field with the herd, I sensed that my attraction to feeling the sensations in my body while focusing my awareness on the closest horse was sign of consent to engage in the connection experience. I began to mirror the actions of the closest horse—attempting to cock my ears to hear better in various directions, stomping my feet as if attempting to gain more attention, shifting my hind-quarters as the horse flicked its tail (which always encouraged a slight smile—from me, that is). Slowly, I became less attached to my thinking and began to focus more on what felt like intuitive feelings. Gradually, I felt like I was a part of the herd (I no longer felt separate or odd); like them, I became ever-vigilant for unknown predators (the hair on my neck stood up for no reason); and, as evidence by my feeling of openness in my chest, I was eager to exchange vibes.

In doing so, thoughts about the value of exercise, the breed of the horses, and what people thought of me communing with horses, gave way rather unexpectedly. Unanticipated messages are one of the hallmarks of the Natural System Thinking Process, along with complexity, variety, and depth of non-linear communication and heart-centered knowing. Instead of attaching myself to my thoughts I became aware of my ease of breathing that, for me, goes along with confidence (a sense of assurance that I had a more intuitive way of feeling the knowledge I acquired). I also felt the raising of my eyebrows—a physical sensation that arises along with the realization of an intuitive heart-felt knowing (but not mentally understanding how I could know such things). Lastly, I experienced the gracefulness of my walking, a gate that simultaneously occurred with the sense that I am somehow acceptable despite periodic thoughts of not mattering (a stride that was not a false display but a naturally self-secure gate). By tapping into the feelings of the horses that coincided with their various obvious and subtle movements, I trust that I was feeling the horses energy vibrations and, by natural extension, the world accepting me, not for what I do, but for who I am. That felt a lot better (and in a nonlinear fashion bigger and deeper, and more surprising) than the notions I had when thinking linearly and narrowly of the horses as models for the importance of human exercise.

By starting in a sense of mindfulness (during which time one focuses on awareness of feelings, the action of breathing, and refrains from attaching themselves to passing thoughts) or by starting a simple linear concept (such as the idea that horses remind us to exercise) one can, with some practice, move to a mode of nonlinear communication with natural attractions that is marked by deep, unanticipated, diverse heart-felt knowings. Below are some examples of linear knowings. Note that they are non-symbolic, free of fabling, and not surprising. Combine these linear knowings with actual experiences outdoors in nature and one will experience the power that comes from a combination of linear and nonlinear knowing.

Other Animals

In addition to the animals highlighted above, there are numerous other traits that humans can learn about by perceiving wildlife. To be loyal, for example, look to the dog. As we all know, a good breed of dog is a cross between a pit bull and a retriever. That way if it bites your leg off it will bring it back to you. Most dogs are faithful, dependable and dedicated. Likewise, be loyal to your commitments, careful about who you are loyal to, and never-ending in your fidelity. To be a team-player, look to the bald eagle. Males and females each do their part and subordinate their own interests to the efficiency of the family unit. They divide up the work load, with the smaller male finding nest materials and the larger female actually building the nest. While the female spends more time on the nest, both prospective parents take time incubating the eggs. As one eagle sits on the eggs, the other maintains a vigil on a nearby branch or searches for food. Both are involved in feeding the young. To be hardworking, look to the beaver; which constantly works to stabilize his dam projects. To be perceptive, look to the solitary bobcat; who spends enough time by itself to hone its perceptive skills which it uses to pay close attention to all that goes on around him. To be patient, look to the grizzly bear, patiently waiting for spring during hibernation and waiting for salmon to fly into their mouths at small waterfalls. To be charismatic, look to the way the elder grey-backed male gorilla commands respect without the need for violence. To be ambitious, look at the way a hedgehog roles over on soft fruit and spears it with its quills and then returns home with a feast. To be bright, notice how a fox can think outside of the box to make the most of its circumstances. To be gregarious, watch a pack of coyotes communicate before the hunt and reestablish ties to each other after the hunt. To be decisive, watch the sure-footed rhinoceros chase a Toyota Land Cruiser (most will need to watch this one on TV). To be properly opportunistic, look to the tree. Taking whatever course is available to them, a tree always seeks the light. In a similar way, seek the light of truth and knowledge. Substitutes leave you hollow and ill-prepared for storms in life. Like a tree, turn light into energy and grow solid and tall year after year. To be helpful, imagine how an elephant can bring down a tree so the small ones in the herd can eat the tender leaves. To demonstrate loyalty, mimic the actions of the members of a wolf pack. To be straight-forward, watch a bighorn ram directly and decisively butt heads with its opponent. To be focused on the present, notice how the horse is constantly alert to events and circumstances in its surroundings. To have confidence, look to the cat eyeing up a jump from a branch of a tree. To be observant, watch a mountain lion patiently eyeing its prey. To be kind or generous, look at the way a doe tends its foal. To have bearing, look to the goose navigating at night during its migrations. To be courageous. watch a squirrel jump from the narrow limbs of one tree to the thin twigs of another. To be unselfish, look to the buffalo which always puts the herd ahead of self. To have endurance, consider the arctic tern which migrates annually from Pole to Pole. To have tact, watch a skunk deftly and diplomatically convince whatever is threatening it to back down and thus avoid the need for spraying. To be devoted, look to the honey bee. They share food, clean the house, feed the babies, remove waste, defend the family, produce a surplus, fix and repair the house, respect and honor their parents (especially the Queen Bee), take responsibility, improve the world around them (by spreading pollen) and even live in a house full of sisters without pulling their antlers out. To be fearless, look into the eyes of a jaguar drinking water from a river that is infested with crocodiles. To be competent look to the spider. This order of arthropods builds all sorts of nests. The strands in these nests are pound for pound stronger than steel yet nearly as light as air. They model competency by taking an idea (the inherent shape of their own species' webs), work hard to build a final product, make repairs as necessary, and secure their goal—their prey. To have commitment, look to the bull, stubborn and committed to the herd. To be flexible, think about the octopus. This animal can change its body shape to fit into all sorts of hiding places and change its color to allude predators. To be persistent, look to the badger. Once determined to achieve a goal a badger will incessantly carry on. Its persistence and tenacity shows the world that it means business. These are not all of the human traits.

To An Unexpected Mirro ...

HumaNatureConnect Activity

Start-up Protocol

If this is not a day when you prefer to spend time in nature without an agenda, do the Heartwood Path Start-up Protocol found in the Appendix. Then return here to do the remaining portion of this activity:

Learning About Personality Traits From Beings In Nature

This activity will explore some of the lessons humans can learn about personality traits from animals not listed in the preceding text. Look around to see how many natural beings you can find to learn lessons about any of the following personality traits: to be passionate, to be a life-long learner, to be modest, to have discipline, to be a leader, to have vision, to be energetic, to be affable, to be reliable, to be giving, to be polite, to be positive, to be rational, to be tasteful, to be sensitive, to be unpretentious, to be witty, to be tenacious, to be innovative, to be creative, to be broad-minded, to be fair, to be optimistic, to be reliable, to demonstrate intelligence, to be a good listener, to be willing to change, to accept responsibility, to be inspiring, to show competence, to be honest, to have integrity, to be just, to show initiative, to remain calm, to apply your will, to be lovable, to be assertive, to have candor, to be sweet, to be humble, and to have empathy and compassion. Write down how you believe you can learn about these personality traits from natural beings in your presence.

Follow-up Protocol

For best results, write down your impressions of this activity in your journal using the Heartwood Path Follow-up Protocol found in the Appendix. Afterwards, consider sharing your interpretations with others.

Heartwood Path Axioms

Key Assertions From Waypoint 5.16

5.16.1.

Find models in nature with valued personality traits.

5.16.2.

Valued traits help you to choose actions that lead to personal happiness, an expansion of perspective that includes compassion for all sentient beings, and a protected environment—all purposes of the Heartwood Path.

5.16.3.

Certain animals can provide important lessons about personality traits.

Nocturnal Pilgrimage 5.16

For best results, write down your impressions of each night's dreams in your journal using the Heartwood Path Dreaming Time Protocols found in the Appendix. Afterwards, consider sharing your Dream Tending with others.

The Natural Law Of Comparisons:

Meaning arises
in our minds
based on the
comparisons we make.

Everything is relative. It all depends on how one thing compares to another. A White Oak, for example, is big until you compare it to a giant Sequoia. When you include yourself in the comparing, make sure to be positive. Your negative reactions and actions as a result of your comparisons can be stifling and obstructive. Additionally, giving yourself a positive reaction when comparing yourself to others can result in a superiority complex. Refrain from judging. Everyone, including yourself, has gifts, talents, and abilities. Compare your uniqueness to the uniqueness of other people but do not pronounce one better than the other. Neutral is the universe. Compare paths, not people.

The Natural Law Of Correlation:

Laws in the physical world
are correlated with laws
in the spiritual world.

When people say "As above, so below" or "As within, so without" they are basing their assessment on The Natural Law Of Correlation. How one feels on the inside is re-elected in one's actions and behavior. For this reason, one cannot be successful until one's inner world is smooth, drama-free, and positive. That is why it is so important to take care of your emotions, thoughts, and perspective. Don't allow yourself to bury your anger, fear, jealousy, or other negative feelings. Conversely, uncover positive inner feelings and they will be reflected in the outer world. For example, if you trust others, they will trust you. Likewise the spiritual realm—the above—is reflected in the physical world—the below. If you want to change the world begin by taking responsibility for yourself. Don't blame others. You can model good behavior, but you ought not try to force someone to alter their path. That is the other person's responsibility. If you are confused about something in the outer world, look for answers in the inner world. Set your sights high and soar.

Pertinent And Instructive Gems From My Dream Tending Journal

As the two of us stood on the bank of the river at Jefferson City, Missouri, I looked her in the eyes and asked:

Don:

"Anything else you need before we set sail?"

Kim:

"No, but thanks for asking," she seemed pleasantly surprised by my attentiveness.

We paddled out to the middle of the river. We moved along at about four mile per hour, with minimal paddling. We both remained quiet. We saw geese, deer, islands, beaches, and bluffs. For the most part, we let the river do the talking.

Several miles downstream, she broke the silence.

Kim:

"So you wrote the book about this part of the river?"

Don:

"Yep, Twenty years ago. It's called "Exploring Missouri River Country."

Kim:

"And now your writing about Eco ... cytology."

Don:

"Psychology...yes...Eco-psychology. What about you? Where have you worked?"

Kim:

"Hold on ... I want to know about your current writing."

Don:

"I thought you didn't want any lectures."

Kim:

"Yeah, that's for sure. How about I ask short questions and you give short answers."

Don:

"OK! See the post along the bank with the numbers on it. Those tell the barges where they are. They are mile markers. I'll only answer one question per mile. It's gonna be a long trip. Does that work for you?"

Kim:

"Deal!" she said, pleasantly surprised again.

Don:

"Ok, shoot."

Kim:

"Before this trip, I looked over your stuff online. Very interesting. But, maybe if I hear you speak the words it won't seem so deep, so over my head. Tell me about trustable information and how that first popped up for you."

Don:

"Ok, since individual experience is the most accurate way to make use of our shared 54 natural senses, it is the most trustable form of information. I first began learning this when, during the summer after First Grade, I began spending my days avoiding family and social meanness by being chest-deep in the waters of the ox-bow lakes (tree-shaded swamps formed by abandoned stretches of the Mississippi) or in the thousand-year-old flooded borrow pits the prehistoric Mound Builders created as they slowly built, one basket of earth at a time, the greatest ancient city and largest mounds of Turtle Island (North America). How's that?"

Kim:

"Heady stuff for a printer!"

Don:

"It gets worse. And, hey, Benjamin Franklin was a printer too, and he had some novel ideas as well."

Kim:

"Ok, Benjamin! I'll wait for the next river mile marker before we continue. You sit back there and plot the next big revolution. And keep an eye out for the next sandbar. I gotta go!"

Lesson Learned: I could tell that Kim, the lady asking me questions in my dream, fresh from a break-up, needed some time for self-reflection. That is why I built in some quiet time during our maiden voyage together. Solitude, hard to come by when sharing a small canoe, would be the best remedy. But, since we cannot separate at the moment, the next best thing, I thought, would be fairly lengthy moments of silence as we moved past one beautiful scene after another.

Tonight, try the Sixty-One Point Relaxation technique, as presented by LaBerge and Rheingold (1990, p. 54-55). After quoting what LaBerge and Rheingold say to do at the first point, the forehead, I will describe the location of each of these points on the body:

"Begin at your forehead. Focus your attention between your eyebrows and think of the number one. Keep your attention fixed at Point 1 for several seconds until you feel that your awareness is clear and distinct. Think of your self being located at this point. Before moving on to the next point, (be sure to) feel a sense of warmth and heaviness at this spot . . . Move through each point in sequence . . . Do not allow your mind to wander . . . (If your mind wanders or you lose your place) return to the beginning or the last numbered point you attended to, and continue. (Practice until) you can do all points without losing your focus" (LaBerge and Rheingold, 1990, p. 54-55). Repeat the process of focusing your attention, locating your self, and feeling the warmth at each point that follows. The second point is near the top of the center of the front of your throat. Point Three is at your right shoulder. Point Four is at the inside of the right elbow. Point Five is at the right wrist, near the base of the thumb. Points 6-10 are the fingers on the right hand, beginning with the thumb. Eleven is back up to the wrist on the right arm. Point Twelve is back up to the right inner elbow. Point Thirteen is at the right shoulder. Point Fourteen is at the middle of the front of the throat. Point Fifteen begins the sequence going down the left arm, beginning at the shoulder. Point Sixteen is at the inner elbow of the left arm. Point Seventeen is at the left wrist, near the bast of the thumb. Points 19-22 are the fingers of the left hand, beginning with the thumb. Point Twenty-three begins the sequence going back up the left arm, beginning with the wrist. Point Twenty-four is located at the inner left elbow. Point Twenty-five is at the left shoulder. Point Twenty-six is located at the front of the throat. Point Twenty-seven is at the sternum. Point Twenty-eight is at the right nipple. Point Twenty-nine is back at the sternum. Point Thirty is at the left nipple. Thirty-one is back at the sternum. Point Thirty-two is at the navel. Point Thirty-three is at the base of the "generative organs" (the genitals). Point Thirty-four is at the point of the right ovary or the right side of the abdomen. Point Thirty-five is at the right knee. Point Thirty-six is at the right ankle. Points 37-41 are right toes, beginning with the big toe. Point Forty-two is back up the right ankle. Point Forty-three is back up to the right knee. Point Forty-four is at the right ovary or right abdomen again. Point Forty-five is at base of the genitals. Point Forty-six is at the left ovary or left lower abdomen. Point Forty-seven begins the sequence going down the left leg, beginning with the left knee. Point Forty-eight is at the left ankle. Points 49-53 are the toes of the left foot, beginning with the big toe. Point Fifty-four starts the series back up the left left, beginning at the ankle. Point Fifty-five is at the left knee. Point Fifty-six is at the left ovary or lower left abdomen. Point Fifty-seven is at the base of the generative organs. Point Fifty-eight is back to the navel. Point Fifty-nine is back to the sternum. Point Sixty is back to the front of the throat. And Point Sixty-one is back to the Third Eye area, the forehead, between the eyebrows. (From Figure 2.1, LaBerge and Rheingold, 1990, p. 56).

With your impressions of these relaxation techniques and your feelings about what you learned in the just-completed lesson foremost in your memory, drift off to dreamland. Upon awakening, tend to your dreams.

In the next activity, expand your world by breaking out of your human clique and by broadening your interspecies contacts and knowledge. By doing the next activity outdoors, you will expand your sense of membership to include not only humans but also the entire world. Pay attention to any developing feelings of affinity with all of the community of life. When ready, head to the next waypoint, entitled "World."

17

World

LEARN FROM THE CIRCLE

Now that the reader has some examples of how nature gives lessons regarding ethos, it is time to see what the symbol of a circle can do regarding not only ethos but also the development of eco-centric elders. Whether this image is used in Buddhist sacred geometry or in Native American dances or in primitive sun worship, the circle is a time-tested symbol for wholeness. Often this circle is divided into four sections, as when the Lakota Sioux are representing the Four Cardinal directions, or the four parts of the Christian Cross, the way a Native American Medicine Wheel is divided (described previously), or the common divisions of a Rose Window in a church.

Help Yourself and Others Move Productively Around The Wheel of Life

To The Sacred Hoop ...

HumaNatureConnect Activity

Start-up Protocol

If this is not a day when you prefer to spend time in nature without an agenda, do the Heartwood Path Start-up Protocol found in the Appendix. Then return here to do the remaining portion of this activity:

Learning From The Circle

Consider the meaning of circles or cycles in nature. Consider how natural cycles, which power the world, go in circles. Look up and the sky seems like part of a circle. Watch the stars over time and you will see a large circle. The same goes for the Sun and the Moon. Most bird nests are circles. From your childhood to your children's childhood, life moves in a circle. So much is round or, like eyebrows and smiles, trying to be. When the wind is most powerful it moves in sorts of circles—spiraling cyclones, hurricanes, and tornadoes. From pupils to bellybuttons, our bodies make use of circles, including the circulatory system and the oxygen/carbon dioxide exchanges that goes on between ourselves and the trees. Find more examples of circles or cycles and ponder their meanings. Write down whether or how you have cycles of moods? Look for ways in your life that the Law of Periodicity is in effect. To do so, look for where effects are rooted in causes and how each cause that produces an effect can be marked in time—the *period* between the generation of the cause and the working out of the effect—which, in itself, is a cycle. Think of activity as a half-circle and rest as the remainder of the half circle. Look for examples of half circles of activity and half circles of inactivity. And do the same for incarnation and its opposite—life in the body and life without a body. Think of another big cycle—the half circle of free will which is fate in its active aspect and the half circle of Karma which is fate in its inactive circle. Ask yourself: how will your active choices affect your inactive receiving of the effects of your choices? You yourself are a cause of effects. Choose who or what you will serve. Using your natural sense of symbol and design, create (using pen, pencil, paintbrush, or computer) an icon or figure—like an avatar used on the Internet—that represents the circle of your service to a person, place, or thing.

Follow-up Protocol

For best results, write down your impressions of this activity in your journal using the Heartwood Path Follow-up Protocol found in the Appendix. Afterwards, consider sharing your interpretations with others.

Heartwood Path Axioms

Key Assertions From Waypoint 5.17

5.17.1.

Learn from the circle—a time-tested symbol for wholeness.

5.17.2.

Often this circle is divided into four sections, as when the Lakota Sioux are representing the Four Cardinal directions, or the four parts of the Christian Cross, the way a Native American Medicine Wheel is divided (described previously), or the common divisions of a Rose Window in a church.

5.17.3.

With continued practice you will be able to have lucid dreams, at will.

Nocturnal Pilgrimage 5.17

For best results, write down your impressions of each night's dreams in your journal using the Heartwood Path Dreaming Time Protocols found in the Appendix. Afterwards, consider sharing your Dream Tending with others.

The Natural Law Of Karma:

The universe
will compensate
for one's behaviors.

The energy you give off eventually comes back to you. For this reason, always give off positive energy. What goes around comes around. That is why it is important to praise more and criticize less, to give off the energy of abundance rather than the energy of lack, and to shift from hoarding to giving. One's energy may return immediately or after many years. I know the energy will return, but I do not know when it will return. The more you give the more you will receive. There is plenty of energy—both positive and negative—to go around.

Pertinent And Instructive Gems From My Dream Tending Journal

After the pit stop on the sandbar,

Kim and I continued our voyage of discovery. In our established pace, we continued to learn about the river, eco-psychology, and each other. A mile or two downstream, long enough for our levels of blood pressure and cortisol to drop, and long enough for the emergence of the sensation of relaxation and peace, we were once again in the mood for the exchange of conversation. Pointing to the upcoming mile marker, which was our next

marker of the transition between quiet time and talking time, she resumed
the questioning.

Kim:

"What is the greatest truth in your life that you can trust?"

Don:

"During my three years of nearly daily amphibious revelry in nearby
wetlands (1960-1963, in and around East St. Louis, Illinois) I learned that
my natural senses operated best during the moments of mindfulness
(heightened awareness of the Now). In my chosen muddy places of peace, to
think of the past or the future meant that I would miss my cherished in-
the-moment encounters with non-human brethren such as the harmless
banded Water Snake (often mistaken for the poisonous and deadly Water
Moccasin, which did not live this far to the North), or the Stevie Wonder-
like head-waving of the nesting American Bittern, or the aptly named
Leopard Frog that sunbathed on the Lily Pad (of the American Lotus)—no
mud, no pad; no pad, no sun-bathing frog or no bright yellow, spectacu-
larly beautiful water lily. I came to appreciate that a day in these waters
beats any day on the violent streets or any day in the tension-filled living
room, filled with un-sympathetic relatives. Nature beats the indoor life or
the city life. That has always been my greatest and most trustable truth.
How about you?"

Kim:

"I don't know, my dad was an unemployed drunk and my mom was a
stripper. I'm not even sure I have Truths. What does that tell ya, Benjamin?
Or maybe I'll change that to Henry, as in Henry David Thoreau, or, better
yet, how about Deepak, as in ... (well, you know), that name fits you better,
I think."

Time for more quiet river therapy, for both of us.

Lesson Learned: There were differences emerging between myself and Kim. Male compared to Female. Over-educated compared to under-educated. And so forth. But, despite our differences, we both were having an experience of the Missouri River. And that leads me to the lesson learned. We know from videos, movies, books, websites, and magazines that nature, and particularly river scenes, are photogenic. This dream trip let me know that nature is, or can be, a destroyer of inequality. For this reason, nature can be called "equigenic." I love how nature levels the status of those in her presence. What was surprising to me in this dream was how this making of equality and this suitability for the making of artistic pictures became arousing sexually. By the time we got to Hermann, Missouri, I was enamored, and sexually attracted to not only my canoe partner but also to the "erogenic" river itself. And, wouldn't you know it, right when my canoe partner was beginning to show me that she had similar feeling about me and the river, my dog barked and woke me up from this dream.

Be sure you are able to recall your dreams. By now, you ought to have recorded at least two dozen dreams in your journal. From these dreams, you ought to have already extracted a number of personal dream signs and built a few Dream Council 3D Figures (I make mine into cairns, small piles of flat rocks). You now know how to have lucid dreams. With continued practice you will be able to have such dreams, at will.

With this and the previous lesson in mind, sleep and dream. Remember to tend to your dreams.

Then, go to the waypoint entitled "Life Stages" to start the next unusually long teaching. Being lengthy, I suggest you linger with a large tree. The shade will comfort you. The trunk will make an excellent back rest. The solidity of the tree trunk, which has within it the wisdom of the ages, will help you to center and ground yourself. With back to tree, rest, meditate, or consider important problems.

The next activity is so long you may decide to return for more than a couple of days. That is why it will be especially important to be a good guest by asking for consent.

18

Life Stages

HELP YOURSELF AND OTHERS MOVE SUCCESSFULLY AROUND THE WHEEL OF LIFE

I recommend a complete understanding of the Wheel of Life because we . . .have to . . . grow according to our stages in life. Created by eco-psychologist Bill Plotkin, the Wheel of Life is a "model of human development that is both eco-centric and soul-centric—that is, a nature-based model that fully honors the deeply imaginative potentials of the human psyche . . . a field guide for growing elders" (Plotkin, 2010, p. 15). On Plotkin's Wheel, the "journey through the stages of life (symbolically) proceeds in a circle—a universal archetypal symbol of wholeness—that is divided into quadrants (another cross-cultural symbol of wholeness)—four main ones, each divided into two.

Nature is the major design influence for the Wheel of Life. It symbolizes the turning of the four seasons and the movement of the sun daily. As we shall see, symbolic colors are associated with each quadrant. Take a quick tour of the Wheel by looking at the illustration below. The main point of including the Wheel of Life in the Heartwood Path is that ...

ideally half of each persons life (depicted in the lower half of the circle) is devoted to the task of determining how to belong. The second half (the top half of the circle) is devoted to determining how to serve one's community.

The rest of the following illustration is a simple way to depict how these determinations proceed, stage by stage.

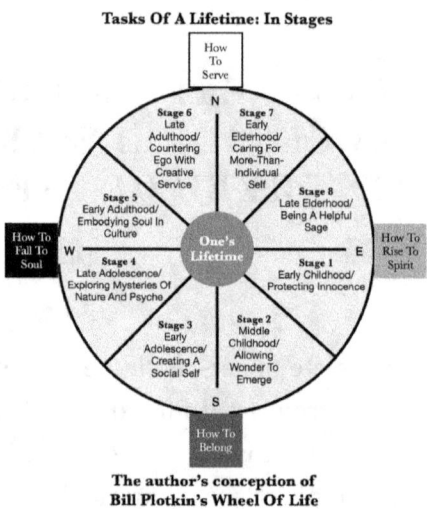

The author's conception of
Bill Plotkin's Wheel Of Life

Beginning on the yellowish-gold, right, or east side of the circle, where symbolically life begins and ends and day begins and ends, one begins one's life and, as one proceeds around the right side of the circle one encounters matters of ascendance to Spirit (similar to the up-ward movement on the Beanstalk of Spiritual development, discussed in previous Heartwood Path books): expansion of perceptions, greater understanding, humor, innocence wisdom, and the "directing of atten-tion and intension beyond ourselves" (Plotkin, 2010, p. 67).

Continue around the circle to its green or red, lower, or south side, where the child matures and begins to grapple with, childhood emo-tions, vulnerabilities, psychological healing, playfulness, spontaneity, a sense of wonder, delight, and emotional connectedness.

On the black, left, or west side of the Wheel, where the sun sets, the young adult faces frightening and bewitching shadows, life transitions into the unknown, introspection, mystery, the occult, the esoteric, self discovery, things that are censored and forbidden, the subconscious and the unconscious, traumatic endings and losses, dreaming, imagining, repressed thoughts or feelings, and other "arisings from the shadowy depths of the soul" (Plotkin, 2010, p. 69).

Moving to the white, upper, or north side of the Wheel, the developing human faces accustomed hardships that are dealt with through knowledge, skill, and fortitude. The overcoming of such challenges leads to strength, endurance, leadership, teaching, care, nurturing, and service.

As one moves back to the east again, the day is almost done and/or the life is almost over. With death comes a returning to the Source. One, metaphorically speaking, goes to seed and begins the life over again. Thus emerges the tender bond between the elder and the newborn.

Movement around the wheel is, as if on a transpersonal axis, from light, ascent towards Spirit, perception, and extroversion (in the East) to dark, descent towards the Soul, introspection, and introversion in the West. Additionally, as if on a personal axis, as one moves from south to north one moves, respectively, from childhood, play, emotion, spontaneity, and delight to parenting, leadership, knowledge, skill, and service.

Of particularly pertinence to those following the Heartwood Path is the Heroic Journey that occurs in life between adolescent stages of development and adult stages of development. As one moves through life, the job is to develop a healthy adolescent ego and then, through trials and tribulations, eventually surrender this ego to the Soul.

In the paragraphs that follow I will not be describing how the mass of common adults are honed, for most people in our society have arrested their psychological development at the stage of an adolescent, even a maladjusted adolescent. For the most part, I will instead be describing how true elders are made.

Toward this end, one undergoes many important passages in life, including:

1. birth;
2. that time of sexual and social flowering known as "puberty;"
3. the shift from "a focus on social belonging and soul discovery to the active embodiment of soul in our community" (Plotkin, 2010, p. 74)—basically, from belonging to serving—known as "soul initiation;" "crowning," or the beginning of "elderhood," wherein one relinquishes one's attachment to the individual soul and, with the strength and endurance that comes with hardships, begins tending to "a more expansive domain, the soul of the more-than-human community" (Plotkin, 2010, p. 75); and
4. Death—the return to Spirit, begin with birth over again.

These events are not tied to chronological age but to the beginning of the developmental stages described below. Each developmental stage is entered into after certain tasks from the previous stage are encountered and after "the center of the individual's psycho-spiritual gravity shifts from one locus to the next" (Plotkin, 2010, p. 76).

We live in a largely egocentric society, but if we did live in a soul-centric society, it would generally not be considered better to reach upper stages of development. Indeed, what is most important is to not quickly or perhaps prematurely skip ahead to higher stages but to fully embrace one's present stage. As mentioned in more detail below, people in each stage offer necessary and valuable gifts to society. Every stages, writes Plotkin, "is the best stage to be in" (2010, p. 84).

As we will see in the subsections that follow, there are numerous ways to determine or identify one's stage (one's psycho-spiritual center of gravity): one's current developmental tasks, resonating with certain archetypes, gifts one effortlessly gives to one's community, one's circle of identity, and, to a degree, the developmental state of one's ego (Plotkin, 2010, p. 88.). In Stages 1 through 3, for example, the ego, if it is progressing in a healthy fashion, is guided by the Spirit and becomes evermore functional. At Stage 4 one's healthy ego aligns with soul and continues this alignment until State 7. At that time the ego surrenders to the Spirit—back where it started. These markings of one's place on the Wheel of Life will become clear in the following description of the eight individual stages.

To Spirit...

HumaNatureConnect Activity

Start-up Protocol

If this is not a day when you prefer to spend time in nature without an agenda, do the Heartwood Path Start-up Protocol found in the Appendix. Then return here to do the remaining portion of this activity:

Reawakening To Spirit

Loosen the Ego's grip upon your self so that you can evolve consciously and flourish. Here's ten ways to do it:

1. **Bridle your Ego.** Recognize your Ego as the false self with the mental conditioning—thoughts and emotions—you typically use to see and act. Your Ego has to be bridled because it is causing you to act in ways that threaten you and other fellow beings. Describe in your journal how you have or need to rein in your Ego.

2. **Uncover the Truth.** During your efforts to grow, do not rely solely on your thoughts. Also rely on deep emotions. More-so than thoughts, feelings will get you closer to the truth. Describe how you have or need to rely on your deep emotions to reveal the truth.

3. **Identify Spirit as the Source of your Identity.** Do not allow your self to identify with your reactions, emotions, stories, thoughts, or possessions. Thinking anything similar to "I have, therefore, I am" is counterproductive to the effort to return to the Source. Describe how you have or need to become unstuck from your possessions, stories, or reactions.

4. **Recognize Impermanence.** Move away from your illusory self image by not identifying with things, conditions, or anything fleeting, such as looks, status, or jobs. Do not bother yourself needlessly by trying to hold on to impermanent things or conditions. Describe how you have or need to detach psychologically from any thing or condition that is short-lived.

5. **Squelch the Voice in your Head.** Recognize that desires and frustrations are all in your head and that most of your thinking is compulsive, recurring, and pointless. Reduce problems by not believing most of what is said by the voice in your head. Do not condemn nor judge your inner voice. Simply listen to it, let it be, let it pass. And refrain from resisting. Doing that is a useless waste of your energy. Feel deeply until you can replace all the negative, recurring thoughts—the chatter—with a few thoughts that lead productively and appropriately to the spiritual dimension. Describe how you have or need to pay less attention to the recurring, unproductive chatter in your mind.

6. **Discern Formless Consciousness.** Be sure not to lose yourself in your gear—your body, skills, mind, and knowledge. Instead, identify with the formless consciousness of all fellow natural beings. Describe how you have or need to connect with your deep sentience (inner awareness).

7. **Center Yourself in the Now.** Accept whatever arises as a way to find peace and joy that is greater than any circumstance or condition in the "Realm of Exteriority"—the so-called "outer world." Know that the present moment is all you have. The future and the past are just thoughts you have in the present.

Stay in the center of the space of Now and let everything fall into place around you. Describe how you have or need to stay in the Now.

8. **Have Mercy**. Your mind is unforgiving. Only you can accept. Agree to receive and forgive so you can see what needs to be done. Describe how you have or need to forgive.

9. **Make Way For Deep Emotions.** Yield to whatever feelings arises within. Describe how you have or need to rely more on your deep emotions.

10. **Meditate**. Dissolve the Ego by listening and being alert to unwanted mind patterns. Describe how you have or need to not just do something, but sit there.

Follow-up Protocol

For best results, write down your impressions of this activity in your journal using the Heartwood Path Follow-up Protocol found in the Appendix. Afterwards, consider sharing your interpretations with others.

Heartwood Path Axioms

Key Assertions From Waypoint 5.18

5.18.1.

Help yourself and others move successfully around the Wheel of Life.

5.18.2.

Nature is the major design influence for the Wheel of Life, which symbolizes the turning of the four seasons and the movement of the sun daily.

5.18.3.

The Wheel of Life shows how one undergoes many important passages in life, including birth, puberty, elderhood, and return to spirit.

Nocturnal Pilgrimage 5.18

For best results, write down your impressions of each night's dreams in your journal using the Heartwood Path Dreaming Time Protocols found in the Appendix. Afterwards, consider sharing your Dream Tending with others.

The Natural Law Of Mutual Support:

One gives
and receives
support from
oneself, the Divine, and others.

Cooperation is working together towards the same result. It involves going under, around, or through obstacles in a coordinated fashion, either with yourself, with the Divine, or with other natural beings—human or otherwise. Being self-aware, learning, and taking independent action is cooperating with yourself. When we share our experiences and knowledge with others, let go, remain flexible, let things happen, go with the flow without worry, and live in the Now, we are cooperating with the Divine. When we listen carefully, seek understanding, share ideas, utilize the variety of abilities, offer encouragement and acknowledgement, and make the work uplifting and fun, we are cooperating with others. Always minimize the drama, turn to the more qualified person to get a job done, allow others to shine, and remain fully engaged.

Pertinent And Instructive Gems From My Dream Tending Journal

On my way back from the bathroom, I set the intention to keep my dream going right from where it ended. That didn't work perfectly. When I dreamt again, Kim and I were about to float past Washington, Missouri, which meant I missed or edited out whatever happened for the last day or so. Still, I was happy to continue with the the present manifestation of my, more or less, ongoing dream. Out in the middle of the Missouri River any canoeist will likely feel a pleasant sense of solitude. For almost all of the time on the water, the river travelers will see either no people or, when towns are passed, the people seen are so far away as to not be able to cause any disturbance. This sense of isolation and security led Kim to turn around in her seat at the bow of the canoe, remove her blouse, face me at the stern, and sunbathe in a way that would gradually remove her tan lines. She even slept like that midday. After she awoke, she was ready to resume our extended conversation. Perhaps to counter her bare breasted overt sexuality, she waxed philosophical.

Kim:

"What is the key factor that makes humanity different or separate from nature? And when did you learn about the difference?"

Don:

"If not immersed in swamp or watery pit, as a child I would be home, watching the reruns of the Three Stooges or 'running the streets,' trying to avoid the oft-nasty stories of the bullies, most being delivered from poorly-educated boys five years older than me. I would later learn that their stories, often about imaginary sexual conquests, were inaccurate and disconnected to the kind of trustworthy information I alone gained in the local swamps and hill-side trails near my family's home. Nobody else wanted to meet face-to-face with my Banded Water Snake companion. Nobody else wanted to hang out with my fellow-in-self-baptism—my oft-maligned Alligator Snapping Turtle friend, whom I considered to be a fellow parishioner of our secret church of nature. And that was fine by me. My solitary daily immersions set me on a different path. I did not want to be like the others I was witnessing, for they were, far too often, too much like all the other people in my sphere. Everyone seemed different and separate from nature. Rather than relying on mindful nature experiences, my family members—some of them less than sympathetic about my presence in "their" home—and the street bullies all blindly operated and related according to what they learned in inaccurate and nature-disconnected stories. To this day, I wager that they still do not know what they are missing."

Kim:

"Nature-disconnect stories? That sounds like the story of my life, until recently."

Don:

"It's that way for most people."

Kim:

"What do we do about it?"

Don, with a smirk:

"Regularly sunbathe topless until your tits turn red, then put on some more sunblock to stop the damage. Here's some, catch! Put it on any exposed skin."

Kim, grimacing:

"I wasn't planning on getting my boobs burnt."

Don:

"Let's get you off of the river, the sun is reflecting off of the water and even your big hat won't protect you."

We will make ourselves comfortable on the next sandbar. And, don't worry. We are far from town. There will be no hoods in these woods. We will be respectful of the resources and thoughtful of whomever might follow.

Kim, with her hands raised in a halting manner:

"Camping without leaving a trace, Boy Scout style. Trust me, I haven't heard much about it. But, tell me no more, paahlease!"

Lesson Learned: This dreamt float trip was doing me—the dreamer —some good. As I have noticed in "real life," nature, the dreamt river had an uncanny ability to reveal conscious and unconscious breaches in the well-being of those who were attentive and appreciative of her; and, just as amazing, the dreamt river lifted the psychological burdens of these breaches. In this dream, Kim and I were each, figuratively speaking, putting our nature-guided fingers in the happiness-draining breach of the dam of our well-being. Additionally, both Kim and I were using this dreamt outing in nature to get to know each other much better. We got some physical exercise—largely through the sporadic vigorous use of our canoe paddles, which, due to the downstream force and speed of the river, really weren't that necessary (except as a means to invigorate our arms). And we gained from the impact nature was having on our senses. The dreamt results of nature's treatment were many, but not yet complete. Although our moods were boosted, we still mutually agreed that we needed more quiet time—both on the sand bars and in the canoe—to solve in our minds any lingering problems, personal or social; to shoo away any mental maladies (I was beginning to think Kim may be fighting depression), to raise each of our levels of creativity, and to exercise each of our capacities for imagination.

Sleep. Dream about something funny you did when you were young. Remember, doing dumb things when we are young gives us something funny to laugh about when we are old. Tend to your dreams. When ready, go to the waypoint entitled "Wheel of Life (Stage 1)" and heed the next teaching point.

19

Wheel Of Life (Stage 1)

PROTECT YOUR INNOCENCE

At Birth, an individual passes into a protective environment Plotkin calls "The Nest." During this stage, the individual is mostly involved with the earliest stages of physical and psychological development. The associated developmental tasks are the preservation of innocence and the formation of a culturally viable ego. Such an ego functions well *in* our egocentric culture yet does not become a "cog" *of* it. Being very young, one is too unqualified to do all these tasks on one's own, therefore, negotiating this Stage is the responsibility of one's parents or caregivers. At this point, one's gift to the community is innocence, luminous presence, and joy. From a "being of spirit and primal innocence" to a "creature who possesses awareness of itself and the world," the human metamorphosis that occurs in Stage 1, nurtured by an environment of people and wild things, creates a little person with "a conscious, relational self still connected with wildness—its own and Earth's" (Plotkin, 2010, p. 03). The learning that occurs during this stage, while necessary, does not need to be done at the expense of innocence or present-centeredness. The innocence of what Buddhists call the "beginner's mind," a birthright in Stage 1, needs to be held onto as a learned skill that one retains as one progresses throughout all stages of life. Examples of this kind of innocent present-centeredness include the feelings one has when watching a waterfall, embracing a loved one, or appreciating fine music. Regularly immersing oneself in the feelings of innocence leads, later in life, to the important job of cooperating—a skill that is very necessary for the jobs of passing on to higher stages of development, successful interpersonal relationships, partnership without ulterior motives, and the survival of both species and ecological systems. The laughable and foolish things children do (and, as we shall see, those in the last stage of life) teaches us all important lessons about not always conforming to convention, worrying about what others think, and impressing others. The Archetype of "The Innocent," so visible in Stage 1, teaches us about the joy of the moment, keeping things simple, and non-attachment. Stage 1 leads to sound development. This can only occur when parents or caregivers are able to answer two of the most important questions that rise half-way through life: "Where am I going?" and "Who is going to come with me?" Once these questions are answered, it is more likely that the caregiver's best hopes for the child lie not in attaining economic excess but in the development of the joy that comes with serving the community and the more-than-human world. The best ways for caregivers to secure the innocence of Stage 1 are to be fully present with the child, to meet the child's requirements for well-being (needs) without anxiety, to not be over-indulgent with the child's preferred outcomes (desires) as a way to help the child learn to be patient and to learn how to cope with disappointment and some discomfort, and to not be preoccupied with the child's future accomplishments.

Innocence is lost by pre-school academic pressures, overindulgence, obedience, anxiety, and the forced development of egocentric social skills—those that end up hurting oneself, other people, or the environment. The natural environment is the outer-most part of the secure Nest one prepares for a child in Stage 1. The caregiver, therefore, ought not be so overprotective as to prohibit a child from having ample exposure to nature. This child needs a chance to consider nature as a fellow caregiver that provides "the interactive nourishment for the child's full development. With plenty of time in nature, the infant learns that her greater mother, the animate world, is always there" (Plotkin, 2010, p. 108).

If you are hoping to regain your own innocence here are some ways:

1. meditation,
2. contemplative prayer,
3. tai chi,
4. yoga,
5. "joyful mindfulness" and solitude in nature,
6. creating works of art (including music),
7. (apprenticing) "yourself to your intuition,"
8. avoiding excessive focus on the past or future,
9. entering into social situations openly,
10. reviewing your day to pick out ways you could have been more innocent,
11. spending time with animals, emulating the behavior of infants, and
12. getting to know the first of the Twelve Archetypes—The Innocent Hero (introduced in the next activity).

Relish your time as a caregiver in the Nest and recover your innocence (Plotkin, 2010, p. 124-129). It is this innocence that fosters the kind of "beginners' mind" that leads un-seasoned amateurs, like those of us who stopped the Meramec Dam in Missouri, to succeed at what seasoned campaigners and longterm professionals know will be very difficult and often say will be impossible. Had we not had beginners' minds, ones that did not know the trials and tribulations that lie ahead, we who fought the ill-considered dam project would not have overcome the odds, we would not have done the impossible, we would not have been such good examples of how it often takes the naive amateur conservationist to get the job done. One way to hold on to this all-important beginners' mind is to encounter the Archetype in the next activity.

To The Innocent Hero...

HumaNatureConnect Activity

Start-up Protocol

If this is not a day when you prefer to spend time in nature without an agenda, do the Heartwood Path Start-up Protocol found in the Appendix. Then return here to do the remaining portion of this activity:

Getting To Know Your Inner Guide—"The Innocent"

Use two of the Natural Senses and Sensitivities—"Sense of self including friendship, companionship, and power" and "Sense of mind and consciousness" (Cohen, website: http://www.ecopsych.com/insight53senses.html)—as you read the follow excerpts from Carol S. Pearson's book **Awaken the Heroes Within** and then answer the questions below, using the perspective of your chosen natural being that you imagine is both informed about all aspects of your self and, unlike you, is fair and objective about your recollections of innocence.

"The Innocent is the part of us that trusts life, ourselves, and other people. It is the part that has faith and hope, even when on the surface things look impossible" (Pearson, 1991, p. 71).

"Innocents ... may pretend to be independent, but underneath, they expect institutions, employers, friends, and spouses to take care of them" (Pearson, 1991, p. 78).

"The journey requires a great paradox. At one level, we (have to) never let go of our dreams and ideals, and in this every hero remains always an Innocent. But at the same time, we need to be willing to sacrifice our illusions, gladly and daily, so that we may grow and learn" (Pearson, 1991, p. 80).

With these statements in mind and with the perspective of your informed, objective natural being, answer the following questions. When doing so, think about the past and the present.

How much or how little are you (and your family, coworkers, and friends) under the influence of the Innocent?

Is there anything about your relationship with the Innocent that you wish were different?

What can you recall about a time in your life when your naiveté, your innocence, or your beginners' mind led you to be able to overcome the odds and to succeed at what other more seasoned folks knew to be difficult, if not impossible?

Follow-up Protocol

For best results, write down your impressions of this activity in your journal using the Heartwood Path Follow-up Protocol found in the Appendix. Afterwards, consider sharing your interpretations with others.

Heartwood Path Axioms

Key Assertions From Waypoint 5.19

5.19.1.

Rather than attempting to go backwards in your development, think about the mission you still need today that was the main job of Life Stage 1: protecting your innocence.

5.19.2.

One's gifts to the community that are developed in Life Stage 1 are innocence, luminous presence, and joy.

5.19.3.

The innocence of what Buddhists call the "beginners' mind," a birthright that needs to be protected in Stage 1, has to be held onto as a learned skill that one retains as one progresses throughout all stages of life.

5.19.4.

The "beginners' mind" enables un-seasoned amateur conservationists to succeed at what seasoned campaigners know to be difficult and claim to be impossible.

Nocturnal Pilgrimage 5.19

For best results, write down your impressions of each night's dreams in your journal using the Heartwood Path Dreaming Time Protocols found in the Appendix. Afterwards, consider sharing your Dream Tending with others.

The Natural Law Of Interpretation:

Every person
has unique interpretations
and points of view.

One's perspective changes as one's beliefs change. Such changes affect one's determination of truth, how one thinks about something, and whether one will take action for or against something. One's point of view affects one's interpretation of reality, one's mood, and whether one's choices are positive or negative.

Adopt another person's perspective to give yourself a fresh look. Doing so is a good way to become unstuck, to develop new ideas, to put forth new interpretations, or to take charge. Ways to see things anew include doing something novel spontaneously and without expectation, purposefully meeting new people outside of your typical orbit, refraining from judging others, temporarily assuming (imaginatively or actually) the roles of people who are different from yourself, and looking for the silver lining in all situations.

Pertinent And Instructive Gems From My Dream Tending Journal

It was hard, after the adult activities of the last day and a half, to restore our child-like innocence, but that is exactly what Kim, in so many words, seemed to need right now.

Kim:

"My life was carefree as a child. I spent most of my time happily with my dad. Then, with puberty, he suddenly pulled away from me, as if he was worried about controlling himself after I ... developed. Now, we barely speak. I wanna go back to my care-free youth, back when I was bathed in my dad's innocent love."

Don:

"Being on an island sandbar, and thus protected from casual visitors, we can frolic here, secretly and innocently; but first we oughta gather up firewood, light the fire, and put up the tent. I don't think the river is gonna come up tonight, but it's always a good idea to place the tent and the canoe on high ground."

After doing so, we agreed to give each other some solo time for self-reflection. As we agreed, I walked upstream, and she down. I found a giant dead tree the river dropped off on the sandbar after a previous time of high water, and used it as a backrest during my nature absorption time. At one point, I looked across the expanse of water-rippled sand—our own private playground and clinic—and saw her lying facedown and naked, on the lowermost tip, in the only patch of sunlight left on our island retreat. Apparently, she felt the need to burn her butt to match her breasts. Or, maybe lying naked in the sand was her way to hasten her absorption of nature's "glad tidings." In time, I noticed that she had returned to the fire where, still naked, she was preparing to put on something warmer for the night. I gave her some more time to arrange herself without interruption.

Don, after our reunion.

"You Ok?"

Kim:

"Couldn't be better! Thank you for asking. And thank you for bringing me here. Can we stay a few days?"

Don:

"As long as you like."

I was gratified by her appreciation (of me and the setting).

It was beginning to feel like Kim, myself, and the island had become a ragtag threesome of lovers. I didn't mind.

Lesson Learned: Sexual love is not restricted to just the two lovers. The setting of the lovemaking is involved, sometimes overtly but usually subconsciously. The multi-dimensional sexual relationshipextends way before and way after intercourse. The individual or the amorous couple, if aware and so disposed, can lovingly interact—physically and emotionally—with an attractive natural setting or a natural being. Sexual events can be conducted with or they can be influenced by non-human leafy or fleshy third parties. The topic of eco-sexuality is presented in Heartwood Path Book Nine: Eros.

Sleep. Dream about moving through the stages of life. Remember that aging and growing old are not necessarily the same thing. You have much leeway regarding aging. Aging is about that refuge in adversity—learning. Growing old, by comparison, is like being a passenger on an airplane. Once you are there, there is nothing you can do. Tend to your dreams. When ready to move forward by going to the next waypoint, entitled "Wheel Of Life (Stage 2)."

20

Wheel Of Life (Stage 2)

ALLOW AWARENESS AND
WONDER TO EMERGE

In the stage Plotkin calls "the Garden," a child goes through a psychological birth—the "emergence of conscious self-awareness" (2010, p. 130). The passage from Nest to Garden is from innocence and spirit to emotions and body. The task now is to discover the enchantment of the natural world and to learn the ways of one's culture. In the Garden, one encounters "The Explorer" Archetype and develops the capability to give the community the gift of wonder. One's sociocentric identity puts the center of one's gravity firmly in the family and nearby nature. This period of "wonder and prolific imagination," (Plotkin, 2010, p. 130) overflowing with emotion, will be one's life stage until Puberty. The Garden is a time for weaving human nature with more-than-human nature. It is a time for one to generate and define "a somewhat distinct world" (Plotkin, 2010, p. 135). This is sometimes done by asking incessant questions or by conducting other forms of exploration. A child's inquisitiveness in this stage is a good model for how anyone beyond the next stage might attempt to likewise observe and be curious. During the second half of Stage 2 and throughout the following stage a developing person learns that one needs to occasionally fend for oneself because of inevitable psychological abandonments that cause with fear, pain, loss, illness, or embarrassment. Such occurrences cause one to feel forsaken by one's caregivers. This is a time of life, which begins early and may never end. This is also a time to come to know the inner guide or Archetype known as "The Orphan." The Orphan helps because during Stage Two the developing person is, in effect, tossed out of paradise. This departure serves to strengthen the Ego, and is another example of how developmental progress coincides with disappointments and hurts—two "catalysts for maturation" (Plotkin, 2010, p. 137). Such inevitable wounds teach one how to express emotions. The gift one gives to one's community during the approach to becoming a soul-rooted adult is the natural exuberance one displays while making discoveries about the givens of the world—one's family, the enchantment of nature, and learning about one's culture. Making such discoveries helps a developing child master the primary task of Stage 2: being able to belong in the world as one finds it. While it is our goal along the Heartwood Path to remake the culture (from egocentric to soul-centric), that job requires an initial belonging before the ultimate transforming. It requires a loving before the saving. This belonging and loving is fostered by an enchantment with HumaNature —wild nature and human nature combined. Wild nature is "the original matrix that gave birth to our species—and the essential catalyst it provides for the healthy development of every human child" (Plotkin, 2010, p. 141). The enchantment needed for healthy development does not occur on outdoor soccer fields or, as when I led my two girls to the Nāpali Coast on Kauai, during forced marches to a predetermined destination. Enchantment requires intimate contact and spontaneous play in nature, more like what occurred for my daughters, when they hid and climbed amongst the sticks, mud, and non-humans found in the woods at our family's ranch. Enchantment is fostered when a child has ample time in nature to see her self reflected back by the natural qualities she encounters. Unstructured outdoor nature play counteracts any leanings towards apathy to the environment and its troubles.

Given these natural benefits, depriving children of nature by diverting them to televisions, video games, computers, iPads, books, and other artificial pursuits is not quite like depriving them of oxygen. Allowing children to spend too much time on such diversions is a way to hamper their healthy development. Stephanie Kaza calls unnatural distractions such as televisions, computers, books, and the like "delusional substitutes for rich, sensory contact with the actual rhythms and textures of the natural world" (1993, p. 7).

Answering questions about the out-of-doors is typically better than flooding the child with unsolicited information. Rather than just providing Narnias and Never-Never Lands in books, also allow a child to have her own natural wonderland, big or small. Such a place allows a child to remove the veil that sometimes perceptually separates people from nature. Private places of natural wonder also help the developing child develop intellectually (through taxonomy or astronomy, for example), empathetically (through caring for plants or animals) and relationally (through being a member of the tribe of fellow Earthlings) and emotionally (through encouraging a child to feel her emotions fully and to learn what her emotions can tell her about herself and the world).

Widespread failure to help children grow positively through this life phase is one reason why we are now, collectively, largely a maladaptive species at twilight. In keeping with the common tendency to fail to develop positively through all of the stages in the Wheel of Life, some people late in life begin to develop a fully ecocentric perspective. The widespread lack of this perspective explains the pervasive tardy rage over the plight of the planet. Despite previous and current widespread pathological development, this rage gives us cause for more than ungrounded hope.

It is never to late to do the nature-bonding task so important to one's development. What works for children in Stage 2 also works for adults who may have never bonded with nature. Without engaging in such tasks one may never come to the important realization that saving the forest or the river is also saving the Soul. In a sense, since one's inner world is determined by one's outer world, outer world abusive development thwarts inner world development. This being the case, it is no surprise that as we make developments that destroy wild nature to an unprecedented extent "truly visionary creativity" becomes "one of the most suppressed human qualities" (Plotkin, 2010, p. 152). The link between outer world development and imagination becomes more understandable as one explores the inter-relationship between Plotkin's "four domains of nature:" body, imagination, emotion, and wild nature (Plotkin, 2010, p. 156-157).

"Diminished opportunities in any dimension impair the child's relationship with each of the other three" (Plotkin, 2010, p. 157). If learning about nature is half of a child's task in Stage 1 exploring the realm of culture is the other half (culture being defined as a person's totality of local stories, practices, knowledge, and values). Given the topic of this section of the Heartwood Path—ethos—we shall focus here mostly on the values aspect of culture. The child's task of exploring ethos is facilitated by how parents and other adults model "a coherent and consistent set of values, a set of ethics and principles for making choices, a system that is authentically lived by the family and its ethnic or social group" (Plotkin, 2010, p. 158). Rather than worrying about forcing a set of values on the next generation, parents need to give the child a set of values because "a child raised in a value-free or value-relevant environment is in danger of lifelong confusion about what's important, and may be unable to decisively choose a life path . . . and may be unable to criticize even the most heinous human tasks . . ." (Plotkin, 2010, p. 158). Concerning values, Plotkin goes on to say:

> "Some shifting of value systems in adolescence and adulthood is inevitable and also necessary for the health of the culture" (2010, p. 159).

When enough individuals are protected from ego-centric influences and opt to shift to soul-centric lifestyles "our culture will shift fundamentally and radically—with or without the support of governments, large corporations, schools, or religious organizations" (Plotkin, 2010, p. 184). To make this shift, more people need to value wanting less good things and more people need to value more good lives. More good lives comes from many sources, including: watching less television, spending less time operating computers, making rather than just listening to music, spending more time in nature, volunteering in the community, celebrating through the use of rituals or ceremonies, attending schools that draw students up rather than fill students up, gathering with a diverse crowd, tending a garden, allowing children to bring you along on outings rather than the other way around, and spending time allowing the world to be new again. Doing such things helps the developing person move from the Garden and a life centered in family and nature to the next major developmental stage: the Oasis (described in the next subsection).

Before reading about the Oasis, explore more fully your relationship with inner guide or Archetype "The Orphan." This is the purpose of the next activity.

To The Abandoned Hero...

HumaNatureConnect Activity

Start-up Protocol

If this is not a day when you prefer to spend time in nature without an agenda, do the Heartwood Path Start-up Protocol found in the Appendix. Then return here to do the remaining portion of this activity:

Getting To Know Your Inner Guide—"The Orphan"

Use two of the Natural Senses and Sensitivities—"Sense of self including friendship, companionship, and power" and "Sense of mind and consciousness" (Cohen, website: http://www.ecopsych.com/

insight53senses.html)—as you read the follow excerpts from Carol S. Pearson's book **Awaken the Heroes Within** and then answer the questions below, using the perspective of your chosen natural being that you imagine is both informed about all aspects of your self and, unlike you, is fair and objective about your recollections of your striving to go it alone.

> "The Orphan experiences the same 'fall' as the Innocent, but to different effect. The Innocent uses the experience to try harder, to have greater faith, to be more perfect and lovable, to be more worthy. The Orphan sees it as demonstrating the essential truth that we are all on our own" (Pearson, 1991, p. 82)

> The goal of The Orphan is to "regain safety." The response of The Orphan is "wish for rescue" and "cynical compliance." The task of The Orphan is to process "pain and disillusionment fully and to be open to receive help from others." The gift of The Orphan is interdependence, empathy, and realism (Pearson, 1991, p. 82).

> "Just as we are all wounded, we are also all raised by wounded parents at various stages on their own journeys . . . The Orphan calls us to wake up, let go of our illusions, and face painful realities . . . If we were not wounded, we would remain in innocence and never mature, grow, or learn" (Pearson, 1991, p. 83-91).

With these statements in mind and with the perspective of your informed, objective natural being, answer the following questions. When doing so, think about the past and the present.

How much or how little are you (and your family, coworkers, and friends) under the influence of the Orphan?

Is there anything about your relationship with the Orphan that you wish were different?

What can you recall about a time in your life when others were delighted in your amazement about some aspect of life?

Follow-up Protocol

For best results, write down your impressions of this activity in your journal using the Heartwood Path Follow-up Protocol found in the Appendix. Afterwards, consider sharing your interpretations with others.

Heartwood Path Axioms

Key Assertions From Waypoint 5.20

5.20.1.

Rather than attempting to regress your development, think about the mission you need today that is the main job of Life Stage 2: allowing awareness and wonder to emerge.

5.20.2.

The gift one gives to one's community, initially secured in Stage 2, is the natural exuberance one displays while making life discoveries.

5.20.3.

The primary task of Stage 2 is being able to belong in the world as one finds it.

5.20.4.

Private places of natural wonder help the developing person develop intellectually, empathetically, relationally, and emotionally.

Nocturnal Pilgrimage 5.20

For best results, write down your impressions of each night's dreams in your journal using the Heartwood Path Dreaming Time Protocols found in the Appendix. Afterwards, consider sharing your Dream Tending with others.

The Natural Law Of Duty:

Meet your obligations.
Respond appropriately.

Make your own decisions. Act independently. Be responsive and responsible. Be accountable. Levy no blame on others. Face difficult circumstances by doing the right thing. Look out for the welfare of others. Pay attention to your emotional, physical, and spiritual needs. Create a budget and stick to it. Prove you can handle responsibilities and you will receive more of them. Accept only your own burdens, not those who can be responsible for themselves.

Pertinent And Instructive Gems From My Dream Tending Journal

Kim:

"I don't want to cover up yet.

I want to feel the contrast between the cool night air

and the heat of the bonfire on my naked skin."

Don:

"Your belly is still covered in sand."

Kim:

"I know. If it doesn't fall off into my food, I was hoping you would brush it off for me when I wrap myself in you as we sit under the stars."

Don:

"It's a tough job, but somebody's got to do it. How do you like the experience so far?"

Kim:

"Are you talking about the sex or the sandbar?"

Don:

"Let's start with the sandbar."

Kim:

"I'm feeling expansive and, as you can see, open and free."

Don:

"Free of...?"

I was hoping I had not led into a discussion about her Ex.

Kim:

"Free from the restrictions of civilization, of narrow-minded people, of controlling men, and...I know, I know, of nature-disconnected stories. What's for dinner, anyway?"

Don:

"The big foil is filled with hamburger and vegetables. They are called Hobo-burgers. The slightly smaller wraps are dessert."

Kim:

"Now we're talkin' Can we start with dessert?"

Don:

"Don't you want to hear what it is?"

Kim

"How soon will it be ready?"

Don:

"In about thirty minutes. They are sweet potatoes smothered in butter and cinnamon, by the way."

Kim:

"Yum, that should give you enough time to rub my belly and any other part of me that you feel sand."

Don:

"Maybe I should spread oil on me and roll around in the sand myself. Would you return the favor?"

Kim:

"Sounds like fun, but only after dessert. I'm starving."

I was too, but not only for food.

Lesson Learned: The effect of nature on this trip was having a bigger impact on Kim than it was on me. Although Kim was a new factor for me, I had floated this stretch of river many times. But for Kim both myself and the river were new experiences. I have noticed that the more novel the nature experience, the bigger the restorative impact. The experience of newness in nature acts like a magnifier of nature's healing resonances. If there is any lingering social stress, or emotional weariness, or mental fatigue, a first time dose of some attractive natural being or the perceiving of a previously unseen natural setting often makes a bigger positive difference than would likely occur after perceiving a well-known being or a familiar setting.

Sleep. Dream about aging. Age now, grow old later. Tend to your dreams. When ready, move to the next waypoint, entitled "Wheel Of Life (Stage 3)."

21

Wheel Of Life (Stage 3)

FOCUS ON YOUR PEER GROUP, SEXUALITY, AND SOCIETY

The major task of the previous stage carries over into Stage 3, which begins with the advent of Psychological Puberty. Thus, neither the life stage task (which is never fully complete) nor the advent of physical puberty marks the beginning of Stage 3.

What does demonstrate that a person has made the transition from Stage 2 to Stage 3 is one's developmental center of gravity. From being centered in nature and family in Stage 2, the person in Stage 3 is centered in one's peer group, sexuality, and society.

Expelled from the Garden by tasting such fruits, the developing adolescent distances himself from nature and parents, a drive that causes some degree of sadness for all involved.

In Stage 3, the Oasis, the new twist on the job of developing a culturally viable ego is "fashioning a social presence" in a way that is (with the help of nature) authentic and (with the help of culture) socially acceptable (Plotkin, 2010, p. 192). One's perspective during Stage 3 is ethnocentric.

As we shall see, the way out of this stage is the "preparedness for the descent to soul" (Plotkin, 2010, p. 192). The road to travel during the Oasis is from being to doing.

Impassioned actions begin to blossom in the warm sunlight of "the urgency to make something of oneself, to plunge into the social world, to fire up new varieties of relationships, to leap into love and heroic adventures, to take on risky and unfamiliar responsibilities, to choose a direction in life, to seek a mate or a lover, to develop a style...(and) a distinctive personality" (Plotkin, 2010, p. 193). All of these occur often with high emotions and strong desires, part of the fuel needed to work towards changing a culture.

Nature, while no longer primary to the developing person, still helps with development. The adolescent needs something beyond her parents and even something beyond culture to serve as a mirror, as a testing ground, and as a place of healing. Since puberty is the first major life transition wherein the developing person has conscious self-awareness on both sides of the passage, celebrating puberty is particularly important.

Doing so does not take the place of doing the main tasks of the developmental stage, but it does help the adolescent gain confidence, pride, and clarity. Puberty rites can include recycling or discarding some of the child's possessions from childhood or that symbolize a more narrow view of life and one or more instructional meetings with same-sex, non-parental adults. Topics for such meetings might include the sacredness of sex, biology, social appropriateness, the maintenance of gender roles, emotional intimacy, conflict resolution, the expression of empathy, and an explanation of the Wheel of Life, perhaps marked out on the ground like a medicine wheel.

Ways to conduct puberty rites include:

1. dancing,
2. music making,
3. immersion in water,
4. sweat ceremonies,

5. smudging,
6. incense burning,
7. prayers,
8. blessings,
9. private or public sacrificing of objects and symbols from childhood,
10. giveaways,
11. gifts to the initiate,
12. statements and ceremonial enactments,
13. question and answer periods about sex,
14. solo time outdoors (perhaps overnight or multiple days) to encounter allies and personal demons,
15. ceremonies in which the initiate claims Earth as primary mother and Sky as primary father but continues to be parented by her human mother and father,
16. a ritual to mark the adolescent's new responsibilities and freedoms,
17. a community feast, and
18. gifts of gratitude to parents.

However puberty rites are conducted, they are a celebration of the initiation of adolescence—the time of more independent youth—not the beginning of adulthood which remains two life stages in the future.

Although called "The Oasis" by Plotkin, this stage of maturation comes with a metaphorical storm on the horizon. Writes Plotkin: "Unbidden disturbances are common emotional tempests, hormonal hurricanes, relationship squalls, and courtship typhoons that sometimes feel like volcanic eruptions from hell" (2010, p. 199).

All of these storms, whether they occur in a few tumultuous years or over a lifetime, are part of the process of growing into wholeness. I say, "over a lifetime" because, in our present egocentric society, adulthood is, more often than not, really little more than an advanced and unhealthy version of adolescence—"adolescence with all the trimmings" (Plotkin, 2010, p. 201).

In the soul-centric society to be created, in part, by the followers of the Heartwood Path, adolescence is something altogether different. EartHearts and their initiates, unlike the mass of people who are passing for psychologically mature adults in our egocentric society, actually become adults psychologically.

EartHearts know that to become such an adult, the adolescent needs to push the limits, she needs to understand personal weaknesses and talents, she has to find a genuine way of belonging, she needs to individuate, and she needs to find an endorsed place in the social world. Always a work-in-progress, the adolescent, regardless of age, wants to feel self-esteem.

At first, she is an apprentice in the art of differentiating a social self, one capable of belonging to an extra-familial social group. In time, most people in Stage 3, because of previous unhealthy development or because of a current wrong turn, fail to continue on their soul-centric pathway of development towards a deeply authentic adult self or, if they go this far, towards being an elder.

This all-too-common continuation of unhealthy development or wrong turn frequently lasts for decades. This unhealthy developmental route is simply a continuation of over-obeying, over-entitlement, or over-socioeconomic training from previous developmental stages or it begins in adolescence as a wrong turn marked by a period of over-conforming or over-rebelling.

Neither of these responses lead one to be particularly good at contributing to a sound society. Finding adult help to move to more productive responses may be difficult, since so few adults who could act as mentors have achieved a soul-centric perspective and are, therefore, unable to lead developing adolescents to levels they themselves have not yet attained.

This catch-22 may partly explain why the transition from adolescence to adulthood is so difficult and why so many contemporary societies are making such a mess of things. To find a worthy mentor in this transition from adolescence to adulthood, make sure you find someone who is not stalled in an adolescent stage of development. One cannot give what one does not have. How a prospective mentor serves the community (rather than how that person carves out an economically viable niche) is a key indicator of that person's level of psycho-spiritual development and worthiness to be a helpful mentor.

Gender roles are most pronounced in the Oasis (Stage 2). When the adolescent continues down the egocentric route or initiates a new bad turn the masculine actor seeks to improve his (or her) position, seeks to find an emotionally safe spouse or social group, seeks to keep up with the Joneses, and seeks to grow the gross national product and die with the most toys. The ego-centric feminine agent seeks to improve her (or his) environment, seeks to secure the border so only similar people are allowed in, and seeks to secure enough consumer goods for her (or his) own kind.

Locked in this unhealthy version of an adolescent beyond the teen years, the egocentric Stage 3 player becomes a "parody of a teenager, a flamer without heat, an aging, surgery-assisted Barbie doll, or a knight in crumbling armor" (Plotkin, 2010, p. 208). In contrast, the healthy masculine player proceeding down the soul-centric route is focused on social advancement, seeks to make things happen, works to create a notable place for himself (or herself) on the socio-economic map, endeavors to attain sex partners and a decent place in the world, and makes sure he (or she) is admired in the world. The healthy feminine soul-centric player seeks compromise over competition; furnishes her (or his) home; says "yes" to resonances that already exist; and seeks social enjoyment, participation, and security.

Given what was just stated and the goals established for those who seek the Heartwood Path, it may seem like the purpose of this course is the feminization of society. This is, in part, true—given that this course is attempting to compensate for the unhealthy masculine bent of our egocentric society. But it is also partial—incomplete because what we who travel the Heartwood path are truly seeking is a better balance between the feminine and the masculine and, more so, a shift from immaturity and ego-centricism to maturity and eco/soul-centricism.

All soul-centric players seek sustainable development, economic fairness, and justice. All masculine Stage 3 players see nature partly as "a context of danger and adventure in which the self can be thoroughly tested." All such feminine players see nature partly as "the standard of a fully fleshed-out self, an inspiration for personal growth" (Plotkin, 2010, p. 226). Whether more masculine or more feminine, soul-centric Stage 3 players see mankind as a part of nature. Healthy Stage 3 players also seek both a fulfilling livelihood and the health of ecological systems.

The fire of enthusiasm, sexual arousal, and innovation are all parts of the gift Stage 3 players give to the community. The other part is the idealism to shake things up.

From the teenage years onward, people in soul-centric Stage 3 work to develop and authenticate the social self. The "authentic" part of this task is the nature-centered aspect of the work. It has to do with one's own attitudes, interests, and other aspects of one's actual nature. The "social" part of this task has to do with fashion, mores, style, and social conventions.

The Stage 3 job is to honor and incorporate both aspects—the natural and the cultural—into one's personhood. Whereas in the Garden the world is *discovered* and *accepted;* in the Oasis the world, by which I mean one's self-in-the-world, is *constructed* and *chosen.*

Noticing that one is no longer striving to conduct the main tasks of Stage 3 and noticing that that one is "no longer prone to feeling like an emotionally abandoned child psychologically fending for yourself without the support of people who really love you and without your own mature psycho-spiritual resources" is an indicator that one is about to complete the tasks associated with Stage 3 development (in which people remain in the ethnocentric stage of development but prepare themselves for entering into the upcoming worldcentric stage) (Plotkin, 2010, p. 229).

The tension-filled job of blending personal intentions with social conventions is the mandatory assignment for those about to face soul initiation. A so-called "first primary personality," developed in the soul-centric stages leading up to soul initiation, is required as parents, teachers, and caregivers give the developing person liberal but well-defined latitude, gradually extended freedoms, and encouragement to explore new values. What is this personality and how is it formed?

Parents rather than schools are the most likely good mentors at this stage; and so, they are helpful in the formation of their child's first primary personality. Less lectures and more questions, less "do it because I say so" and more role modeling and personal authenticity are good ways caregivers can help the developing person through this difficult period. For now, the job for the developing teenager (at whatever age) is to walk the line between acceptance and authenticity while also exploring values before the pressures of career, marriage, and other midlife obligations cause entrenchment.

For those who have not properly negotiated earlier stages, finding membership in a suitable group, getting in touch with one's present-tense body, emotions, and imagination, or all of the above, will provide the soothing nurturance that will foster growth. So will taking walks in nature.

Too controversial for some professional and all underage audiences, the topic of sexuality is not covered in great detail in this course. It is, nevertheless, too important to be left out so it is covered in detail in a separate Heartwood Path course and covered in this section in sufficient detail to help describe the important passage through the sexually-charged Oasis.

Teenagers need a suitable introduction to sex. They need an understanding of the relationship between the genitals and the heart. They need to know that sex, in addition to being a means to physical pleasure and procreation, is also a portal to the mysteries of seduction, soul, shadow, self, and separateness. They also need to understand the relationship between sex and union, sex and death, and sex and joy. Once one advances to later stages of development, such as "The Cocoon" or "The Wellspring," each described subsequently, one will be ready for the information included in the Heartwood Path for Couples: Connecting Sexually to Reconcile Self and Other. But first, there is more work to be done in the Oasis, namely acquiring the ability to get by in the world by earning a livelihood, by defining oneself culturally, and by studying human-nature reciprocity and ecological responsibility.

One needs to learn that social belonging requires an understanding of "the systemic relationships that make up our more-than-human world" (Plotkin, 2010, p. 224). Such learning occurs best, "not in a traditional classroom experience divided into one-hour intervals, but through more progressive educational models and in the course of genuine, wholehearted living outside of classrooms" (Plotkin, 2010, p. 241).

Some consideration needs to be given to whether all teens need so much algebra and physics at the expense of cosmology, mythology, and eco-literacy. Given the ecological and spiritual nature of many world problems today, a more varied curriculum might be in order. In an eco/soul-centric society there is a requirement that participating members behave well ecologically.

If one has successfully done the tasks of all developmental stages previously discussed one has learned how to think abstractly using formal operations—that is, one can think not only about oneself but also about oneself thinking about oneself. By the end of Stage 3, one has also learned how to "become a competent, proactive protector of nature" (Plotkin, 2010, p. 22). One has learned how to become comfortable "celebrating and expressing gratitude for the generosity and abundance of nature. These ceremonies include those associated with gardening, farming, hunting, eating and observances of the seasonal cycles (anchored in the solstices and equinoxes)" (Plotkin, 2010, p. 224).

To facilitate the development of eco-centric youth and, by extension, an eco-centric society, schools need to provide more experiential field research into matters of the human-nature relationship and to "cultivate language, math, and science skills within a core ecological curriculum" (Plotkin, 2010, p. 225). Such a curriculum would show that environmentalism "is a foundation to all else" (Plotkin, 2010, p. 225).

The oft-rebellious teenager, who often seeks to "cut a wide swath as he finds his way of belonging in the world" is typically reined in by his egocentric society—itself alienated from nature, "insecure, competitive, vigilant, defensive, aggressive when threatened, chronically hungry and often depressed" (Plotkin, 2010, p. 251-253). "When people lose their sense of belonging to circles," writes Macy and Johnstone, "they lose not only their motivation to act for their communities and environment but also valuable sources of support and resilience" (2012, p. 91). The best countermeasure for the developing person, one very difficult to find, is the help of a soul-centric mentor.

Many religious institutions (distinguished from religion itself) in an egocentric society such as ours discourage parishioners from using their imagination and exploring their depths by claiming that their leaders, sometimes developmentally immature, are the only ones who can interpret what is morally right. Many religious organizations use the prospect of heaven to fill the pews. They "keep the individual developmentally arrested by preying on his fear of abandonment" or going to hell (Plotkin, 2010, p. 255). If one feels the desire for religious fellowship, seek a congregation that allows a high degree of self-determination and social engagement. Likewise, egocentric psychotherapy, particularly therapy constricted by the demands of insurance-influenced, shallow-managed care, serve to help clients conform to the egocentric society by going quickly back to work without work inefficiencies but do not particularly help clients develop into developmentally mature elders.

If you seek psychotherapy, find a therapist with the proper credentials, one that uses a soul-centric approach (not focused on only fixing the insulated individual but also helpful with transforming the world), and has a history of social activism. Such activism provides the much needed modeling. "Contributing to positive cultural change can be one of the most potent means of generating one's own positive personal change" (Plotkin, 2010, p 256).

Without the help of soul-centric religious institutions or soul-centric psychotherapy, it is no wonder the overall society is stuck in the mud of "social acceptability, materialism, self-centered individualism, and superficial security rather than authenticity, intimate relationships, soul-infused individual service, creative risk and adventure" (Plotkin, 2010, p. 257).

From a variety of angles we who love in an egocentric society are discouraged from becoming free thinking, psychologically mature adults who might not choose to fill the pew, productively occupy the workstation, spend too much money at the cash register, buy the house with a double garage, or vote the restrictive party line. It is safe to say that about three-quarters of the people living in your neighborhood are stuck in a patho-adolescent stage of psychological development. That means most people nearby are addicted to our egocentric society with all of its problems. They will not be good role models.

To help us get out of this mess, the first step is to personally admit how you have been part of the problem. Then, after getting your own developmental house in order, figure out how you can help others mature psychologically so that they can join you in effectively working for solutions.

If you are beyond your teen years but still in a healthy state within stage 3 there is still plenty of ways you can be of service. You can be a good spouse or parent. You can grow an organic garden, drive a hybrid car, and send money to environmental organizations.

Make sure you have full-bodied present centeredness. If not, spend more mindful time in nature.

To determine when you are ready to move beyond the Oasis—the adolescent stage of development in Stage 3:

1. notice if you feel fairly good about yourself most of the time,
2. notice whether you have accepting friends,
3. notice whether you can communicate your feelings without aggression even in the course of a disagreement,
4. notice whether you accept and take care of your body,
5. notice whether you are apt to apologize when needed,
6. notice whether you are able to determine what sorts of people are best for you,

7. notice whether you can earn a living,

8. notice whether you can celebrate the good and grieve over the bad,

9. notice whether you feel a sense of belonging to the earth,

10. notice whether you recognize that there is more to life than making a big splash socioeconomically,

11. notice whether you think about death and divinity,

12. notice if you are looking to get more out of romance than sex and social standing,

13. notice if you are attentive to the dream world (which most don't because they keep sleeping through it), and

14. notice if you are beginning to be fascinated with the hidden depths within.

Awareness of such occurrences is a sign that a new stage may be imminent. Those transitioning to Stage 4 will likely feel reluctant to move out of the Oasis. If you can overcome your reluctance and if you are lucky (or if you contact an eartHeart at www.heartwoodpath.com), an elder, sent by the Earth in her own defense against the planetary crisis, will be waiting to help with the transition. It will be a transition wherein self-interest is extended to embrace the whole. In the next stage, authenticity will be a higher priority than acceptance.

Paradoxically, the embrace of one's present stage—or one's engagement in the key tasks associated with one's stage—is the only way to move to the next stage. For this reason, there is no room along the Heartwood Path for prejudice towards any one stage. It may be the goal to help people move to higher stages but any disregard or lack of respect for earlier stages is nonsensical—since we all have to be babies before we can become adults, for example. Such disregard is also unethical.

Those who favor higher levels over lower levels are being "stagist." Each level is equally important and ought to be equally valued, both in its own right and because it is the only way to move to higher stages.

No stage can be skipped. One can only occupy one stage at a time.

The successful work on the tasks of one stage determines the success one might achieve in the next higher stage. This work at each level is never really totally done. One can work on tasks from a previous stage but cannot do the tasks of succeeding stages until one is ready.

Add "stagism" to your list of "isms." Like racism, "stagism" is beneath your own dignity.

Also, note the other paradox of human development: as one grows more unique, during one's development, one's focus does not become self-centered. Added personal uniqueness leads to a more wide-ranging concern for others. As Plotkin says: "As our way of belonging to the world becomes more particular (unique) our sense of community becomes less particular. We fall in love, outwardly and progressively, with the universe" (2010, p. 85).

From this description of what it takes to successfully move through Wheel of Life Stage 3 one can see that there are many metaphorical dragons to slay. For help with battles of self development turn to inner guide and Archetype "The Destroyer" by doing the next activity.

Successfully confronting one's own outdated notions and behavioral habits and confronting one's own death are, along with learning to let go and turning things over to others, a task guided by the Archetype Pearson calls "The Destroyer" (1991, p. 137). The fears of annihilation, stagnation and death without rebirth propel those under the influence of The Destroyer to seek to the goals of growth and metamorphosis. Without a relationship with The Destroyer one is more likely to destroy or be destroyed. Beyond survival, the gifts of The Destroyer are humility and acceptance—two aspects of human growth fostered in the following activity.

To The Destructive Hero...

HumaNatureConnect Activity

Start-up Protocol

If this is not a day when you prefer to spend time in nature without an agenda, do the Heartwood Path Start-up Protocol found in the Appendix. Then return here to do the remaining portion of this activity:

Getting To Know Your Inner Guide—"The Destroyer"

Use two of the Natural Senses and Sensitivities—"Sense of self including friendship, companionship, and power" and "Sense of mind and consciousness" (Cohen, website: http://www.ecopsych.com/insight53senses.html)—as you read the follow excerpts from Carol S. Pearson's book **Awaken the Heroes Within** and then answer the questions below, using the perspective of your chosen natural being that you imagine is both informed about all aspects of your self and, unlike you, is fair and objective about your recollections of your destructions that lead to humility and acceptance.

"Entering the mysteries almost always requires an encounter with fear and recognition that the ultimate reality of the universe is not pretty and neat and in human control" (Pearson, 1991, p. 139).

"At some point in our lives, the Destroyer within or without strikes, and hollows us out, humbles us. It 'wounds' us, and through that opening we are able to experience new realities" (Pearson, 1991, p. 142).

"The Destroyer begins to become our ally when we recognize the need to change or give up something with denying the pain or grief involved" (Pearson, 1991, p. 142).

The shadow sides of the Destroyer are self-destructiveness and/or destruction of others. The impetuses to follow the sunny side of the Destroyer is pain, suffering, loss, and tragedy. A Level One Destroyer brings confusion, the grappling with the meaning of death, loss and pain. A Level Two Destroyer brings an acceptance of loss, mortality, and "relative powerlessness." A Level Three Destroyer helps one choose to let go of "anything that no longer supports your values, life, and growth, or that of others" (Pearson, 1991, p. 146).

With these statements in mind and with the perspective of your informed, objective natural being, answer the following questions. When doing so, think about the past and the present.

How much or how little are you (and your family, coworkers, and friends) under the influence of the Destroyer?

Is there anything about your relationship with the Destroyer that you wish were different?

Next, review and "remember" the major events of your life, including those that have not yet happened. When you visualize your own death imagine saying goodbye to everyone and everything that brings you pleasure. After your burial or cremation, visualize how you will be reborn in a way that is "consistent with your philosophy or theology" (Pearson, 1991, p. 147).

What can you recall in your life about a time when you were praised for a personally developed aspect of your self that is both authentic and socially acceptable?

Follow-up Protocol

For best results, write down your impressions of this activity in your journal using the Heartwood Path Follow-up Protocol found in the Appendix. Afterwards, consider sharing your interpretations with others.

Heartwood Path Axioms

Key Assertions From Waypoint 5.21

5.21.1.

Rather than attempting to regress or compromise your development, think about the mission you need today that is the main job of Life Stage 3: focusing on your peer group, sexuality, and society.

5.21.2.

From being centered in nature and family in Stage 2, the person in Stage 3 is centered in one's peer group, sexuality, and society.

5.21.3.

One's gift to the community that is forged in Stage 3 is one's development of a culturally viable ego that is authentic and acceptable.

5.21.4.

Whereas in the Garden of Stage 2 one's self-in-the-world is *discovered* and *accepted;* in the Oasis of Stage 3 one's self-in-the-world is *constructed* and *chosen.*

Nocturnal Pilgrimage 5.21

For best results, write down your impressions of each night's dreams in your journal using the Heartwood Path Dreaming Time Protocols found in the Appendix. Afterwards, consider sharing your Dream Tending with others.

The Natural Law Of Forfeiture:

> One has to
> give up something
> to obtain something new.

All gains are paid for by a loss. Give first to obtain something of greater value later. One cannot move forward without leaving some things behind. To obtain what you want you have to give up something in return. To resist making sacrifices is to block your forward momentum. You cannot have both what you want and what you have to give up. You have to make a choice by determining if the sacrifice is worth the achievement. Remember, once you have what you want you will have to pay continuously for its maintenance and protection.

Pertinent And Instructive Gems From My Dream Tending Journal

After dinner, we threw a few more pieces of wood on the fire and walked down to river's edge, about twenty feet away. We held each other as we enjoyed the reflection of the moon on the churning water. The bigger fire lured us back to camp, where we set about the task of throughly removing sand from each other's naked body. This was not eco-tourism, although we did manage to half-fill a large garbage bag with junk carried onto the island by the river. This was eco-sexual tourism, for lack of a better name. Something indefinite and odd was emerging—a three-way respectful and intimate relationship in which the island was an equal partner. When it came time to curl up in the big sleeping bag, for example, we decided to pull it out of our tent so we could include nature—the night sky, the sounds of beavers slapping the water with their tails in the backwater behind the island, and the ever-present sand in our adult playtime.

When I asked Kim if she wanted to sleep under the stars or in the tent she said, unhesitatingly:

"Let's linger out here for a while, so nothing comes between us and the river."

Warmed by the fire, we used the down sleeping bag only as a cushion beneath us. Our inter-twined skin glowed orange against the blackness of night. The exact positioning of the tarp and sleeping bag was determined by three factors: safety, warmth, and enough darkness to see the meteor shower. As in all relationships, compromises had to be made.

Lesson Learned: A separate Kim, a separate me, and a separate island was not the way it was. The most important thing was the way we perceived of the relationship between our own individual selves, between each other, and between us and the sandy island. We found higher meaning there because our perceptions had become interwoven with the setting. Just as my body fit well with hers, we both fit well with the setting. When one becomes fully conscious, it becomes apparent that the World is fitted to the Mind, and vice versa. The island— including the water around it and the sky above it—was affecting our thinking and our active bodies. We were in the heat of the setting, a fever we did not want to break.

Sleep. Dream about your time in adolescence. We all know that was the time of your life when being hot did not come in flashes. Try to remember now at least three good things about your youth. That way you will at least remember one of them later. Tend to your dreams. When ready, go to the next waypoint, "Wheel Of Life (Stage 4)."

22

Wheel Of Life (Stage 4)

LEAVE "HOME" TO EXPLORE THE MYSTERIES OF NATURE AND THE PSYCHE

Beginning typically with the rite of passage known as "Confirmation," the developing person enters a sort of tomb if she is still an adolescent and a sort of womb if she is an adult. The main task for this stage is leaving the "home" of the adolescent personality (the cultural task) and exploring the mysteries of nature and psyche (the natural task)" (Plotkin, 2010, p. 264).

Inspired by the Archetype of the Wanderer, the developing person in State 4 offers as gifts to the world darkness and mystery. Understandably, one's center of gravity is the underworld mysteries of soul and nature, a centering that enables one to obtain a world-centric perspective or Circle of Identity.

Assuming healthy development, one falls more under the influence of the Soul. The siren call of mystery and the depths of wild nature cause a temporary loss of one's focus on contemporary society. Both spooky and alluring, this call causes a shift from one's peer group, sex, and society to a drawn out experiential meeting with the darker aspects of nature and psyche.

In these depths one enters a sort of Cocoon where one's perspective on life shifts. In the metamorphosis that occurs in the Cocoon, one shifts from social, academic, economic, and religious projects to a search for a greater story about what one is destined to live, a more pronounced search for the Soul, and a completion of an adolescent personality capable of handling the expanded significance of one's life. Unlike the restrictive silk bag for the metamorphosis of moths, the human developmental Cocoon, woven from one's dreams and examinations of previous wounds and allurements, is a task that is the alternative to conformity and rebellion: wide wanderings in Nature—both inner world and outer world.

So important is drifting with no apparent purpose that it is not considered wasteful if half of your time along the Heartwood Path is devoted to unstructured wandering (even at the expense of doing the Activities).

Within the Cocoon the metamorphosing person uses her own path (that might take her to dream work, wilderness excursions, initiatory literature, or the arts) to seek her Authentic Self and, upon finding her Soul (her ultimate role in the world), emerges a true adult. If one is afraid of undertaking such an adventure, for fear of the pain of the existential crisis that might emerge, know that the attractive beauty of nature will provide enough distraction to counter the angst.

Along with the archetype of "The Wanderer," the Archetype "The Visionary" has a role to play in the Cocoon and beyond. The Visionary "is in conversation with the mysteries of the world, on the lookout for signs and omens" (Plotkin, 2010, p. 282). The Visionary helps the developing person see into the unknown, borrow ideas from one discipline and apply them to another, pull what is mysterious and precious about one's Soul into the light of everyday life, and allow one's vision and dreams to take precedence over tradition.

Whether you find this Visionary in yourself, in another person, or in nature the Archetype will help you with answering two key questions: "What is my life about anyway? What do I live for?" (Plotkin, 2010, p. 285).

Answers will be found by wandering, figuratively and actually, until one finds a life to call one's own, one's Soul, and, to quote theologian Frederick Buechner, that place where one's "deepest gladness and the world's hunger meet." Such answers are determined by a Stage 4 person with a "particular set of skills, ideas, sensitivities and values" (Plotkin, 2010, p. 266).

A healthy Stage 4 individual has the qualifications for a significant descent towards greater significance, towards the Soul, and towards one's destiny. Like all the previous tectonic developmental shifts that a healthy developing person undergoes, the transition that occurs in Stage 4 is both an *ending* (a Confirmation) without repentance for past sins but with a surrender of old pillars of support and beliefs about how oneself and one's world are supposed to be and a *beginning* (a Commencement) of "a surrender to the desires of (one's) truer human nature . . ." and (one's) "deepest and wildest passions" (Plotkin, 2010, p. 267-268).

One may or may not feel the need to quit one's job, sell one's house, or leave one's marriage, and one ought not abandon one's children, but it is necessary to surrender what no longer supports the exploration of one's deepest nature. To most who go through it, the quest is precipitated by a death of a loved one, a failed business, a near-death experience, or other calamities.

Many undertake the quest not so much for the seeking of mature adulthood, which is often associated with drudgery, but rather for adventure or freedom. One begins to yearn to explore both the "enigmas and raptures of life" (Plotkin, 2010, p. 290). This time of one's life is both exciting and daunting.

There is also a mixture of encouragements. If you are on a quest, culture encourages you to leave home, but not for too long. Nature encourages you to explore the mysteries, however long that takes.

The passage that occurs on such a quest is often accompanied by vow-making, leave-taking, appearance-changing, loose-ends-tying, wild oats-sowing, and, most significantly, community gift-giving. This gift may be simply the confirmed State 4 person's presence, with all her mystery, newness, embodied affirmation of darkness, psychic turbulence, originality, irreverence, and emergence into the future.

The key jobs of the journey are "honing your skills of self-reliance" and "relinquishing your attachment to your adolescent, or first adult, identity" (Plotkin, 2010, p. 291) and establishing your means of survival. Such endeavors are part of one's "survival dance." They make it possible for one to more fully wander inwardly and outwardly (one's sacred dance). If one is progressing in a healthy manner, this latter sacred form of "dance" eventually makes the survival form of dance less needed.

This transition is often made possible by finding what the Buddhists call "right livelihood"—work that is "psychologically sustaining, economically adequate, socially responsible, and environmentally sound" (Plotkin, 2010, p. 293) One's sacred dance is the real work of Stage 4. This real work may require:

1. catching-up from previous developmental stages,
2. remedial work in reclaiming one's innocence,
3. becoming more eco-literate,
4. not becoming fixated on healing emotional wounds as this is a never-ending job and doing so may prevent further development which requires one to make too big a deal regarding one's small personal story,
5. accepting some degree of suffering,
6. wanting to feel more, and
7. wanting to not be mired in the past.

When most people in a society are centered in a particular stage, that society will take on the attributes associated with that stage of individual development. One can tell what is important to a society by how much attention the members of that society give to any aspect of that society.

One can determine if a society has failed to collectively reach a center of gravity that has its locus in Stage 3 (or lower) in the following ways:

1. when shopping is the main freedom,
2. when entities are less important than commodities,
3. when the highest value comes from technology,
4. when profits are more important than people,
5. when natural resources and Third World people are discarded so the world's elite can buy techno-gadgets and other toys,
6. when money is more important than meaning, and
7. when "us" reigns supreme over "them."

Sound familiar?

Such patterns are the result of the collective wounds of the people in the society, the lack of development of the bulk of the people in the society, and the mass avoidance of psychological wounds. Knowing that trauma fosters genesis, the Soul fosters psychological wounds so that, in the Cocoon, the developing person can work on her sacred personal challenges and, in so doing, become a unique individual. In this way, one's wounds become the keys to one's destiny. Such teachings occur only if one faces the pain rather than denying it by shopping or overeating, or having impersonal sex, or doing the other things that serve as a distraction.

Facing the pain at the heart of one's psychological wounds is not about healing the adolescent ego. It is rather about opening the psyche so that one can replace stewing over the old wounds that occurred during one's small story (personal history) with going into action to solve the wounds from the larger story (cultural history).

One's old life dies in the metaphorical small-story death chamber of the Cocoon. One dis-identifies with the old narrow, personal patterns and, after becoming like the goo in the Cocoon, one undergoes a metamorphosis and then, like an emerging butterfly, launches one's new self into the world. This metamorphosis occurs at its own pace. One cannot rush or help a butterfly emerge from its cocoon.

Finding one's core wounds without indulging or repressing the pain that is found there is slow work. Self-blame, self-pity, and playing the victim is not only not called for it is also a pathetic way to miss the treasure at the heart of one's ruins. Such treasures are excavated by:

1. certain forms of bodywork,
2. dream work,
3. creating or engaging with sacred geometry,
4. certain ceremonies (rites of passage, for example),
5. meditation,
6. the practice of mindfulness,
7. vision quests,
8. fasts,
9. responding to signs in nature,
10. trance drumming,
11. council or circle meetings,
12. conversing with the Spirit,
13. prayer,
14. dialogues with more-than-human beings,
15. sensitive nature observation,
16. myth making and telling,
17. service work that helps one delve more deeply into the world and the heart,
18. sacred sexuality (that demonstrates that one's innate sexual nature fosters membership into the natural world),
19. soulful music making or listening,
20. ceremonial sweats,
21. shadow work,
22. the joys and pains of romance,
23. life coaching,
24. praising the world enough to realize the one's Greater Self is full of resplendence, and

25. certain nature-based rituals.

These practices are different from and can be adjuncts to psycho-therapy, which helps the conscious self grow its ego and improve its emotional life and functioning in society. Psychotherapy helps people get in touch with themselves emotionally and bodily, feel more cen-tered and calm, function in a less conflicted way socially, increase their capacity for empathy and intimacy, and become more secure econom-ically. Typically psychotherapy does not lower the veils of separation that keep one from developing a "relationship with the mysteries of the soul and spirit" (Plotkin, 2010, p. 330).

While psychotherapy helps with the narrow individual self (and has encouraged complacency, conformity, and narcissism) it does little to help meet the urgent needs of the Greater Self that is the world (Plotkin, 2010, p. 330). Sometimes the best therapy is actively working to improve the world.

Service work "provides a respite from self-obsession . . . builds self esteem . . . and reshapes us as part of the solution" (Plotkin, 2010, p. 331). A well-adjusted conformist is not going to help solve the world's problems as much as a sad and angry engaged visionary.

What is needed is a set of practices aimed at helping people abandon their social stability and "me-only" psychological composure. The kind of soul work done along the Heartwood Path is not about job satis-faction, narrowly defined psychological comfort, or blending in better with a pathological society. It is rather about creating psychologically mature elders who are capable of post-conventional criticism of the culture.

Such elders work to make a better world through the help they give to those willing to transform the world by transforming themselves. This work is not done as a form of compromise, or compliance, or imposed morality. It is done because world-centric love is beautiful and attractive.

The rewards of being an eco-centric elder come in a variety of forms, including:

1. making peace with the past;
2. being able to know the difference between shallow and deep loyalty (between enablers and true helpers, for example);
3. avoiding the creation or absorption of all deception;
4. ending unhealthy involvements;
5. giving up the old life story that was both enabling and limiting;
6. living more fully in the present;
7. savoring the gifts of the world;
8. finding solitude in nature;
9. enhancing the feeling of gratitude for one's experiencing of richness and opportunity;
10. developing an ongoing meeting with the Soul and, in so doing, discovering "the gift you were born to carry to others" (Plotkin, 2010, p. 304);
11. obtaining nature's atypical news while wandering in nature;
12. successfully confronting one's own death; and
13. choosing authenticity over social acceptance.

Choosing authenticity over social acceptance and receiving the above-mentioned other rewards from the practice of Soul work is made more understandable and fruitful if one gets to know the inner guide Plotkin calls "the Wanderer," which is very similar to the Archetype Pearson calls "the Seeker." In the following activity, I will combine these two names and call them collectively "The Seeking Sojourner."

To The Pilgrim Hero...

HumaNatureConnect Activity

Start-up Protocol

If this is not a day when you prefer to spend time in nature without an agenda, do the Heartwood Path Start-up Protocol found in the Appendix. Then return here to do the remaining portion of this activity:

Getting To Know Your Inner Guide—"The Seeking Sojourner"

Use two of the Natural Senses and Sensitivities—"Sense of self including friendship, companionship, and power" and "Sense of mind and consciousness" (Cohen, website: http://www.ecopsych.com/in-sight53senses.html)—as you read the follow excerpts from Carol S. Pearson's book **Awaken the Heroes Within** and then answer the questions below, using the perspective of your chosen natural being that you imagine is both informed about all aspects of your self and, unlike you, is fair and objective about your recollections of your wandering searches.

"The quest always begins with yearning. We feel discontented, confined, alienated, or empty. Often we do not even have a name for what is missing, but we long for that mysterious something" (Pearson, 1991, p. 123).

The urge to seek the grail, to climb the mountain in search of visions, to seek wisdom, to cross new frontiers, to achieve the formerly unachievable in all area of life seems endemic in the human race. The Seeker responds to the call to Spirit—to ascend" (Pearson, 1991, p. 123).

The goal of the Searching Sojourner is "for a better life or a better way." The fear of the Seeking Sojourner is conformity and become entrapped. The shadow side of the Searching Sojourner is to leave, escape, and take off. The task of the Searching Sojourner is to be "true to a deeper or higher truth." The gift of the Seeking Sojourner is ambition and autonomy (Pearson, 1991, p. 123).

"The call to the quest can come at any age, but it is clearest and most distinct in late adolescence and early adulthood." This is the time of exploration, "new experiences, study, travel and experimentation" (Pearson, 1991, p. 125).

"It is never too late to respond to the Soul's call to adventure . . .The Seeker experiences the call as a rite of passage, an initiatory experience of the transpersonal without which the real Self cannot be born" (Pearson, 1991, p. 129).

"To some degree, all the forms of the quest reduce to a basic desire to encounter authenticity—in oneself, in the world outside, and in the cosmos as a whole" (Pearson, 1991, p. 129).

Quoting Abraham Joshua Heschel: "We have in common a terrible loneliness. Day after day a question goes up desperately in our minds: 'Are we alone in the wilderness of the self'" (Pearson, 1991, p. 129).

"If we do not respond to our inner Seeker's call, we may experience it in its shadow forms. The shadow Seeker manifests itself as an obsessive need to be independent that keeps us isolated and alone. If the urge is totally denied, it will be expressed through physical and mental symptoms" (Pearson, 1991, p. 131). Thus, the Shadow side of the Seeking Sojourner is "excessive ambition, perfectionism, pride, inability to commit, and addictiveness" (Pearson, p. 132).

The call of the Seeking Sojourner, that which gets her going, is alienation emptiness, dissatisfaction, and opportunity. Level One Seeking Sojourners focus on exploring, experimenting, studying, and wandering. Level Two Sojourners become the best they can be and climb "the ladder of success," Level Three Sojourners focus on transformation and "spiritual seeking" (Pearson, 1991, p. 132).

With these statements in mind and with the perspective of your informed, objective natural being, answer the following questions. When doing so, think about the past and the present.

How much or how little are you (and your family, coworkers, and friends) under the influence of the Seeking Sojourner?

Is there anything about your relationship with the Seeking Sojourner that you wish were different?

What can you recall about your journey of soul work thus far that helped you, if at all, become a thoughtful post-conventional critic of culture?

Follow-up Protocol

For best results, write down your impressions of this activity in your journal using the Heartwood Path Follow-up Protocol found in the Appendix. Afterwards, consider sharing your interpretations with others.

Heartwood Path Axioms

Key Assertions From Waypoint 5.22

5.22.1.

Rather than attempting to backslide or compromise your development, think about the mission you still need today that is the main job of Life Stage 4: leaving "home" to explore the mysteries of nature and the psyche.

5.22.2.

Inspired by the Archetype of the Wanderer, the developing person in Stage 4 offers as gifts to the world darkness and mystery.

5.22.3.

Having no agenda and following one's joy leads to unforeseen lessons about self-reliance and establishing one's means of survival.

5.22.4.

The kind of soul work done along the Heartwood Path is about creating psychologically mature elders who are capable of helpful and necessary post-conventional criticism of the culture.

Nocturnal Pilgrimage 5.22

For best results, write down your impressions of each night's dreams in your journal using the Heartwood Path Dreaming Time Protocols found in the Appendix. Afterwards, consider sharing your Dream Tending with others.

The Natural Law Of Affixing and Unfastening:

"Affixing"
is attaching one's happiness and self-worth
to the attainment of something and
"unfastening"
is detaching from the suffering
that accompanies desire.

Such attachment and detachment applies to any person or thing one wants or admires obsessively. Obsession leads to imbalance and is, therefore, unsustainable.

The antidote is self-love. We cannot love another person fully until we love ourselves unconditionally. Obsessive affixing requires the kind of "unfastening" that brings forth understanding of one's inner self, self-compassion, a loss of control and power, a release of past conditioning, and detached observation. If a thing or a relationship does not serve you let it go.

Pertinent And Instructive Gems From My Dream Tending Journal

Kim:

"What was that?"

Don:

"A beaver slapping its tail on the water. Probably letting its mate know of its whereabouts."

Kim:

"I wish all men were like that."

Don:

"We all need to be needed."

Kim:

"Before your after-sex "snoremones" kick in, should we sleep out here or move into the tent?"

Don:

"What do you prefer?"

Kim:

"It's funny, but I feel like we would be abandoning our island partner if we moved inside together."

Don:

"If we take off the rainfly the mesh layer beneath will let in our partner's scent. We can also leave the door unzipped, if you like."

Kim:

"What's the downside to sleeping out here, in full island embrace?"

Don:

"Insects will buzz our ears. And the early morning commercial fishermen out on the river will get a kick out of your sunburnt ass, assuming they have binoculars."

Kim:

"I may have to pull the bag over me. My mom made me vow to never to become a Stripper."

Don:

"We will wake up drenched in morning dew, but that's OK. The Sun, after it burns off the morning river fog, will dry the dew on our sleeping bag— thus sterilizing our bed clothes."

Kim:

"I vote to get drenched, to get sun-cleaned, and to entertain the fishermen in the morning (Sorry, Mom!). Let's stay out here and keep our three-way going, for now."

Don:

"I won't tell your mom."

Lesson Learned: Just as one cannot take the mountain out of the mating mountain lions, or the stream out of the spawning salmon, despite all of one's ill-informed efforts to live according to nature-disconnected stories, one cannot remove the human couple from their natural setting. Between lovers there is always a third partner—the personified setting of the love affair. This third party makes the loving as much about transformation as it is about gratification. It not only adds zest to the coupling, it also reconciles the incongruities between what is masculine from what is feminine. As a testimony to the importance of this topic, a full book and course is devoted to eco-sexual erotic relationships later in the Heartwood Path series. This book/course will transform the notion of Mother Earth—which leads to the abusive and humiliating infantilization of the human—into a much more realistic, helpful, and pertinent personification—that of Lover Earth.

Sleep. Dream about your early adulthood. We all know that was a time when chest pain was not about someone standing on your nipples. Don't worry about aging. You are never gonna be old enough to know better. It's all a cycle anyway. Take friends for example. When you are old and senile they become new friends again. Tend to your dreams. When ready, to move another step closer to Gladandgreen Junction, proceed to the next waypoint, entitled "Wheel Of Life (Stage 5)."

23

Wheel Of Life (Stage 5)

BRING VISIONARY ACTION, HOPE, AND INSPIRATION TO YOUR COMMUNITY

Now comes the time in the human development cycle to learn how to embody the soul in culture. With the help of the Visionary, the Archetype of the western section of the Wheel of Life, one uses the archetypal model of the Soul Apprentice to give visionary action, hope, and inspiration to one's community.

Throughout the Wheel of Life, one is carried along, consciously or unconsciously, in the enduring spring. At Stage 5, one enters into a sort of fount, "the Wellspring." Immersed in this metaphorical source of the Enduring Stream, one is aware for the first time of its nourishing and sustaining flow. This new awareness bubbles up like spring water from one's inner depths, becomes overt, and rouses one's thoughts and actions in a seemingly magical fashion. At the Wellspring—the transfer zone between the underworld and the everyday world, between mystery and manifestation, and between the enigmatic and the formed— the developing person applies for the first time deep cavernous mysteries to her service in the middle world of everyday society. As if in the spell of attractive wet sirens at the westward-most part of the Wheel of

Life, whose songs make formerly invisible secrets plainly evident, the developing person now seeks to embody the Sirens at the Wellspring through creative actions.

Elders—those who have already heard and responded to the Siren's song—are needed at this point to spur the developing person to take real world actions that are also inspired by the Sirens' songs. The Elders ensure that the developing person retains a mixture of magic and nature; and, in so doing, secure the emergence of right action—the elixir of life. Henceforth, dripping in what Plotkin calls the "enigmatic creativity of the unfathomable depths" one's personality, formed earlier on the Wheel of Life, becomes "rooted firmly in the soul's desire" (Plotkin, 2010, p. 343).

Thus, at the Wellspring, one finds one's ultimate place in the world, one's mysterious mystical mark, and one's particular way to engage in visionary action. Such embodying is a powerful political act for it marks the transition from individual existence to collective action.

At the Wellspring, one is no longer centered on being an individual agent. One becomes also a mediator of Mystery and the more-than-human Self. At the Wellspring one becomes bonded to one's own particular destiny. Destiny is a sense of purpose we are born to bring into the world through our own bent on art, raising children, politics, or any other cultural doing. Like the tasty watercress plant rooted in a spring branch, old styles, strengths, and abilities may linger at the Wellspring. Despite such resiliency, one's status changes irreversibly as one makes a promise broken only by death.

With no excuses, one now has an obligation that is both joyous (because one feels on track) and terrible (because of the magnitude of the burden). This obligation is one's own role in the unfolding of the world's Soul that is marked by communion between people, landscapes, and non-humans. The Wellspring provides water for "one's soulful seed of quiescent potential," a seed that blooms as "soulful service" (Plotkin, 2010, p. 346 and 348). This service begins after an Initiation, public or private, that may include the giving of vows, the consecration of symbols, and the giving of prayers.

After such Initiation, which has nothing to do with elitism or disreputable cults or membership in hierarchical organizations, one undertakes a journey that is best done without boasting, for one is not on a heroic but delusional mission to save the world but rather "simply participating in the world" in one's own fashion (Plotkin, 2010, p. 349). During this journey one engages in true service to one's community in a way that is also fulfilling personally and sustainable. One shifts from concerns about acceptance to a more mature form of authenticity that is rooted in an allegiance to something greater and deeper than one's own desires, emotions, opinions, and personal comfort.

As if demonstrating that being a visionary is not restricted to only those who are extraordinarily gifted, one undertakes one's own concentrated and fresh brand of engaged, on-the-ground, creative artistry. One takes what was formerly invisible and unformed and gives it a new apparent shape. One becomes the change one seeks. Loyal to both the essence of nature and the form of culture, one walks a metaphorical tightrope while balancing mystery with practicality, essence with form, imagination with embodiment, and the mysteries of the underworld with beneficial serviceable trades in the middle world. In brief, one balances idealism and a useful delivery system.

This balancing leads to instabilities, false turns, and occasional falls. It usually results in more-than-individual and more-than-human self-discovery. At the Wellspring, egocentrism dies as one adopts an eco-centric perspective. One begins to identify with all species, landscapes, and ecosystems. One remembers one's original fidelity to the earth. One remembers a long lost interweaving as one imagines being a thread in the tapestry of the earth. This imagining and remembering —sometimes holy, sometimes horrible, and sometimes both—propels one into action, but this carrying out of one's vision is beyond typical altruism. It is self-love and, more accurately, love of Greater Self.

One experiences the pain of the earth—pain that is, like all pain, a warning to take remedial action. The result is one's standing up for one's more-than-human community, armed with deep emotional responses to symbols, dreams, myths, visions, and other mysteries of the underworld.

Even if one is rewarded and fulfilled in one's soul mission, there comes a time, inevitably, when one feels the need for redirection. Like a hermit crab that has outgrown its home and needs to move to a new place, one will someday again need to make a change, delve into the depths, die to one's current ways, and launch one's self in a new direction.

As you continue in your own fashion, the Soul is revealed to you. You will likely notice that it is not a "ghost," but a "place"—one's deepest purpose. As one moves around the western half of the Wheel of Life, far enough to move into the upper half, one begins to realize that the first half of one's life has been shaped so it can best serve the Spirit and the World in the second half of life.

The Soul Initiation that occurs at this point is not marked by any badge of honor or status symbol but is made quietly evident by sustainable Soul-inspired service. Unlike some earlier strivings, such Soulful service is not debilitating. Instead, one does what can in one's own way. Whether in or out of work and whether one's dealings are directed at family or strangers, one's actions are enough.

One becomes skilled at balancing good challenges against doing too much. In this way, if all goes well, perseverance becomes the norm.

If one has not succumbed to capitulation, and has not reverted to conformity, but is following one's Soul purpose, one has finally conquered burnout. The still-developing person at the Wellspring has become an attentive apprentice to the Soul.

At the Wellspring I discovered how I averted burnout and, with that knowledge, I am, at last, able to write that piece, now nine books long, that David Brower asked me to produce over two decades ago.

I am hearing long-horned trumpets: dat-dah,dah-dahhh!! Are you?

At and after the Wellspring callings from the Soul become more important than social approval or one's own opinions and desires. Giving up egocentric or socio-centric perspectives is not total, for these are not sacrificed. Such less mature perspectives just become subordinate to deeper forms of genuineness that coincide with the desires of the Soul.

From striving to find a good fit between community and one's individual personality one begins to arrive at a good fit between one's individuality, one's more-than-human community, and one's Soul. Bolstered by this fit, one is prepared to embody the mysteries from the depths.

Embodying these mysteries is a way of living that is both *blessed* by Soul-imparted ways of seeing how to make possibilities manifest and *burdened* by inevitable vulnerabilities and melancholia. Making possibilities manifest stems from being now able to have "the largest possible conversation she can have with life" (Plotkin, 2010, p. 352). The vulnerabilities and melancholia occur in the following ways:

1. as one begins to contemplate the inevitability of one's own death;
2. as one engages in soul-discovery;
3. as one frets over the risks that go along with the adventure of embodying the mysteries of the Underworld;
4. as one causes misunderstandings;
5. as one examines deep but sacred inner world wounds;
6. as one feels greater empathy for the plight of humans, non-humans, and the earth; and
7. as one more fully begins to feel the pain of the Earth itself.

Despite these emotional challenges, one begins to feel more grateful of the blessings of the earth. This expanded sense of gratitude spurs the developing person to give back to the world the gifts of her vision and action.

Knowing herself better now, the developing person is able to bring greater authenticity to her relationships, and to own her " projections of shadow and of anima and animus . . . She also discovers that her relationship to the wild world mirrors her romantic relationships, and, even more, that nature becomes the context within which she experiences her loving. Her longing for her lover resonates with her love of nature. Perhaps they become indistinguishable" (Plotkin, 2010, p. 374). Learn more by doing the following activity.

To The Loving Hero...

HumaNatureConnect Activity

Start-up Protocol

If this is not a day when you prefer to spend time in nature without an agenda, do the Heartwood Path Start-up Protocol found in the Appendix. Then return here to do the remaining portion of this activity:

Getting To Know Your Inner Guide—"The Lover"

Use two of the Natural Senses and Sensitivities—"Sense of self including friendship, companionship, and power" and "Sense of mind and consciousness" (Cohen, website: http://www.ecopsych.com/insight53senses.html)—as you read the follow excerpts from Carol S. Pearson's book **Awaken the Heroes Within** and then answer the questions below, using the perspective of your chosen natural being that you imagine is both informed about all aspects of your self and, unlike you, is fair and objective about your recollections of your love life.

"Without love, the Soul does not engage itself with life" (Pearson, 1991, p. 148).

"Attachment and bonding come under the protection of Eros (the Lover). Such attachments are deeply primal, sensual, physical." The " . . . sexual intimacy of lovers carries that quality of extreme physicality, vulnerability, trust, and the slaking of desires—for closeness, for sexual expression and release, for knowing and being known" (Pearson, 1991, p. 149).

"The challenge of Eros is literally the key today to the survival of our species and to our cultural recovery from an epidemic of workaholism, consumerism, drug and alcohol addiction, and the widespread denial of both Spirit and Soul" (Pearson 1991, p. 152).

"Agape differs from Eros in that the loving union is initially with oneself, not a lover, friend, or child. It is this inner union that allows us to develop the capacity not just to love our own loved ones, but to love humanity and the cosmos" (Pearson, 1991, p. 156).

"Eros smiles on those who see it as sacred." Quoting Matthew Fox: "All lovemaking (as distinct from having sex) is Christ meeting Christ. Love beds are altars. People are temples meeting temples, the holy of holies receiving the holy of holies..." Go beyond 'being in love' to being the presence of cosmic love embodied and reflected in two human lovers" (Pearson, 1991, p. 155).

"Eros often attends the creative process" (Pearson, 1991, p. 157).

The shadow side of the Lover is envy, jealousy, an "obsessive on a love object or relationship, sexual addiction . . . promiscuity, obsession with sex or pornography, or (conversely) puritanism." The call of the Lover is yearning, seduction, and "falling in love (with a person, an idea, a cause, a work)" (Pearson, 1991, p. 157). A Level One Lover helps one follow bliss and love. A Level Two Lover helps one become bonded and make commitments. A Level Three Lover helps one give birth to the Self, connect the personal to the transpersonal, and connect "the individual with the collective" (Pearson, 1991, p. 157).

With these statements in mind and with the perspective of your informed, objective natural being, answer the following questions. When doing so, think about the past and the present.

How much or how little are you (and your family, coworkers, and friends) under the influence of the Lover?

Is there anything about your relationship with the Lover that you wish were different?

Follow-up Protocol

For best results, write down your impressions of this activity in your journal using the Heartwood Path Follow-up Protocol found in the Appendix. Afterwards, consider sharing your interpretations with others.

Heartwood Path Axioms

Key Assertions From Waypoint 5.23

5.23.1.

Rather than attempting to backslide or short circuit your development, think about the mission you need today that is the main job of Life Stage 5: bringing visionary action, hope, and inspiration to your community.

5.23.2.

Life Stage 5 is the time to learn how to embody the soul in culture through powerful political acts that mark the transition from individual existence to collective action.

5.23.3.

During Stage 5 one shifts from concerns about acceptance to a more mature form of authenticity that is rooted in an alle-

giance to something greater and deeper than one's own desires, emotions, opinions, and personal comfort.

5.23.4.

Perseverance becomes the norm at the Wellspring of Stage 5 as one becomes skilled at balancing good challenges against doing too much.

Nocturnal Pilgrimage 5.23

For best results, write down your impressions of each night's dreams in your journal using the Heartwood Path Dreaming Time Protocols found in the Appendix. Afterwards, consider sharing your Dream Tending with others.

The Natural Law Of Focused Awareness:

Paying attention to something
makes it grow in one's life.

Everything you do requires focused awareness. Be careful not to pay too much attention to negativity. Focus your awareness instead on what you want in life. Where there is doubt, change your attention back to what you know will be successful.

Pertinent And Instructive Gems From My Dream Tending Journal

After a brief walk with the dog, I rushed back to bed with the intention of seamlessly continuing my dream. Seems that my dream character partner wanted me to skip in my dream to the following morning. I often seem to edit out the juicy parts.

Stretching her arms out into the morning air, my sleeping bag partner opened the day with the salutation:

Kim:

"Good morning, Love."

Don, with a gravely voice while still buried deep within our dew drenched sleeping bag.

"Good morning."

Kim:

"I wasn't talking to you, but 'Good morning.'"

Don:

"Who were you talking to, then?"

Kim:

"Our River Island Lover."

Don:

"In your mind's eye, is our mutual lover a man or a woman?"

Kim:

"Hmmmm? It's a 'What's It?'"

Don:

"Huh?"

Kim:

"It's both male and female, not transgendered or transsexual though."

Don:

"So it's happy with the way it was born."

Kim:

"It's a 'she-he.'"

Don:

"A what?"

Kim:

"A herman... herman...herman..."

Don:

"Hermaphrodite"

Kim:

"Easy for you to say."

Don:

"So it's an intersex being."

Kim:

"If you say so. Ain't it weird to kinda think of a river island as a lover, like a mythological person."

Don:

"Not really, there's a long history of widely accepted personifications."

Kim:

"Oh yeah? Name three."

"Don:

"God, Jesus, and Mother Nature."

Kim:

"You're getting kinda controversial, now. I like it when you go rogue."

Don:

"Was our third partner just this Island River or was it all of Nature?"

Kim:

"Yes, both. It morphed back and forth, with each climax?"

Don:

"River to Nature or man to woman?"

Kim:

"Don't worry, Stud, you're still a solid woman-loving man. I'm sure you noticed, however, that Lover Nature is a chick with a ...."

Don:

"Oh, my God!"

Kim:

"Just kidding. Apparently, s/he can be whatever s/he wants, whenever s/he wants, with whoever s/he wants. I hope to see him/her again."

Lesson Learned: Cultures don't normally go where they don't want to go. They are the way they want to be, often symbolized as some sort of personification—the incarnation of something nonhuman into a human form. The classic image of Mother Nature, for example, is a personification in the form of a mother figure who provides for our needs, who is endlessly nurturing, and who is usually tolerant of our greediness and lack of gratitude. We wanted to take whatever we wanted from nature so we personified it into an all giving mother, cruel when irked, but generally tolerant. We also made it so we did not have to pay dues to Mother Nature by also creating the Jesus personification—a man on a cross who died to forgive us for our sins. Once forgiven, we behaved as if we were free to take and take without displays of gratitude. Given the magnitude of our taking and destroying, the endlessly forgiving Mother Earth personification no longer perfectly fits our needs. Now we want a sustainable environment so a new personification—that of Lover Earth—is gradually taking form. Unlike Mother Nature, who would never abandon her offspring, Lover Earth can take off at anytime or destroy us, perhaps with an intolerable climate. The shaping and appreciating of Lover Earth will be addressed in a subsequent Heartwood Path course.

Sleep. Dream about your middle years. If you start having hot flashes just tell your Inner Child to stop playing with matches. Remember, the meaning of rock and roll now by recalling the lyrics of Chuck Berry and the Beatles. We all know that later in life rock and roll will mean you have two choices: the rocking chair and the wheel chair. Kinda depressing? Naps will prevent old age, especially if you do them while driving. Andy Rooney says life is like toilet paper, the closer you get to the end the faster it goes. Don't worry. You are not old yet. Flowers still don't scare you. When ready to head to the next learning post, move to the next waypoint, "Wheel Of Life (Stage 6)."

24

Wheel Of Life (Stage 6)

COUNTER THE EGO WITH
CREATIVE FORMS OF SERVICE

Confirmation that one has mastery of a delivery system for embodying soul powers is the beginning of a developmental stage Plotkin calls the "Wild Orchard" (2012, p. 391). In this stage the developing person has an eco-centric perspective and is most influenced by what Plotkin calls "the Artisan" Archetype and what Pearson calls "the Creator" Archetype. These archetypes, by whatever name, help the developing person give to one's community the seeds of cultural renaissance.

This may be a time when one's Ego, eager to hold on, throws out bones as relatively shallow suggestions as an attempt to gain one's attention. Beware. Such inducements are ways to hold you to past patterns, previous perspectives, and prior priorities.

To counter such distractions, find that place (your Soul) where you can express yourself through the giving not of things but of unique and creative forms of service (writing, organizing, composing, singing, listening, helping, or caring, for example). These novel forms need to arise from a mysterious place of depth. They probably do not come from the people of one's everyday life, people who may have shallow perspectives or agendas of their own.

The source of the ideas for the gifts that you will now give to your community is that peculiar place of depth that oddly seems to be, at once, both something conceived in one's own inner, intangible, noumenal depths and something from the tangible, phenomenal world of nature. This mysterious place is one's most heartfelt sense of purpose, a muse unshaken by such great contradictions as eastern or western religions, or mind and body, or essence and form, or hope and despair, or feminine and masculine, or joy and death.

The muse of the Wild Orchard speaks through dreams, visions, and gifted visionary coaches. This muse, this deep place (a purpose, not a geographic location), allows one to be publicly the way one experiences one to be privately.

You are now the doer of your soulcraft, worthy of induction into a circle of artisans. The old "you" has died, or, better said, made a positive disintegration. The the new "you" has new obligations and responsibilities. It is time to quietly give up old roles and items, make new vows, and undergo a solo fasting ritual in the wild. After such rituals, one's greatest longing is to practice what Plotkin calls the "art of the cultural giveaway" (2010, p. 399).

The forms one gives away may shift over time but the function—the essence of one's Soul—remains steadfast. In the Northwest Quadrant of the Wheel of Life, one blends community (a theme of the North quadrant) with action (a theme of the West quadrant). One also blends the calling of nature (to embody the Soul) with the pleas from culture (to create effective ways to deliver one's gift to society). This blending causes one to have a new appreciation for how there is weal in the wild (meaning something good in Nature, a source of ethical direction that goes beyond—deeper than—religious restrictions or cultural codifications).

The surge of Nature's enduring stream does not lead to bedevilment but to the Soul's wild intentions which always gives one a new voice, a new way of expression, a freshness that is also fair, a newness that does not compromise rightness, and an originality that does not displace decency. As one is and acts from such inspiration, Spirit becomes shown, the Soul's singular productions and the world of infinite possibilities are fulfilling each other, and the mysterious becomes manifest. One not only experiences "a radiant presence in nature that most people largely overlook" one might also lead people on wilderness journeys or help people with plant medicine (Plotkin, 2012, p. 414).

In such ways, one's soul craft becomes who one is in the world. Along with blending action and pleas from culture with callings from nature, the muse/archetype the Artisan in the Wild Orchard blends the four intra-psychic resources from the four quadrants of the Wheel of Life: the leadership of the North, the innocence of the East, the sensual wildness of the South, and the imaginative and visionary capacities of the West.

Through all these blendings and by not identifying with any single Archetype one carries on their energies in ways that serve the more-than-human community. As if all these blendings and dis-identifying is not enough, the developing person in the Wild Orchard needs to spend time working on any unfinished developmental tasks from earlier stages.

A continuation of meditation will help with all of these chores. And help you will need.

In the Wild Orchard, more than in any other stage, one comes to the realization that culture, like an ecological system, remains healthy only through fresh inputs, through an openness of feedback loops. The developing person is likely to experience despair and frustration as one's freshness may not be accepted, at least at first. As one offers "seeds of organic, wild innovation" and as one attempts to "bring mystery, wildness and deep imagination, and praise of the sacred (the natural) to a society obsessed with security, comfort, material wealth and the ownership of things" one's innovations become regarded by members of that society as irrelevant, odd, crazy, or immoral (Plotkin, 2010, p. 423).

For this reason, a sign that you are on the right track may be your initial obscurity. In an egocentric society there will not be many people willing to accept and legitimize one's soul-rooted gifts. This lack of support is one reason why perseverance is both difficult and necessary. Society will likely make you appear to be a fool, but you have a foil.

Turn to your Inner Child. Its innocence will carry you through until you begin to find sympathetic others. Your nature-inspired soul gifts are needed most in a society that honors you the least. Your long period of rejection keeps you from self-inflation, which, along with self-doubt, is too excessively self-centered for a person who has developed the more-than-individual and, indeed, more-than-human perspective. You are rocking the boat filled with people who are accustomed to control. You are attempting to present essences to those who only see objects. You have subjects for those who mainly value objects.

Out of frustration or predisposition, one may turn to earnestness as a way to force the society to take heed. There is danger in this approach. One may become even more discounted and, therefore, prone to burnout. Do not become too serious or heavy. Remember that Joy is the oft-obscure bride of Death and Love is their offspring. One's work need not be burdensome or gloomy. Keep it light and fun. We all know . . . (I'll spare you).

With the fresh energy from the Enduring Stream pulsing through you, people in our egocentric society may likely find you unique, pleasant, yet unsettling. When others view you as a fool think of their condemnations as an ineffective form of sabotage, their attempt to keep you from loosening the bonds of control so valued in their society. Naysayers are likely to be jealous of your level of maturity.

Many of those who will hold you and your gifts in disregard may be those who have not succeeded in passing through an earlier stage of development. Instead, they may have become a conformist and will likely be highly compensated for sticking to the ideals of their egocentric society. While perhaps more financially secure than you, their success may not be rooted in the pathway of eco-centric development and "their intentions and labors are not sourced in the Earth's unfolding or rooted in the soul's desires" (Plotkin, 2010, p. 428). Your naysayers are either, figuratively speaking, likely to be prisoners doing hard time breaking up stones or, at best, they manage the other prisoners in their patho-adolescent society. They are likely to be controllers accustomed to domination and, therefore, cannot appreciate your "power with" and "service to others" approaches. Pay no attention to these managers of the managed, these cogs of the corporate wheels, these lords of the flies. Looking a little deeper: you will see their discontents.

Likewise, pay no heed to those few who will regard you as a god, goddess, or sage. Your distinctiveness blinds them from seeing that you are simply a person participating in the world the best you can. Grow your humility commensurate with your beauty, broad prospective, and uniqueness. Be, therefore, neither a robber baron who makes her money on the backs of the disadvantaged nor a caretaker who, at each moment of service, digs her "hole of low self-esteem a spadeful deeper" (Plotkin, 2010, p. 431) Be sure to balance caregiving with caretaking, but even if you do, it is likely that eventually you will come to a time when your desire for material success wanes, when interest in accomplishment ebbs, when striving gives way to arriving.

"Something new now calls. It is not so much about doing as it is about being . . . It is sad to leave the Wild Orchard with all its imaginative and fulfilling busyness, with all its magical, soul-infused inventions of things, ideas, crafts and expressions never before seen or heard" (Plotkin, 2010, p. 432).

To The Creative Hero...

HumaNatureConnect Activity

Start-up Protocol

If this is not a day when you prefer to spend time in nature without an agenda, do the Heartwood Path Start-up Protocol found in the Appendix. Then return here to do the remaining portion of this activity:

Getting To Know Your Inner Guide—"The Creator"

Use two of the Natural Senses and Sensitivities—"Sense of self including friendship, companionship, and power" and "Sense of mind and consciousness" (Cohen, website: http://www.ecopsych.com/insight53senses.html)—as you read the follow excerpts from Carol S. Pearson's book **Awaken the Heroes Within** and then answer the questions below, using the perspective of your chosen natural being that you imagine is both informed about all aspects of your self and, unlike you, is fair and objective about your recollections of your creativity.

"When we become aware of our connection with the creative source of the universe, we also begin to become aware of our part in creation" (Pearson, 1991, p. 162).

"Most modern thinkers stress the ways we are being created by our environments. Many contemporary New Age leaders, however, assert that at the deepest Soul level, we choose everything that happens to us, and in this way, we are the authors of our destinies, even their most tragic or difficult parts of them" (Pearson, 1991, p. 162).

"If what we create, in the artworks of our own lives, comes authentically from our Souls, the product will inevitably be beautiful" (Pearson, 1991, p. 167).

The goal of the Creator is the "creation of a life, work, or new reality of any kind." The fears of inauthenticity, mis-creation, and failure of imagination propels the developing person to self creation and self-acceptance while enabling the developing person to bring to her community the gifts of creativity, vocation, and identity. (Pearson, 1991, p. 164).

The shadow side of the Creator urges the creation of "negative circumstances, limited opportunities, obsessive creation, (and) workaholism." Called by daydreams, fantasies, and flashes of insight, the person influenced by a Level One Lover Archetype will be open to receive visions, images, hunches, and inspiration; the person influenced by a Level Two Lover Archetype will allow themselves to know what she really want to have or what to create; the person influenced by the Level Three Lover Archetype will let her dreams come true. (Pearson, 1991, p. 169).

With these statements in mind and with the perspective of your informed, objective natural being, answer the following questions. When doing so, think about the past and the present.

How much or how little are you (and your family, coworkers, and friends) under the influence of the Creator?

Is there anything about your relationship with the Creator that you wish were different?

What can you recall from your life about a time when you considered how you formed, if ever, an ethical direction for your life?

What are your recollections of a time, if ever, when you shared the gift of revealing the weal in the wild to others?

What are your recollections, if any, of times in your life when you had to disregard the criticisms of others?

Follow-up Protocol

For best results, write down your impressions of this activity in your journal using the Heartwood Path Follow-up Protocol found in the Appendix. Afterwards, consider sharing your interpretations with others.

Heartwood Path Axioms

Key Assertions From Waypoint 5.24

5.24.1.

Rather than attempt to regress or jump ahead prematurely in your development, think about the mission you need today that is the main job of Life Stage 6: countering the Ego with creative forms of service.

5.24.2.

Confirmation that one has mastery of a delivery system for embodying soul powers marks the beginning of Life Stage 6.

5.24.3.

In Life Stage one's gift to the community is the revelation that there is weal in the wild (meaning something good in Nature, a source of ethical direction that goes beyond—deeper than— religious restrictions or cultural codifications).

5.24.4.

Many of those who will hold you and your gifts in disregard may be those who have not succeeded in passing through an earlier stage of development.

Nocturnal Pilgrimage 5.24

For best results, write down your impressions of each night's dreams in your journal using the Heartwood Path Dreaming Time Protocols found in the Appendix. Afterwards, consider sharing your Dream Tending with others.

The Natural Law Of Pardoning:

Forgive those who have done wrong
and send them love.

Forgiving someone allows love to overcome negative feelings and release animosity. Pardoning, another word for forgiving, does not mean acceptance of bad behavior. Forgiving someone is for your own benefit. It heals and empowers as long as you also forget the transgression. It allows you to grow spiritually, reach your desires, and honor your own path. Forgiveness mends broken hearts, fixes relationships, and bring forth peace and harmony. It often takes time to be ready to forgive earnestly, but rest assured that pardoning is worth the effort.

Pertinent And Instructive Gems From My Dream Tending Journal

As predicted, while we were lingering inside our sleeping bag, still in the shadow of the huge bluff across the river, downstream came a johnboat, filled with nets, and driven by a commercial fisherman. Our camp was in plain site, but he was traveling on the opposite side of the largest river in North America, so he posed no imminent threat to our serenity. Kim, delighted, stuck her bare leg and arm outside of the sleeping bag, imitating those tantalizing last photos of Marilyn Monroe. As he passed, she waved and yelled, "Good morning!" several times. There was no response, possibly due to the distance or the loudness of his outboard motor. After he could no longer be heard, Kim took the opportunity afforded by the stillness to ask another of her weighty questions:

"What message did Lover Nature say to you last night?"

Don:

"Hello, let me introduce myself. I'm the bigger part of you."

Kim:

"I thought I heard her talking to you just before daybreak.

Care to share what s/he said?"

There was a long pause.

Don:

"Get over yourself. Your problems are tiny when compared to all the other problems of the world."

Lying their together for a long period of silence, I could feel my empathy growing along with her self-reflecting.

Eventually she sat up, holding the sleeping bag across her bare breasts. She looked up and down the big river, which, despite a historical mistake in the naming, stretched from the Northern Rockies to the Gulf of Mexico.

Eventually, she whispered as she shook her head and wiped away tears.

Kim:

"Awesome, frickin' awesome."

Lesson Learned: Awe is inspired by the vastness of extent and the difficulty it takes making sense of the matter. It was a privilege to be there and watch Kim get out of her life and into the river.

Sleep. Do not fret about growing old. Sixty will look great when you are Seventy. You are now old enough to remember when the Dead Sea was only sick. I know its a bit scary. After all, people from your high school years are running the country. We all know that it is not a good idea to give up something just to gain three more years in the geriatric ward. Keep up your daily number of steps. Soon you will be too old to go anywhere anyway. Go outside now before your back goes out more than you do. Tend to your dreams. When ready to move forward, go to the next waypoint, "Wheel Of Life (Stage 7)."

25

Wheel Of Life (Stage 7)

ENTER INTO THE GROVE OF THE ELDERS

As one's propensity for busyness wanes one tends to enter into the next stage of life, called "Grove of Elders" a developmental step characterized as a time for caring for the more-than-human community (Plotkin, 2010, p. 433). This stage is when a person reaches their most esteemed time of life. Wholeness, the positive disintegration of the autonomous sense of self (individual identity), and the switch in one's primary perception from eco-centric to cosmo-centric characterizes one's center of gravity. By cosmo-centric I mean that one's center of gravity is informed by the universe, by Spirit, and by all of space and time as one begins to partner with the cosmos. Rarely achieved in Western culture, this stage comes after you have supersaturated the world with one's striving and now "your presence causes your whole environment to crystallize in a certain way. One's presence alone (and not one's intention or striving) allows possibility to materialize through what seems like synchronicity—unexplainable circumstance, the coinciding occurrence of events that appear strikingly linked but have no apparent causal relationship. Consequently, there is a release from having to try so hard and one tends to feel that one is being played by an unseen hand, the grace of the earth itself. Without choosing, one's attentions turn beyond one's own life to the life of the earth. From the . . .

> "half of life focused on doing (striving, aspiring, convincing, insisting, struggling, competing, contending) and manifesting your uniqueness (West, soul) one develops into the half devoted to being (accepting, enjoying, celebrating, receiving, submitting, enduring) and reflecting the universal (East, spirit). As if returning to an odd form of childhood marked by mature innocence, worldly accomplishments become less important, celebration becomes more important, actuality becomes more astonishing than possibility, and one becomes "more like an expression of life than a fashioner of it" (Plotkin, 2010, p. 438).

One focuses more on one's social and ecological context than on one's individual goals that have nothing to do with one's relationship to the whole. As such, one's inspiration comes from the Soul of the community and one allows rather than pushes one's World Soul-inspired contribution. Your soulcraft still happens, but now it is through you in an automatic fashion. As this is a time for "surrendering nothing less than your unquestioned belief in your own personal agency, your sense of individual accomplishment" this is often a difficult stage to launch. There usually occurs a crisis of identity, dealt with best by a protracted time of withdrawal during which the developing person intently observes her mind and the natural world. Following the crisis of identity, the developing person, now momentarily secure in Stage 7, tends to find herself deliberating about decisive concerns with a council of elders, whose job it is to make sure that, beyond the needs of a society, the whole world is taken into account before final decisions are made. Without such councils, the transition to the Ecozoic Era is stalled. Those who partake in such councils have successfully moved through the apprentice-artisan-master sequence, have achieved some virtuosity in their soulwork, have shifted from the honing of skill and struggle to "centered non-striving" and are now fully equipped to serve as ecocentric mentors to those still learning how to tend to the web of life (Plotkin, 2010, p. 442). The challenge now is to get out of the way of deep-rooted magic so that the essence of nature can be manifested through the self of the Elder, now, at once, both individuated and more-than-individual. One now knows what to do and how to do it. The current challenge is to find a balanced place to apply one's brilliance for the good of species, habitats, and people in the web of life, if not to deliver them, then to, at least, be with them in their struggles, toil, and, dismay. Her core value is that every being, human or otherwise, finds its place, its healthful relationship to the whole, and its "comprehensive destiny" (Plotkin, 2010, p. 444). In her advanced state of confirmed wholeness, she is simultaneously:

1. Wild Self, an Anima/Animus Muse, and Innocent Sage, and a Generative Adult;
2. more particular than universal;
3. neither perfect nor a conformist to standard behavior;
4. a highly developed person who beholds, understands, and speaks for both her human community and her more-than-human world community;
5. a lender of an air of mastery, completeness, rightness, tolerance, forgiveness, and compassion as she carries on her main task—caring for the soul of the more-than-human world community; and
6. a saver of life.

With all of these qualities, she at once cultivates a viable society (free of war, poverty, disease, and starvation) and preserves wildness and diversity by:

1. defending the innocence of children,
2. caring for the disabled,
3. mentoring adolescents,

4. helping adults in their soulwork,
5. reassuring adolescents and adults as they move into new stages of life by helping them see the death of old stages as positive disintegration,
6. guiding the transformation of culture, and
7. maintaining a balance between nature and culture.

These are ways to engender and embrace wholeness. Having been through all but one life stage, the developing person at this point in the Wheel of Life has transcended (carried onwards and given a new twist to various attributes) the innocence of the child and the arrogant but so needed crazy confidence of the young adult innovator and the seriousness of the responsibility-burdened older adult. She exhibits in Stage 7 a lightness, a playfulness, but also an enormous ability to be compassionate, as if, paraphrasing Joanna Macy, the thinking heart has broken open enough to contain the whole universe (Plotkin, 2010, p. 456). Adolescent politics, military adventurism, the rapidly deteriorating environment, and the loss of respect for older persons make the work of the developing person—now a Master in Stage 7—necessary but difficult.

Think of the enormous unused potential of the millions of older persons. They are perhaps depressed in their belief that they are no longer valued in society. They are perhaps bored by their playing of inconsequential games. They perhaps feel pitiful for being put out to pasture. They are perhaps tired of cultural leadership positions. They may not yet see how they can serve the world as Cooperators of the mysteries from the deep, Guardians of deep time-tested traditions, Master Elders, and Eco-centric Sages. They may not see what they can teach us about meditating, gardening, experiential nature study, walking in nature, spending time with children, learning new skills, and marveling at the world of nature.

Although included here so participants can see the whole picture, the last of the developmental steps is beyond the scope of the Heartwood Path and beyond the experience of its author. When one is in the last stage, described next, one is a sage. The Heartwood Path, which leads its followers to saintliness, can get you about seven-eighths of the way to sageness. To get all the way to Stage Eight requires following one's own course beyond the Heartwood Path.

Though you may not be a Sage yet, there is still usefulness in being influenced by the last two of Pearson's Archetypes, which seem to work best when operating in tandem: the Ruler (described earlier) and the Magician (described next). Learn to identify and use the Magician by doing the next activity. Review the whole Wheel of Life by doing the activity after the next.

While the power of the Ruler from the last activity helps you create and maintain a prosperous and peaceful life, the power of the Magician, described more in the activity that follows, helps you to transform reality by changing consciousness. It often takes the help of these last two archetypes to evoke a respectable kingdom. Sometimes the Ruler becomes wounded or misguided. In case this happens, the Magician stands ready to set things right.

To A Good Standing In The Grove Of The Elders...

HumaNatureConnect Activity

Start-up Protocol

If this is not a day when you prefer to spend time in nature without an agenda, do the Heartwood Path Start-up Protocol found in the Appendix. Then return here to do the remaining portion of this activity:

Getting To Know Your Inner Guides—"The Ruler" And "The Magician"

Use two of the Natural Senses and Sensitivities—"Sense of self including friendship, companionship, and power" and "Sense of mind and consciousness" (Cohen, website: http://www.ecopsych.com/

insight53senses.html)—as you read the follow excerpts from Carol S. Pearson's book **Awaken the Heroes Within** and then answer the questions below, using the perspective of your chosen natural being that you imagine is both informed about all aspects of your self and, unlike you, is fair and objective about your recollections of your decrees and rulings.

"In modern life, we become the Ruler by taking complete responsibility for our lives–not only for our inner reality, but also for the way our outer world mirrors that reality. This includes the ways our individual selves affect our families, our communities, and our societies. When we have very likely become too comfortable and stopped growing, our kingdoms feel like wastelands; we (have to) allow the budding of new life—the new hero—within us to take a new journey" (Pearson, 1991, p. 182).

"The Ruler's job is to promote order, peace, prosperity, and abundance. This means a healthy economy, wise laws that are honored and enforced, an environment that promotes the development of each individual, and the wise use of resources, both human and material" (Pearson, 1991, p. 182).

"The Ruler archetype helps us to see that to spend our time blaming others for our problems takes away our own dignity" (Pearson, 1991, p. 186).

"Shadow Rulers are ogre tyrants operating out of a scarcity mentality, believing that there is not enough, so my gain (has to) be your loss" (Pearson, 1991, p. 187).

Seeking a "harmonious and prosperous kingdom (life)" but fearing chaos and "loss of control." the Ruler shows you how to take "full responsibility for your life" and, using the gifts of sovereignty, competence, and responsibility, to "find ways to express your deeper Self in the world" (Pearson, 1991, p. 181).

The Shadow side of the Ruler Archetype encourages us to be controlling, tyrannical, rigid, and manipulative. The sunny side of the Ruler at Level One is concerned primarily with you (the individual) and your family. She helps you "take responsibility for the state of your life;" and seek "healing of wounds or areas of powerlessness." The Level Two Ruler, concerned now with groups and the community, helps you develop skills and create structures "for manifesting your own dreams in the real world as it is." A Level Three Ruler, helps you utilize "all resources–internal and external." She helps you to be "concerned with the good of society and the planet" (Pearson, 1991, p. 189).

With these statements in mind and with the perspective of your informed, objective natural being, answer the following questions. When doing so, think about the past and the present.

How much or how little are you (and your family, coworkers, and friends) under the influence of the Ruler?

Is there anything about your relationship with the Ruler that you wish were different?

Now shift your focus to the Magician Archetype by answering the questions below, using the perspective of your chosen natural being that you imagine is both informed about all aspects of your self and, unlike you, is fair and objective about your recollections of your inexplicable achievements or magic.

"When the Magician is active in our lives . . . we begin to notice synchronistic events—that is, meaningful coincidences, such as when we need to know something and a book containing what we need practically falls into our lap . . ." (Pearson, 1991, p. 196).

"Private rituals are often essential for keeping the Magician connected and in touch with the deeper aspects of his or her nature and hence the cosmos. Ritual prayer, meditation, and centering meditations help unify conscious so that work can be done with internal static" (Pearson, 1991, p. 203).

With these statements in mind and with the perspective of your informed, objective natural being, answer the following questions. When doing so, think about the past and the present.

How much or how little are you (and your family, coworkers, and friends) under the influence of the Magician?

Is there anything about your relationship with the Magician that you wish were different?

What can you recall about a time in your life, if ever, that you stopped striving and focused more on arriving?

What can you recall about a time in your life, if ever, that you were so esteemed that your mere presence changed the environment for the better?

Follow-up Protocol

For best results, write down your impressions of this activity in your journal using the Heartwood Path Follow-up Protocol found in the Appendix. Afterwards, consider sharing your interpretations with others.

Heartwood Path Axioms

Key Assertions From Waypoint 5.25

5.25.1.

Rather than attempting to regress or jump ahead prematurely in your development, think about the mission you need today that is the main job of Life Stage 7: caring for the more-than-human community.

5.25.2.

Rarely achieved in Western culture, Life Stage 7 comes after one has supersaturated the world with one's striving and now one's presence causes one's whole environment to crystallize according to one's own essence.

5.25.3.

Beginning in Life Stage 7 one focuses more on one's social and ecological context than on one's individual goals that have nothing to do with one's relationship to the whole.

5.25.4.

In Stage 7 and beyond one's core value is that every being, human or otherwise, finds its place, its healthful relationship to the whole and its destiny.

Nocturnal Pilgrimage 5.25

For best results, write down your impressions of each night's dreams in your journal using the Heartwood Path Dreaming Time Protocols found in the Appendix. Afterwards, consider sharing your Dream Tending with others.

The Natural Law Of Assistance-giving:

Clearly and specifically, ask for assistance when you need
it,
accept solicited assistance when offered, and,
except for random acts of kindness,
do not offer assistance to those you think need help
or to those you think you can help better than they are
helping themselves
unless you are asked to deliver it.

To offer unsolicited help to people you feel are inferior to your-self in status or skill is to interfere with the problem-solving lessons being offered by the Absolute. For the sake of the development of your own best psychological outlook, refrain from meddling, judging, or giving unwanted advice or assistance. Such giving creates unacceptable power-over relationships that result in resentment and uncrossable chasms between the giver and the receiver. By contrast, helping name-less natural beings is usually appropriate because, being nonsensical, the relative status of the recipients is not typically under consideration and the assistance is usually solicited on behalf of the voiceless anawim—the myriad of natural beings—by informed and thoughtful conservation leaders. Always allow the receiver to make his or her own decisions or risk being an imposing preventer of someone else's learning. For these reasons, the best payoff comes by helping those you do not know.

Universal help is given to those who ask for it and are grateful for it. Be thankful to those who give solicited help.

Pertinent And Instructive Gems From My Dream Tending Journal

Together in the sleeping bag,

waiting for shadow of the bluff across the river

to move off of our private riverside campsite,

we laughed at something that happened the night before.

It happened in the twilight that happens right after sunset.

Not an experienced camper, Kim was off on her own gathering firewood for our

bonfire. Nearby some squirrels scampered across the dry leaves. Not knowing what the sound was, Kim's imagination ran wild. Frantic, she came running back to camp, screaming.

Kim:

"The cavemen are coming! The cavemen are coming!"

The funniest part of this recollection is the look on Kim's face the instant she recognized the implausibility of her sounded alarm.

Lesson Learned: Sometimes people, speaking while in a state of fear or anger, say things they do not mean. Actions speak louder than words.

Sleep. As we all know, you are old when people say, "My, you look good." Now your Inner Child is saying "What the Hell happened?" At least before breakfast, you ARE as old as you look. Now, when you commune with nature, you will be able to lean up against some trees that are younger than you. To make the most of your Silver Years, be childlike. People past Eighty die when they act their own age. So live it up. You deserve it. You have paid a high price for your maturity. When ready, keep going. Move to the next waypoint, entitled "Wheel of Life (Stage 8)."

26

Wheel Of Life (Stage Eight)

ARRIVE AS A SAGE

Once found, the Sage, in a simple way, will "help us appreciate and live in resonance with the cosmological patterns, to educate us with her wisdom, her love, her humor, her way of being still" (Plotkin, 2010, p. 472). Instinctively attuned to the universe, the task-free role of the Sage is to be a sharer of wisdom (such as the notion that profit follows justice), the coordinator of the human and cosmological realms (human "consciousness provides a way in which the universe...(reflects)... on itself and celebrates itself in a special mode of conscious self-awareness"), and mentoring through imaginal presence. After her death, people remember the now departed but shape-shifted Sage as an exemplar, a potent force, and a source of guidance, particularly about how there can be no survival unless we begin to see that an integral earth is more important than an individual person—thus tending the universe, and preparer of death (surrounded by loved ones who see what it is to have a good death).

All of this glorious being is not a given, nor does it occur for the majority. Most aged have not followed a lifetime on the soulcentric path

302 | DON PIERCE

I have been describing. Instead, they have unfinished business, unfelt emotions, and unrealized potential; and so, they withdraw from life, perhaps years before their physical death. The last stage of life can be a blessing or a time of failure, when the aged person becomes a burden on family and the healthcare system. Other than offering distractions, the remedy for the depression and dementia that accompanies those who have aged and not abandoned their egocentric perspectives is to make it possible for people to retain their innocence as children, resist being conformist in adolescence, and transform society into a eco/soul-centered nest. Failing that, it is never to late to correct developmental missteps, those developmental choices and opportunities that, for most people, occur well before the end of life. In fact, as death approaches most people can "no longer biologically or neurologically sustain an egocentric agenda" (Plotkin, 2010, p. 495). There comes a mellowing of attitudes, the emergence of a sense of peace, the expressions of love, the occurrence of forgiveness or the asking of forgiveness, and a drive to share natural astonishments with others. If enough of these sorts of occurrences happen on the brink of death, the last days are filled with the anticipation of death as an aspiring event, filled with light, and arrival (rather than departure alone).

It takes an eco/soul-centric village to "raise a child well. It also takes a more-than-human community to have a healthy village" (Plotkin, 2010, p. 500). The health of the whole is the foundation for the health of individuals. And vice versa.

The wheel of human development turns over and over, It spins from innocence to grace to innocence to grace . . .

Industrialization, on average, seems to promote egocentric development rather than eco/soul-centric development. A healthy natural environment is necessary for a healthy cultural environment. And vice versa.

Neither is possible without the healthy psycho-spiritual development of all peoples, beginning at birth and not ending until death. Our culture's attention to spiritual development in the post-adolescent years began in the Sixties. That has to continue but real psycho/social/ecological/spiritual progress will not occur unless more attention is also given to the early stages of development, for these become the foundation for the emergences of the eco/soul centric perspective that is so needed for a magnificent future.

This better future requires a balancing of culture and nature, as described above, in each stage of human development along with pervasive plunges into the depths of the instinctive resources of people. Balancing nature and culture and plunging into the depths of the inner world will cause a shift from egocentric consuming to ecocentric communing. And that is precisely what is needed.

But it will not happen unless we take care of peoples' developmental needs at each stage in the Wheel of Life: in Stage 1, protection of innocence; in Stage 2, protection of the wonder of free play in nature; in Stage 3, protection of authenticity and creativity; in Stage 4, encouragement of the exploration of nature, appropriate sex, and the psyche; in Stage 5, the development of self-reliance; in Stage 6, the innovative giving of soul-inspired gifts to the community; in Stage 7, protection of the more-than-human community; and in Stage 8, tending the universe by sharing wisdom, mentoring through imaginal presence, coordinating the human with the cosmological realms, and preparing for death. Without the completion of such tasks, the suggestions that come from the Muse or the Soul will be discounted, for one will not have developed the requisite personality to accept them.

Given that most of us are not yet fully developed in a healthy way, dream the impossible dreams. These are the one's that count. If the subject of the dream seems evident or possible, continue dreaming until what seems impossible emerges. Possible dreams are the dreams of people not fully whole. Impossible dreams are the dreams needed to become perfect in the sense of being whole and healthy. With the inspiration of such dreams, act as if you can make a difference which, of course, you can. Particularly if enough people join you.

To A Fast Review Of One's Life...

HumaNatureConnect Activity

Start-up Protocol

If this is not a day when you prefer to spend time in nature without an agenda, do the Heartwood Path Start-up Protocol found in the Appendix. Then return here to do the remaining portion of this activity:

Moving Quickly Around The Wheel Of Life

Use your natural sense of time by converting the eight stages of time, which normally last about eighty years into eight five minute sections of time, each representing a stage on the Wheel of Life.

For the first five minutes, recall how in Stage One of your life you were innocent, how your innocence was preserved or taken away from you, and what you can do to recover some of the benefits from being innocent.

During the second five minutes, ponder the emergence in Stage Two of your conscious self-awareness, conscious awareness of your emotions, and conscious awareness of your body. Contemplate your own gift of wonder, how in the early years of your life the center of your life was family and nearby nature. Think about how, if at all, this center fostered your imagination. Think about your early times of deep imagination and wonder. Think about how your center, your imagination and your wonder developed your ego. Remember what you did (or did not do) to help yourself belong in the world as you found it. Think about the enchantment you found in family and outdoor experiences and what, if anything, this enchantment did for you in a lasting way.

During the third five minutes, recall how in Stage Three your center of gravity shifted (or did not shift) around the time of puberty from a centering in nature and family to a centering in one's peer group, sexuality, and society. Recall any sadness you may have felt at this time,

how you endeavored (or did not endeavor) to make a socially acceptable and authentic direction for your life, how you leapt (or did not
leap) into love and unfamiliar responsibilities, and how you developed
(or did not develop) the style of your distinctive personality. Note how
you turned (or did not turn) to nature to give you what your parents
and your culture gave (or did not give) you—a reflective testing ground
and a place of healing. Recall how, and if, you celebrated the onset
of puberty. The last thing to recollect regarding your development
(or lack of development) in Stage Three is how any added personal
uniqueness led to a more wide-ranging concern for others, how your
belonging to the world becomes more particular (unique) and how,
over time, your sense of community became (or did not become) less
particular. In what ways, if any, did you around the time of the onset of
puberty "fall in love, outwardly and progressively, with the universe"
(Plotkin, 2010, p. 85)?

During the next five minutes recall the time of your life just after
puberty—Plotkin's Stage Four on the Wheel of Life. Beginning sometimes with the rite of passage known as "Confirmation," the developing
person enters a sort of tomb if she is still an adolescent and a sort of
womb if she is an adult. The main task for this stage is leaving the
"home" of the adolescent personality (the cultural task) and exploring
the mysteries of nature and psyche (the nature task)" (Plotkin, 2010, p.
264). Were you during this time of your life inspired by the Archetype
of the Wanderer? In what ways, if at all, did you offer as gifts to the
world darkness and mystery. How, if at all, did your center of gravity
turn to the underworld mysteries of soul and nature. In what ways, if at
all, did you develop a centering that now enables you to have a world-
centric perspective or Circle of Identity? More specifically, in what
ways, if at all, did you: 1) make peace with the past, 2) come to know the
difference between shallow and deep loyalty (between enablers and true
helpers, for example), 3) learn how to avoid the creation or absorption
of deception, 4) learn how to end unhealthy involvements, 5) give up
the old life story that was both enabling and limiting, 6) learn how to
live more fully in the present, 7) savor the gifts of the world, 8) develop

the habit of finding solitude in nature, 9) begin the habit of enhancing the feeling of gratitude for one's experiencing of richness and opportunity, 10) develop an ongoing encounter with the Soul and, in so doing, discover "the gift you were born to carry to others" (Plotkin, 2010, p. 304), 11) learn how to obtain nature's atypical news while wandering in nature, 12) successfully begin the process of confronting one's own death, 13) begin to see one's own qualities in natural things, and, 14) begin the process of choosing authenticity over social acceptance. In short, compared to earlier times of your life, in what ways, if at all, did you fall more under the influence of the soul, causing a temporary loss of one's focus on contemporary society. In what ways, if at all, did you meet with the darker aspects of nature and psyche?

In the next five minutes, focus on one's passage (or lack of passage) through Stage Five of the Wheel of Life. Recall whether you began to learn how to embody your soul in culture. You can determine if you made this important life transition by assessing whether you significantly brought visionary action, hope, and inspiration to your community. More specifically, in what ways, if at all, did you begin a more expansive conversation with life? Did you push through any feelings of vulnerability and melancholia as you contemplated the inevitability of your own death? In what ways, if at all, did your soul-discovery reveal the fretful risks that go along with 1) the adventure of embodying the mysteries of the Underworld; 2) the causes of misunderstandings; 3) the examination of deep but sacred inner world wounds; 4) the feelings of greater empathy for the plight of humans, non-humans, and the earth; and 5) the feeling of the pain of the earth itself?

In the next five minutes, recall any former battling you did with your ego that marks one's passage through Stage Six. How, if at all, did you counter the Ego with the giving of creative forms of service based on imaginative ideas that arise, not from one's everyday life, but from, at once, one's own intangible noumenal depths and the tangible offerings from nature? How, if at all, did these fountainheads of creativity yield a sense of purpose for you? How, if at all, did private dreams, inspired coaches, and nature allow you to have the integrity that comes from being on the outside what one feels on the inside? How, if at all, did your gratitude for such offerings inspire you to give to your community? How, if at all, did you blend the community with action? In what ways, if at all, did you blend the callings of nature with the pleas of culture? In what ways, if at all, did you discover any greater appreciation for how there is weal in the wild—something good in Nature, a source of ethical direction that goes beyond—deeper than—religious restrictions or cultural codifications? If the answer to many of these questions is "No" you may not have progressed through Stage Five. This is not uncommon. There is still time to continue your development, a process necessary if one is going to truly become soul-centric beyond egocentric.

The next five minutes may help you determine if you have entered Plotkin's name for Stage Seven: the "The Grove of the Elders." To find out, ask yourself the following set of questions: In what ways, if at all, are you less fulfilled by busyness? In what ways, if at all, do you spend time caring for the more-than-human community? Did, or does, this time feel like the esteemed time of life? In what ways, if at all, did you know that you have progressed through ego-centricism and eco-centricism to cosmo-centricism? By cosmo-centricism I mean that one's center of gravity is informed by the universe, by spirit, and by all of space and time as one begins to partner with the cosmos. In what ways, if at all, did or does one's presence alone (and not one's intention or striving) allow possibility to happen through what seems like syn-chronicity—unexplainable circumstance, the coinciding occurrence of events that appear strikingly linked but have no apparent causal relationship? In what ways, if at all, did or do you experience a release from having to try so hard? In what ways, if at all, do you instead feel like you are being played by an unseen hand, the grace of the Earth itself? Have your attentions turned beyond your own life to the life of the earth? In what ways, if at all, are you moving or did you already move from a life of doing (striving, aspiring, convincing, insisting, struggling, competing, contending) and manifesting your uniqueness (West, soul) to a life of being (accepting, enjoying, celebrating, receiving, submitting, enduring) and reflecting the universal)? In what ways, if at all, are worldly accomplishments becoming less important? In what ways, if at all, are celebrations becoming more important? In what ways, if at all, is actuality becoming more astonishing than possibility? Are you feeling more like an expresser of life rather than a fashioner of life? In what ways, if at all, are you focusing on your social and ecological context more than on your individual goals that have nothing to do with one's relationship to the whole? Have you surrendered nothing less than your unquestioned belief in your own personal agency, your sense of individual accomplishment? In what ways, if at all, have you undergone a crisis of identity? Do you find yourself frequently deliberating about decisive concerns with a council of elders, whose job it is to make sure that, beyond the needs of a society, the whole world is taken into account before final decisions are made? In what ways, if at all do you recognize that without such councils the transition to the Ecozoic Era is stalled? Do you feel like a Wild Self, a Muse, an Innocent Sage, or a Generative Adult? In what ways, if at all, do you resist standards of behavior? In what ways, if at all, do you behold, understand, and speak for both the human community and the more-than-human world community? In what ways, if at all, are you a lender of an air of mastery, completeness, rightness, tolerance, forgiveness, and compassion as you carry on your main task—caring for the soul of the more-than-human world community? How, if at all, are you a saver of life? Have you carried along with you the innocence of childhood, the crazy confidence of the young adult innovator, and the seriousness of the responsibility-burdened older adult while at the same time maintaining or developing a lightness and a playfulness that colors your ability to be awed with and compassionate towards the whole of the universe?

In the last five minutes of this activity, unless you are in the final stage of life, your assignment is to look forward rather than backward. Stage Eight in the Wheel of Life is a time for no more developmental tasks other than tending to the universe without deliberation but with grace, gratitude, generosity, fellow-feeling, and untrammeled freedom. To determine if you are in Stage Eight, or, more likely, to prepare yourself for entry into Stage Eight, ask yourself the following questions: Have you, or are you, prepared to celebrate the mysteries of the universe? Do you know your collective place in the cosmos? Are you ready to enter into a time for the easing of striving, the release from the ego, the detachment from outcomes, the alleviating of the tensions of opposites, the serenity of a fully developed character, and the end of life that is a beginning? Are you prepared to make the adjustment from leadership and the giving of gifts to one's world one to a focus on the present moment, eternity, and a celebration of the sacred and the inspiring? In what ways, if at all, are you prepared to be an oracle, a prophet, or a humble consultant? In what ways, if at all, do you have unfinished business, unfelt emotions, and unrealized potential? Have you withdrawn from life? Will you become a burden on your family and the healthcare system? In what ways, if at all, are you willing to correct developmental missteps, those developmental choices and opportunities that, for most people, occur well before the end of life? Do you anticipate death as an aspiring event, filled with light, and arrival (rather than departure) alone? Are you able to retain a mixture of magic and nature; and, in so doing, secure the emergence of right action—the elixir of life?

With the whole Wheel of Your Life in mind, think about how time, among other things, is the period between causes and the emergence of the effects of the causes. Also think about how these effects then recycle to become new causes. What does thinking about time in this way tell you about your life, time, and the universe?

Follow-up Protocol

For best results, write down your impressions of this activity in your journal using the Heartwood Path Follow-up Protocol found in the Appendix. Afterwards, consider sharing your interpretations with others.

Heartwood Path Axioms

Key Assertions From Waypoint 5.26

5.26.1.

Rather than attempting to jump ahead prematurely in your development, think about the difference between your mission to become a saint and the main job of those few who make it to Life Stage 8: being a sage (helpful consultant).

5.26.2.

There comes In Life Stage 8 a mellowing of attitudes, the emergence of a sense of peace, the expressions of love, the occurrence of forgiveness or the asking of forgiveness, and the drive to share natural astonishments with others.

5.26.3.

In Life Stage 8 there will be a shift from egocentric consuming to ecocentric communing.

Nocturnal Pilgrimage 5.26

For best results, write down your impressions of each night's dreams in your journal using the Heartwood Path Dreaming Time Protocols found in the Appendix. Afterwards, consider sharing your Dream Tending with others.

The Natural Law Of Sanctioning:

Allow for the natural flow of energy.

It is best to allow for the unfolding of situations, if only for the sake of learning and growth. No one can be aware of all the karma involved in the development of circumstances. Let go of control so that the unforeseen can take place. Allow people to be who they are. Rather than resist—which is hard—allow—which is easy.

Pertinent And Instructive Gems From My Dream Tending Journal

Luckily the cavemen did not take away our pile of firewood.

After her illogical alarm the nite before, Kim seemed to want to do something redemptive.

She asks if I would let her rebuild the fire and cook breakfast—her first time—by herself.

I watch as Kim, dressed only in my old, long-sleeve and unbuttoned shirt, throws wood on the fire.

Down on her hands and knees, she blows on the old embers.

Some sparks flare-up enough that, for safety reasons, she has to hold my over-sized shirt closer to her body. She looks in the cooler and pulls out eggs and milk. The pancake flour is in a separate container.

She keeps looking at me for reassurance.

She yells as she shows me the thickness of the batter:

Kim:

"Do you like your pancakes thin or thick?"

Don:

"Thin."

Kim:

"So more milk then?"

Don:

"Yeah, and another egg to help hold it all together."

Kim cooks a big pile of thin pancakes.

We eat breakfast while straddling a big dead tree,

deposited on our sandbar during the last flood.

Kim smiles and kisses me as I congratulate her

on the making of her first outdoor meal.

Kim's response:

"I cooked, so you clean."

Lesson Learned: Allow your loved ones to take appropriate risks. Make sure there is a safety net.

Do not be discouraged if you cannot yet succeed in having lucid dreams. Your ability to do so will improve with practice. Here's a couple of good tips, quoting LaBerge and Rheingold: "One way to become lucid is to ask yourself whether or not you are dreaming while you are dreaming. In order to do this, you can make a habit of asking the question while you are awake . . . Asking the question at bedtime and while falling asleep is also favorable" (LaBerge and Rheingold, 1990, p. 59-61). More techniques follow.

With this and the just-completed teaching in mind, sleep, dream, and tend to your dreams. When ready, head to the "Health Pipeline," the next waypoint.

This time, when instructed to head outdoors to find a natural attraction, consider looking for an atypical form of vegetation. Consider making friends with a fern, a large bush, or a patch of moss. Begin to diversify your floral acquaintances. Become comfortable with a bigger variety of beings. Seek to belong in new landscapes. In these ways your nature-connect experiences will be more interesting and fulfilling.

27

Health Pipeline

MAKE YOURSELF A CONDUIT OF OPTIMAL HEALTH

This instruction may require a change in perspective, especially if you think bodily symptoms of pain and discomfort are to avoided at all cost. Symptoms, including headaches, diarrhea, nausea, fatigue, depression, panic, anxiety, and cancer, are the body's way to telling you that it is time to stop suppressing feelings and to start paying more attention to your body. Of all that one needs to pay attention to, one's emotions are high on the list.

Emotions can be thought of as energy motions, a flow that needs to be unimpeded so that the body can go through the necessary processes of detoxification and purification. "Symptoms," writes author and chiropractor Dr. Darren R. Weissman, "are the result of stored poisons, toxins and blockages caused by the subconscious internalization or denial of—and disconnection from—emotions" (2005, p. 6). Weissman, who contends that the "greatest obstacle to your health and well-being is the subconscious disconnection from your emotions" has developed a form of healing that uses, among other things, gratitude to create "a more harmonious connection between the body and the universe" (Weissman, 2005, p. 6).

This connection will be expanded upon as we focus on Weissman's Five Basics for optimal Health, beginning with . . .

1. Water

As an electrical being, you need to drink plenty of water to foster conductivity.

2. Food

Shop from a sensible grocery list, eat every two hours (use the substitute of protein snacks when on the run), keep a food log, and eat apples or cashews when appetite flairs. Permitted foods include:

1. fresh fruits;
2. juiced or fresh vegetables;
3. small amounts of meat and dairy products;
4. whole-grain rice, sprouted-grain bread, and cold-pressed olive oil;

Prohibited foods include:

1. sugar,
2. natural and artificial sweeteners,
3. wheat products,
4. seeds,
5. grains,
6. white rice,
7. cauliflower,
8. canned or frozen vegetables,
9. canned or frozen fruit,
10. potatoes,
11. sweets,
12. tofu,

13. soy milk,

14. legumes, and

15. cooking spray and condiments such as ketchup or margarine.

Stick to this list eighty percent of the time and indulge twenty percent of the time (Weissman, 2005, p. 185-188).

3. Rest

Recommendations include:

1. sleep 7-9 hours per day;
2. avoid caffeine before retiring;
3. do not take work to bed; and
4. reserve time for 15-minute naps.

When awake, focus on present time consciousness (Weissman, 2005, p. 184).

4. Exercise

Recommendations include:

1. working out at least fifteen minutes everyday,
2. finding a partner to help with the regularity of exercise, and
3. practicing mindfulness during exercise.

Weissman also shares my fondness for a Qigong exercise called "Standing Like A Tree": "Stand with your feet about hip width apart. Position your spine on top of your hips . . . Verify your alignment in from of a mirror. Rest your head at the center of the gravity that runs through your spine. Drop your chin, and free the back of your neck. You may feel like falling forward, but you won't. Make sure your palms are parallel to the ground.

As you stand, breathe deeply, expanding your stomach as you inhale and pulling your nave to your spine as you exhale. The goal is to connect to an open state of awareness while doing nothing else. Do this for one minute, and work on extending the time to ten....It allows you to become accurately aware of what's going on in your mind and body and expand your ability to use (present time consciousness), which will help heal your body at a much quicker rate. The longer you hold the tree posture, the more grounded and stronger your mind-body-spirit connection" (Weissman, 2005, p. 202-203).

5. Owning Your Power

This means living with infinite love and gratitude; embracing all aspects of life with passion purpose and courage; living in the "Now;" and reconnecting with your emotions, especially those that lie dormant in your subconscious mind. It also means learning to feel so you can heal and imagine yourself healed (Weissman, 2005, p. 207-229).

To Become A Transformer Of Positive Personal Change...

HumaNatureConnect Activity

Start-up Protocol

If this is not a day when you prefer to spend time in nature without an agenda, do the Heartwood Path Start-up Protocol found in the Appendix. Then return here to do the remaining portion of this activity:

Making Yourself A Conduit Of Optimal Life

Use your natural sense of intuition or subconscious deduction to make yourself into a conduit of optimal health. As you are outside with your chosen attractive being, pay attention to your own gut feelings or hunches. This may be hard for some people to achieve but doing so is important because, as psychiatry professor and practicing intuitive Judith Orloff M.D, says, "finding your inner voice can give you the confidence and wisdom to face anything; following it is key to living a passionate, high-energy life" (Orloff, Website, 2003). Here are a few pointers for you to try to develop your intuition and improve or maintain your health:

1. Clear your mind. Sitting outside alone in silence meditate to remove inner chatter. Do so by closing your eyes and allowing your mind to calm down. Focus on your breath rather than on your thoughts. Once your mind slows down, in the presence of your attractive natural being, ask a question pertaining to improving your health. After doing so, you may experience your answer as an inner image or a sudden realization.

2. Be psychologically attuned to your body as you remain close to your attractive natural being. Doing so can be a deep form of self care. Clearing the mind counter-acts the common practice of functioning only from the neck up which, says Orloff, is "counterintuitive and cuts off vital energy reserves" (2003). Being in the body allows you to notice body signals and, in so doing, "recognize early signs of pain or fatigue instead of pushing yourself to injury or illness" (Orloff, 2003).

3. Sense the energy both in your natural setting and throughout your body. Subtle energies from the natural environment surround and penetrate the body. "Tuning in to this energy can significantly impact your mood and your well-being. Positive energy feels invigorating, compassionate and supportive, but negative energy is tiring, unkind and critical. By intuiting these differences in friends and colleagues, you'll be clear about who is nurturing and who saps your strength" (Orloff, 2003). You have already chosen your attractive natural object (being), presumably, at least in part, because it gives you positive energy. Spend more time with people and objects that bolster your energy.

4. Pay attention to your day dreams as you sit near your attractive natural object (being). Enter such day dreams immediately into your journal so they can be retained and put to use later.

5. Let go of defeatist attitudes. Every organ in the body is affected by one's thoughts. To help your attitudes make you a conduit of optimal health, replace negative attitudes with positive affirmations. Such reframing will be good for your health.

Follow-up Protocol

For best results, write down your impressions of this activity in your journal using the Heartwood Path Follow-up Protocol found in the Appendix. Afterwards, consider sharing your interpretations with others.

Heartwood Path Axioms

Key Assertions From Waypoint 5.27

5.27.1.

Make yourself a conduit of optimal health.

5.27.2.

Symptoms, including headaches, diarrhea, nausea, fatigue, depression, panic, anxiety and cancer, are the body's way to telling you that it is time to stop suppressing feelings and to start paying more attention to your body.

5.27.3.

Emotions can be thought of as energy motions, a flow that needs to be unimpeded so that the body can go through the necessary processes of detoxification and purification.

5.27.4.

Drinking plenty of water, shopping from a sensible grocery list, sleeping at least eight hours per day, daily exercise, owning your power through being in touch with your emotions, being grateful, and living in the Now all lead to optimal health.

Nocturnal Pilgrimage 5.27

For best results, write down your impressions of each night's dreams in your journal using the Heartwood Path Dreaming Time Protocols found in the Appendix. Afterwards, consider sharing your Dream Tending with others.

The Natural Law Of Appropriate Prosperity:

We all prosper
when any one of us
reaches a goal.

There is enough possibility for success to go around to each and every one of us. Trade the mentality of lack for the mentality of appropriate abundance, and abandon poverty consciousness for appropriate prosperity consciousness. Success, abundance, and prosperity are appropriate when you take no more than you need.

It will likely take hard work to become successful. Through due diligence, obtain enough and no more.

There is enough for all needs, but not for all wants. Some of the things you have no longer serve you. Sell or give away the degenerated to make way for the regenerated.

Hoarding is a sign to the Absolute that you have enough. Your hoarding will block the acquisition of additional needed objects.

322 | DON PIERCE

Think how nice it would be to have a living space with nothing stored under anything or behind anything. Purge until your stuff no longer interferes with your spiritual well-being. Gain more by sharing more.

Pertinent And Instructive Gems From My Dream Tending Journal

Kim meditates nude

in the morning sun

at the downstream tip of our secluded sandbar.

I finish cleaning up everything from breakfast.

The lucid dream continues.

Kim returns from her naked meditating,

takes my hand, and leads me back to the sleeping bag,

where we slept the night before under the stars.

The bag is now spread out in the sun

to dry from the morning dew.

She pulls off my gym shorts and shirt,

and wraps me in the old shirt of mine that she is holding.

Sitting on my lap, facing me, she asks me to hold her.

I immediately feel the warmth

of her soft breasts upon my bare chest.

Kim:

"Do we have a Heartwood Path activity planned for today?"

Don:

"No, I was thinking of slowly moving downstream without any agenda.

The river will work its magic on us."

Kim:

"Sounds good, but let's linger here for a while..."

Lesson Learned: As often as you like, rather than doing a predetermined Heartwood Path activity, just amble through nature without a plan. Nature always has something good in store for you.

Another way to help you prepare for entering into lucid dreaming is to test the state of our consciousness at five to ten different locations in any given day. Whenever you find in what appears to you to be your waking state a condition that resembles a dream sign, whenever encountering something surprising or unlikely, whenever you experience something that is powerful, or whenever you experience anything that is dreamlike, ask yourself: "Am I dreaming or awake?" "Do not just automatically ask the question and mindlessly reply, 'Obviously, I'm awake.' or you will do the same thing when you are dreaming. Look around for any oddities or inconsistencies that might indicate that you are dreaming" (LaBerge & Rheingold, 1990, p. 61-62). Do not take anyone else's advice about whether you are dreaming. Just hop up in the air and if it takes you longer to descend than normal, you are dreaming.

With these words and your impressions from the present lesson, prepare to fall asleep. Dream and then tend to your dreams.

When ready, turn your attention to "Eco Codes," the next waypoint. Make sure you have not fallen into the habit of simply going out and becoming an uninvolved onlooker.

Since you will be using nature to de-stress or seek guidance, it is only fair that you seek consent. You will not be establishing this sense of fairness for the tree's sake only.

Creating a state of justness leads to optimal functioning because the evenhandedness feels good psychologically and keeps one free of disturbing distractions. The feeling of being attracted to the natural being or landscape will help you feel sanctioned. This implicit approval will help you make a connection. The connection will help you feel better psychologically. Feeling better psychologically will help you function more optimally. Better functioning helps you do the activities better. These activities lead to the attainment of guidance from nature. Note how the whole life-enhancing chain reaction begins with the seeking of consent.

Sleep. Dream. Tend to your dreams. When ready, turn to the next waypoint, entitled "Eco Codes."

28

Eco Codes

DEVELOP AND USE
ENVIRONMENTAL ETHICS

I predicate this discussion with a brief examination of the nature of right and wrong. Humans have a moral instinct that interfaces with the social landscape; grows as "an inevitable outcome of normal growth" (Hauser, 2006, p. 25); and is "a part of nature" (Hauser, 2006, p. 61). We have four types of moral emotions:

1. other-condemning (which includes anger, contempt, and disgust);
2. self-consciousness (which includes shame, embarrassment, and guilt);
3. other-suffering (which includes compassion) and
4. other-praising (which includes gratitude and elation) (Hauser, 2006, p. 53).

These tell us what is right and wrong, including how we ought to relate to and protect the environment.

To follow the instruction to develop and use environmental ethics, one needs to answer thoroughly the question posed over and over in Moore and Nelson's book **Moral Ground: Ethical Action for a Planet in Peril**: Do we have a moral obligation to take action to protect the future of a planet in peril? (Moore and Nelson, 2010). Here is why Moore, Nelson, myself, and others contend that the answer is "Yes."

Act to save the Earth because it has instrumental value to humans. We need not here dwell in much detail on the instrumental value of nature to human welfare. The argument that nature ought to be protected because it serves humans is universally accepted. Despite this acceptance, there is not sufficient other-praising.

Act to save the Earth because it is real. Thanks to the efforts of Cambridge University philosopher G.E. Moore, who "led a rebellion against the philosophies of Kant and Hegel at Cambridge University, which brought about the end of idealism as mainstream philosophy and permitted the rehabilitation of the external world" (Hargrove, 1988, p. 37), we can rely on our common sense to establish that the Realm of Exteriority exists and, as such, is important foundational fodder for how we humans evoke reality and the future. The contention that nature is not real frees those who have this belief from other-condemning moral emotions.

Act to save the Earth because it is beautiful. Just as many people enjoy the works of art created by man, so too do many people enjoy nature as "God's work." "If this is the way the world is—beautiful, astonishing, wondrous, awe-inspiriting—then this is how we ought to act in that world—with respect, with deep caring and fierce protectiveness, and with a full sense of our obligation to the future, that this beauty shall remain" (Moore and Nelson, 2010, p. 330). Valuing the beauty of nature is an example of the moral emotion of other-praising.

Act to save the Earth because we humans love the world. "Because we love the world we were born to, a world now so deeply imperiled, we have a responsibility to come to its defense" (Moore and Nelson, 2010, p. 355). Success in this defense depends on our political will. The direction and fervor of our political will depends on our moral commitment. We need a moral commitment that goes beyond prohibitions of one individual hurting another. We need also prohibitions against taking small parts from the many, taking from beings far away, and taking from future beings. We need to cheerfully protect specimens and species, communities and ecosystems, previous relics, the present moment, and the future. We need to go beyond agreements, treaties, and laws that afford mere symptom relief to confront underlying causes of ecological distress, particularly those causes having to do with our emotions, intellect, morals, and spiritual needs. Social ecology professor Stephen R. Keller asserts that if "we lack a diverse base of physical and mental connection to nature, we rarely strive after its conservation" (Moore and Nelson, 2010, p. 376). There can be no cleanup without first having the motivation to act. Negative can't-of-mind prevents positive can-of-body. Writes Aldo Leopold:

> "There (has to) be some force behind conservation, more universal than profit, less awkward than government, less ephemeral than sport, something that reaches into all times and places . . . some thing that brackets everything from rivers to raindrops, from whales to hummingbirds, from land-estates to window-boxes . . . I can see only one such force: a respect for land as an organism . . . out of love for and obligation to that great biota" (1949, p. 198).

This sense of love and obligation grows as one applies the moral emotion of other-suffering to nature.

Act to save the Earth because it is interesting. This argument seems to hold more sway when the aspect of nature is not particularly picturesque or beautiful. One's interest in nature piques elation, an aspect of the moral emotion of other—praising.

Act to save the Earth because to do otherwise will cause pain and suffering to humans and animals—a clear example of the moral emotion of other-suffering.

Act to save the Earth because all species have an inherent right to exist. An important "step in moral development is to expand the sphere of moral concern to include other forms of life" (Moore and Nelson,

2010, p. 98). Violations of the rights of other earthly beings engenders the moral emotion of other-condemning.

Act to save the Earth because it contains all the parts. Quoting Aldo Leopold: "If the land mechanism as a whole is good, then every part is good, whether we understand it or not. If a biota, over aeons, has built something we like but do not understand, then who but a fool would discard useless parts? To keep every cog and wheel is the first preoccupation of intelligent tinkering" (Hargrove, 1988, p. 139). Tinkering with nature and thereby losing its parts is so unwise, it leads to the moral emotion of self-consciousness.

Act to save the Earth because the real thing is better than renderings of it. Following philosophical arguments development by G. E. Moore, "the existence of the qualities in nature constitutes an additional element that makes the natural landscape aesthetically superior to a representation of it..." (Hargrove, 1988, p. 173). This appreciation of aesthetics is an example of the moral emotion of other-praising.

Act to save the Earth because of the authenticity of its creativity. Writes Hargrove:

"Nature is not simply a collection of natural objects; it is a process that progressively transforms those objects, retaining some, altering and discarding others, as it selectively unfolds and actualizes its possibilities . . . Although many natural objects are destroyed in this way, the loss is not complete, for they remain part of the ongoing natural history that constitutes the essence of nature. When we interfere with nature, regardless of whether our intentions are good or not, we create a break in that natural history . . . Historically, manipulation of nature, even to improve it, has been considered subjugation or domination. Such manipulation limits the freedom of nature, which, in turn reduces its ability to be creative . . . The authenticity of nature arises out of the fact that its existence precedes its essence" (Hargrove, 1988, p. 195.).

Praising authenticity comes from the moral emotion of other-praising. Thus, when we disturb nature's places their "ontological status (have) been altered; they have become objects whose essence has preceded their existence" (Hargrove, 1988, p. 196).

Act to save the Earth because, without doing so, humanity will not survive. We humans "have an obligation not to destroy our own kind . . .and a corresponding moral obligation not to destroy the ecological and geological foundations of our lives and the future of humankind . . ." (Moore and Nelson, 2010, p. 2). This call to action demonstrates compassion for all of humanity, an example of the moral emotion of other-suffering.

Act to save the Earth for the well-being of children. "A life sustaining planet . . . will be our last and greatest gift to the ones we love the most" (Moore and Nelson, 2010, p. 66). An example of other-suffering.

Act to save the Earth because it has intrinsic value. "Some people argue that the Earth itself is a living, sensate being" and therefore, like our obligation to protect humans, "we owe respect and protection to the Earth" (Moore and Nelson, 2010, p. 68). This obligation entails sacrifice (which can be interpreted to mean to make sacred) and some renunciation. "It is exactly this renunciation of self-interest that brings a person into closer relation to the divine" (Moore and Nelson, 2010, p. 96). An example of other-praising.

Act to save the Earth for the well-being of animals. Ways include not buying or using poisons, not building a house on unspoiled land, not shopping in stores built on undisturbed land, not owning or tolerating outdoor cats that prey on birds and skinks, joining environmental groups and making donations to environmental causes, buying only materials harvested sustainably, refraining from planting exotic species, taking only what is needed from nature, and acting on behalf of nature before scientists prove the point of its jeopardy beyond a reasonable doubt. An example of other-suffering.

Act to save the Earth to demonstrate "gratitude and reciprocity" (Moore and Nelson, 2010, p. 131). An "important part of gratitude is reciprocity, the responsibility to give in return" and "gratitude for our abundant gifts (from nature) is the root of our moral obligation to the future to avert the coming environmental calamities and leave a world as rich in possibilities as the world that has been given to us" (Moore and Nelson, 2010, p. 132). Gifts of gratitude "will follow the circle of reciprocity and flow back to you again" (Moore and Nelson, 2010, p. 142). An example of other-praising.

Act to save the Earth because doing so helps one become a better person. "Ask not, 'What shall I do.' Ask, 'What kind of person do I want to be?' Then act as that person would act. Some of the valued traits, virtues or 'habits of the mind and heart' acting to save the Earth engenders include a sense of wonder, compassion, imagination, independence of mind, integrity, justice, and courage" (Nelson and Moore, 2010, p. 192). An example of an attempt to avoid shame, and therefore an example of self-consciousness.

Act to save the Earth because not doing so is a sin. Nature is "God's gift of love to us, and we (have to) return His love by protecting it and all that is in it" (Moore and Nelson, 2010, p. 136). Such a restriction stems from the moral emotion of other-condemning.

Act to save the Earth as a steward of God's creation. If "God is perfect, and God created the world, it might be reasonable to conclude that His Creation has value beyond what humans can create. To maintain that value, to protect and steward it—that is the work and privilege of humankind" (Moore and Nelson, 2010, p. 142). An example of the moral emotion of other-praising.

Act to save the Earth "because compassion requires it" (Moore and Nelson, 2010, 268). We "who call ourselves virtuous have an inescapable obligation to the future to avert the effects of the coming ecological storm" (Moore and Nelson, 2010, p. 268). An example of other-suffering.

Act to save the Earth "because justice demands it" (Moore and Nelson, 2010, p. 292). "No one would freely choose to pay, in the currency of their suffering and the suffering of their children, in famine and disease and the risk of human life on Earth, the costs of the reckless adventures of the wealthy nations" (Moore and Nelson, 2010, p. 293). Justice is fueled by the moral emotion of other-condemning.

Act to save the Earth to demonstrate moral integrity. "So much human unhappiness is caused by the fracturing of the self . . .the dishonest stories we tell ourselves...the anger at ourselves, the consequent frantic striving after something (anything!) . . ." (Moore and Nelson, 2010, p. 419). To do otherwise would lead to the unwanted moral emotion of guilt, an aspect of the moral emotion of self-consciousness.

To The Use Of The Dictates Of Conscience...

HumaNatureConnect Activity

Start-up Protocol

If this is not a day when you prefer to spend time in nature without an agenda, do the Heartwood Path Start-up Protocol found in the Appendix. Then return here to do the remaining portion of this activity:

Developing And Using Environmental Ethics

Use your sense of survival by joining a more established organism as you develop and use environmental ethics. Think of you being inseparable from the whole natural environment. With this perspective, true but atypical, create a grid in your journal. Down the vertical axis on the left side of the sheet list ten environmental concerns— these may be both the beings you wish to see conserved, preserved, protected, improved, or restored (i.e. rain forests, whales, rivers) and the issues you wish to see solved (i.e. ozone depletion, solid waste). On the horizontal axis across the top of the sheet wright down the reason for the consternation about each being or issue of concern. These may include extinction preventions, cruelty, ecosystem value, animal rights, human survival, etc. Place an X in the grid where the vertical axis of concerns intersects with the horizontal axis of reasons for the concern.

Since we are trying to create a personal code of environmental ethics, make your inputs your own. To help with the generation of concerns and reasons for concern, consider who, what, when, where, and why. Remembering that you are perceiving this activity through the eyes of the whole natural environment the "who" will be a part of the greater you, the "what" will be a part of the greater you, the "where" will be a part of the greater you, and the "why" will take on a wide ecosystem perspective. For "who" ask "Who are the stakeholders?" For "what" ask about wholes: "How can we protect whole populations or the whole ecosystem?" Also, "How can I solve the whole solid waste issue?" This may sound like a tall order. But sometimes it is easier to take a broad brush to an issue than it is to attempt to solve it piecemeal. For "when" adopt the perspective of both today and the future, at least several generations out. And for "how" consider the whole spectrum: ideological, scientific, intuitive and opinionated perspectives. Another way to flesh out the concerns vs. reasons grid is to recall at typical day in your daily life. Examine what natural resources you use? What impacts do you have on the environment? What choices do you make that have an impact on the environment? What would you change about your daily life? For more help, develop a "mind map" pertaining to your ecological impacts and your ecological values. After doing such things, create a sentence, paragraph, or poem that might capture the essence of your own "Personal Code of Environmental Ethics." After completing this Code in proximity to your chosen attractive natural being, wait for ten minutes or more to determine if you receive any emphatic resonant feedback from your natural being and then from the natural area around you and your chosen natural being.

Follow-up Protocol

For best results, write down your impressions of this activity in your journal using the Heartwood Path Follow-up Protocol found in the Appendix. Afterwards, consider sharing your interpretations with others.

Heartwood Path Axioms

Key Assertions From Waypoint 5.28

5.28.1.

Develop and use environmental ethics.

5.28.2.

Humans have four types of moral emotions: 1) other-condemning (anger, contempt, and disgust); 2) self-consciousness (shame, embarrassment, and guilt); 3) other-suffering; 4) and other-praising (gratitude and elation).

5.28.3.

Ethical reasons to save the earth include its value to humans (including children), its actuality, its beauty, its function as a storehouse, its interesting quality, its right to exist, its intrinsic value, and its ability to make us better people.

5.28.4.

To become lucid during dreams it is helpful to practice testing your state of consciousness while supposedly awake.

Nocturnal Pilgrimage 5.28

For best results, write down your impressions of each night's dreams in your journal using the Heartwood Path Dreaming Time Protocols found in the Appendix. Afterwards, consider sharing your Dream Tending with others.

The Natural Law Of The Proscribed Course:

Do what you know
you have to do
even if you do not want to do it.

Overcome weakness and control your feelings by doing the right thing. Do not abandon your goals. Adopt a regimen and stick to the proscribed course. Hold yourself to high standards. Discipline allows you to achieve more. Create the reality you desire. Allow for distractions that sharpen the mind or encourage you to exercise or rest Do your chores now. Do not wait until you feel like doing them. That time may come too late. Eliminate your excuses. Getting started is usually the hardest part. Do the least desirable tasks first. That way later assignments will seem like rewards.

Pertinent And Instructive Gems From My Dream Tending Journal

My dream with Kim on the Missouri River continues.

There is still no sign of Great Blue.

Kim works on her upper body strength

by paddling very hard.

After a spell, I offer to trade places

so she can get some practice

controlling the canoe by herself.

Kim, confidently:

"I bet he's waiting for me around the next bend,"

"What shall I ask him?"

Don:

"Perhaps...Is there anything you would like me to know?"

Kim:

"Oooh, I like that. Not too directing."

Kim paddles the canoe by herself, around three river bends.

"I'll be so glad to see him."

I turn around in my seat and lean back on the bow.

Kim practices turning left and then right.

Watching Kim and the river, I think to myself:

"I couldn't ask for more."

Lesson Learned: Always count your blessings. Be grateful for what you have.

Dreams "can seem as vividly real as waking life" (but they are) "much more changcable." To become lucid during dreams it is helpful to practice testing your state of consciousness while supposedly awake. "You may discover that anytime you feel the genuine need to test reality, this in itself is proof enough that you're dreaming, since while awake we almost never seriously wonder if we're really awake" (LaBerge & Rheingold, 1990, p. 65).

With this and the previous teaching in mind, sleep, dream, tend to you dreams. When ready, move to the next waypoint, "Daily Actions."

29

Daily Actions

PROVIDE A SOLUTION TO THE
PROBLEM EVERYONE HAS MADE

Humanity, collectively, achieved astonishing results from its development and use of fossil fuels. The industrial development, the greater transportation capabilities, and the widespread affluence fossil fuel development brought to the world is epic in its proportions.

But, along with the spoils of fossil fuel development came the massive spewing of carbon dioxide and other so-called greenhouse gases. These pollutants caused the specter of global climate change. Within my own lifetime, humanity has gone from widespread enthusiasm for the use of fossil fuels to the thinking that excessive combustion—in factories, in power plants, and in automobiles—has to be curbed substantially to prevent intolerable conditions all over the world. Despite the huge amount of consumption that nursing on the breast of fossil-fuel burning made possible, our largely unrestrained and continuous suckling amounts to an enormous failure of human imagination. It is not very imaginative to ask people to cut their carbon consumption to the point where the restrictions are painful. That won't work. We may think that carbon offsets are the answer, but the planting of trees in the rainforest, for example, while better than doing nothing, largely allows the consumers of the products of big polluters to think that enough is being done and to continue in their destructive ways.

It will take the collective imagination of humanity to wean ourselves off of the fossil fuel nipple. Everyone is called to pitch in. Your ideas and actions count.

The next four waypoints are devoted to helping you think and act in ways that forge a significant contribution to the effort to hammer out significant solutions. I call this the path of love because in the activities I am not looking for you to come up with burdensome solutions. Rather, we are looking for personal changes that add pleasure and happiness to your life.

The fate of humanity and the future of untold numbers of other natural beings depends on what you and others do to extinguish the fossil fuel fires. Is it really all that fun to stay on the present dirty fuel causeway? What better solutions—ones that favor love over fear, fun over despair, concrete changes over pie-in-the-sky remedies—can we forge? Do the following activity. Let's see what you can unearth?

To The Dousing Of Unsatisfying Daily Actions...

HumaNatureConnect Activity

Start-up Protocol

If this is not a day when you prefer to spend time in nature without an agenda, do the Heartwood Path Start-up Protocol found in the Appendix. Then return here to do the remaining portion of this activity:

Walking On The Path Of Love, Part One

Before you begin your nature communing, read the following ideas for what you can do to stamp out humanity's addiction to fossil fuels:

1. Add solar collectors to your home.

2. Sign-up for a home energy audit.
3. Switch to LED lightbulbs.
4. Request that your utility company purchase clean energy.
5. Replace or clean the filters on your heater or air conditioner.

Use you head to ponder how these solutions can be a part of your own path of love. Then, look for ways that natural beings are inspiring you to put your head, hands and heart to use in the effort to smother the fossil fuel inferno. Focus most on solutions that are more pleasurable than your present daily fossil fuel-guzzling actions. And, remember that the components of a plan amount to who is going to do what by when.

1. I can ride a bicycle instead of driving a car, at least for short trips. My plan for bringing this solution to fruition is...
2. I can tell five people that, while their individual actions will not solve the climate change problem, their changed behavior patterns will be important pieces in the puzzle. My plan for bringing this solution to fruition is...
3. I will go without predetermined solutions to a natural area and use my natural senses to glean valuable inspiration and information. Once a nature-inspired solution becomes evident, here is my plan for bringing it to fruition.

Inscribe your nature-inspired solution(s) in your journal. Log related plans.

Follow-up Protocol

For best results, write down your impressions of this activity in your journal using the Heartwood Path Follow-up Protocol found in the Appendix. Afterwards, consider sharing your interpretations with others.

Heartwood Path Axioms

Key Assertions From Waypoint 5.29

5.29.1.

Provide a solution to the problem everyone has made.

5.29.2.

Despite the huge amount of consumption that suckling on the breast of fossil-fuel burning made possible, our largely unrestrained and continuous suckling amounts to an enormous failure of human imagination.

5.29.3.

It will take the collective imagination of humanity to wean ourselves off of the fossil fuel nipple.

Nocturnal Pilgrimage 5.29

For best results, write down your impressions of each night's dreams in your journal using the Heartwood Path Dreaming Time Protocols found in the Appendix. Afterwards, consider sharing your Dream Tending with others.

The Natural Law Of Rotation:

The energy of the universe
ebbs and flows
at different rates at different times.

All things are powered by universal energy. This power does not remain stable. It behaves as a grand rotation: around and around, up and down. It will always eventually increase or decrease.

Use times of stability and decrease for planning. It's wise to hold back during times of lessening, as it is in Wintertime.

Don't give up hope. Projects have a greater chance of success when universal momentum is on the increase, as it is during Springtime.

Be aware of the cycles and prepare for times of decrease. Everything in life has its time. Coordinate your projects with the cycles to help insure financial success, needed policy changes, harmony, creativity, and spiritual growth.

Forward motion is facilitated by your recognition that everyone and everything changes. During hard times—which typically coincide with universal times of decrease—it is reassuring to know that better times are coming.

Pertinent And Instructive Gems From My Dream Tending Journal

Floating on the Missouri River, as we do in the next dream, is a fantastic activity for nature lovers. Only on a few occasions is the scenery marred by intrusive man-made eye-sores.

After many glorious hours without overt signs of global destruction, I could see Kim's bubble burst as we floated around the bend and passed the behemoth of Labadie, one of the nation's largest sources of air pollution. As we passed the power plant, Kim kept turning around to face me, glaring.

Kim:

"Let's have lunch on that sandbar over there, and talk about this."

As her feet touched the sand, she exclaimed:

"That is horrible! That monster is harming the planet. It's gonna take something really big to shut that thing down."

My reply:

"I don't think there is one big magic bullet, but there are many little things that can be done."

Kim:

"It makes me despair. And what it symbolizes—industrialization—makes me afraid. Aren't you pissed?"

Don:

"I don't have despair about it. That comes from fear. I do, however, have anger. And I grieve over the losses such polluters are causing."

Kim:

"How do you personally keep from despairing?"

Don:

"I try to, on a daily basis, experience lovely beings in lovely places."

Kim:

"Like me, with you, on this beautiful beach?"

Don:

"Yes, this is a perfect example of what I mean. Being alone with you and Lover Nature on this deserted and beautiful stretch of sand shows me how much there is to love. And that love propels me into action in creative ways that fear prevents."

Kim:

"Wait, you love me?"

Don:

"Yes."

Kim:

"Hmmph?... I want that polluter shut down."

Don:

"So do I. The utilities always seem to place these ugly beasts in the most scenic areas. Actually, I want Labadie; it's sister plant on the Mississippi—Portage Des Sioux—; all powerplants, really; and the culture of industrial civilization—the petroculture—all phased out as soon as possible."

Kim:

"Why the whole culture?"

Don:

"Because of what it whispers to us day and night, throughout the year. Petroculture tells us, on the subconscious level, that, to be happy, we all need more money, more stuff, and more convenience. Satisfying these wants is rendering the planet unlivable. I'm angry about that. And I grieve. But, I'm not in despair—can't afford to be. I use my anger and grief, tempered by the joy I feel, to move me into action. I don't think I could do that if I was both fearful and in despair."

Kim:

"So it's love rather than despair that moves you. I did not see much about love in your various published words about sustainability. Compared to what I read on your website, and certainly compared to the love I feel in our three-way forays—with you, me, and Lover Nature—your expressions about sustainability are rather blasé."

Don:

"I think that's because I am still working that out in my mind. The thought of merely 'sustaining'"love or the environment leaves me a bit..."

Kim:

"Flaccid?" she said with a big laugh.

Don:

"I was gonna say 'flat'. I need a word that conveys more about the experience of healing and how that healing leads to transformation. Shall we think about that in our respective corners?"

Kim:

"If you like.vBut I want the upstream end of the sand bar this time, if you don't mind."

Noticing that her chosen end is where the last rays of today's sunshine were still warming the sand, I agreed. She immediately started running upstream, leaving a trail of clothes as she proceeded. Separated from me for about ninety minutes, and having recovered her clothes, crumpled and dirty, she returns to our camp and stuffs her threads into a trash bag. She is nude and standing where she can receive the heat of the fire. She says nothing. Nothing except, while looking direct at me:

"Regeneration."

Lesson Learned: Sustainability means to stop the growth and to find the balance. It means to bring global consumption and population growth down to a level that the earth can endure. Kim's "regeneration," she informs me, is about doing more than merely sustaining. It is about healing. And it is about making our lives expressions of love for all sentient beings. Nothing would depend on fossil fuels. Energy use would be dependent on how much could be retrieved from the sun, which includes from the wind. Much of the planet would be allowed to rewild. Technology would focus on doing more with less. Even the amount of recycling would go down, as this practices creates the false impression that there is a place where things go away. In this way, recycling makes people feel that, since they are recycling, they can ethically continue to consume as much as they like. It creates confusion over the impacts of our consumption. By keeping us from blindly chasing after things that ultimately increase our wanting and our suffering, regeneration leads to a sense of peace, to a sense of wellness, to a reduction in anxiety and craving, to an increase in gratitude, to the eagerness to help others, and to the spreading of happiness that is authentic, abundant, and abiding.

Sleep. Dream. Tend to your dreams. When ready, turn your attention to the next waypoint, entitled "A New Level."

30

A New Level

LIVE A NEW LIFE SO YOU CAN CHANGE THE WORLD

Those of us who care about the environment need to make some changes in our strategy and in the words we use. Doing so will not only be good for the environment. It will also be good for us, mainly because most of the suggested changes are not external to us. These changes will give us valued traits. By succeeding in becoming better, we will feel good about ourselves, we will become better advocates, and, beginning with those closest to us, the positivity will spread. The result will be the regeneration of nature, an increased number of effective environmental advocates, and increased human happiness.

Making these changes are simply the right thing to do, which means they are ethical—a major topic of this part of the Heartwood Path. Science gives us a clear picture of the reality we face. But clarity alone is not enough. We also need a way to guide our behavior. That is where ethics come into play.

And some questions too:

Are we to care most about individuals? Or, are we to care most about natural systems? Since many future problems are dependent on how we act today, what are we to do about future generations? Do we care about our family only? Or, do we also care about our friends, our neighbors, our fellow citizens. Are we really expected to care about all sentient beings? Where do we cut off our concern? Do we need to stop all suffering? Who decides, the majority? Do your own individual actions matter? How can we expect to affect the larger society, if we cannot make even small changes in ourselves?

These questions will likely be answered automatically as we work to make important changes in ourselves. Here are few simple suggestions (more will follow):

Each one of us need to:

1. focus on solving problems proactively,
2. stop shaming others,
3. refrain from making people fearful, and
4. discontinue making people feel guilty.

These last three tactics don't work. They need to be replaced with:

1. helping people live their lives in alignment with the biosphere,
2. being appreciative of the gifts of nature;
3. cultivating love;
4. doing no harm to natural beings or natural landscapes;
5. recognizing that buying "green" perpetuates the consumer mind-set and allows people—who falsely feel like they are responding to the environmental predicament—avoid making meaningful changes—those that go beyond shopping; and
6. showing people that a low-energy lifestyle can be fun and satisfying.

To Continue Walking On The Path Of Love...

HumaNatureConnect Activity

Start-up Protocol

If this is not a day when you prefer to spend time in nature without an agenda, do the Heartwood Path Start-up Protocol found in the Appendix. Then return here to do the remaining portion of this activity:

Walking On The Path Of Love, Part Two

Before you begin your nature communing, read the following ideas for what you can do to stamp out humanity's addiction to fossil fuels:

1. Use a smart thermostat to prevent excess energy usage (like when no one is home).
2. Wash clothes in cold water.
3. Repurpose your furniture instead of buying new.
4. Recycle your clothes.
5. Buy new appliances with the Energy Star label.

Then look for ways that natural beings are inspiring you to put your head, hands, and heart to use in the effort to smother the fossil fuel inferno. Focus most on solutions that are more pleasurable than your present daily fossil fuel-guzzling actions. And, remember that the components of a plan amount to who is going to do what by when.

1. I can focus on improving the world rather than on the implausible and discouraging task of saving the world. My plan for bringing this solution to fruition is...
2. I can live in a historic (recycled) house in an urban neighborhood and walk to where I need to go for goods and services. My plan for bringing this solution to fruition is...
3. I will go without predetermined solutions to a natural area and use my natural senses to glean valuable inspiration and information. Once a nature-inspired solution becomes evident, here is my plan for bringing it to fruition.

Follow-up Protocol

For best results, write down your impressions of this activity in your journal using the Heartwood Path Follow-up Protocol found in the Appendix. Afterwards, consider sharing your interpretations with others.

Heartwood Path Axioms

Key Assertions From Waypoint 5.30

5.30.1.

By succeeding in becoming better, we will feel good about ourselves, we will become better advocates, and, beginning with those closest to us, the positivity will spread.

5.30.2.

Replace making people feel shameful, guilty, and fearful, with helping them feel appreciation for nature, aligned with the biosphere, and feel loved.

Nocturnal Pilgrimage 5.30

For best results, write down your impressions of each night's dreams in your journal using the Heartwood Path Dreaming Time Protocols found in the Appendix. Afterwards, consider sharing your Dream Tending with others.

We all know...

The (Un)Natural Law Of Expounding:

Anything is possible
if you don't know your subject.

The Natural Law Of Comparisons:

Meaning arises
in our minds
based on the
comparisons we make.

Everything is relative. It all depends on how one thing compares to another. A White Oak, for example, is big until you compare it to a giant Sequoia. When you include yourself in the comparing, make sure to be positive. Your negative reactions and actions as a result of your comparisons can be stifling and obstructive. Additionally, giving yourself a positive reaction when comparing yourself to others can result in a superiority complex. Refrain from judging. Everyone, including yourself, has gifts, talents, and abilities. Compare your uniqueness to the uniqueness of other people but do not pronounce one better than the other. Neutral is the universe. Compare paths, not people.

Pertinent And Instructive Gems From My Dream Tending Journal

Kim's word—regeneration—hit the mark.

She makes a beautiful source of words.

Don:

"Thank you for the better word."

Kim:

"Maybe sometime you'll tell me how each person can help us get there."

Don:

"Not tonight. I don't want to tax nature's inspirational abilities; or, should I say, my ability to make sense of patterns, vibes, and behaviors in nature. Is that how you came up with 'Regeneration', from Nature?"

Kim:

"I think so, I just know that being quiet and mindful in nature's presence makes me think differently, deeper, or better."

Don:

"When you show your appreciation, your gratitude; and when you don't force yourself or your words onto Nature, but instead wait for Her continuing appeal, which is how consent is granted in the Wild, more comes from the nature communing."

Kim:

"I've read what you mean by consent. Do you realize that you are already changing yourself in ways that lead to regeneration?"

Don:

"How so?"

Kim:

"Giving away your printing company. Voluntary poverty. Being attuned to the needs of others, like when you asked me how I'm doing or whether I need anything—I love when you do that. The way you spread your sense of self out to include all of nature. The way you devote yourself to bringing the issues and solutions to a wider audience. The way you don't leave it all up to God but instead combine His blessings with your own atypical participation."

Don:

"Sheesh! Astute observations. Such eloquence!"

Kim:

"I didn't know you were noticing. I love the way you don't call attention to yourself."

Hugging me from behind, Kim spun us around and warmed her bottom, one side at a time, on the raging fire. Staring out into the darkness, I thought I was hiding my emotional response. Instinctively, without ever looking, Kim reached up to wipe away my tears of joy. Lowering her moistened hands, I'm not sure if she was checking for sand, which really hurts when it's in the wrong place, or for my amorous readiness. In any event, she used my tears for lubrication as she performed a full manual inspection. Having found me both free of granules and suitably disposed, we were good to go. And the night was still young.

Lesson Learned: Each of us have four things we need to do if we are to become the change the world needs:

1. Voluntary poverty.
2. Being attuned to the needs of others.
3. Developing a sense of oneness. And

4. Bringing the message to others.

Sleep. Dream. Tend to your dream. When ready, go to the next waypoint, "Three Steps To Ethos."

31

Three Steps To Ethos

BEGIN IN MOTIVATION AND END IN ACTION

Ethos—the characteristic spirit of a culture based on its aspirations and beliefs—transforms from undeveloped motivation to effective action by employing the three-legged stool of causality. The first leg is the culture's most prevalent view—that is to say, its dominant outlook. The view we shall seek is formed by science, not dogma. The way a culture sees the world determines what it becomes. That brings us to the second leg: meditation. The outlook becomes familiar to the members of a culture by the way it becomes, by the way it is made, or by the way it is cultivated. Each of these ways are reinforced through meditation, which results in the internalization of good habits and the strengthening of the will. The individual and collective development of determination, strength of character, commitment, and tenacity allows a culture to lean on the third leg: action. We cannot just jump to action. Any attempt at transformation without the three legs of view, mediation, and action will be both short-sided and short-lived.

To Continue On The Pathway Of Love...

HumaNatureConnect Activity

Start-up Protocol

If this is not a day when you prefer to spend time in nature without an agenda, do the Heartwood Path Start-up Protocol found in the Appendix. Then return here to do the remaining portion of this activity:

Walking On The Path Of Love, Part Three

Before you begin your nature communing, read the following ideas for what you can do to stamp out humanity's addiction to fossil fuels:

1. Organize or participate in a peaceful demonstration.
2. Show others how consuming less can be pleasurable, fulfilling, and health-producing.
3. Give your own environmental version of an "I have a dream" speech, making sure it does not morph into an "I have a nightmare" speech.
4. Keep your solutions practical. And
5. Engage in right development of your character so that your actions lead to ethical action. Chance favors right development.

Then look for ways that natural beings are inspiring you to put your head, hands and heart to use in the effort to smother the fossil fuel inferno. Focus most on solutions that are more pleasurable than your present daily fossil fuel-guzzling actions. And, remember that the components of a plan amount to who is going to do what by when.

1. I can repair something rather than discard it and buy something new. My plan for bringing this solution to fruition is...
2. I can get rid of stuff. My plan for bringing this solution to fruition is ...

3. I will go without predetermined solutions to a natural area and use my natural senses to glean valuable inspiration and information. Once a nature-inspired solution becomes evident, here is my plan for bringing it to fruition.

Follow-up Protocol

For best results, write down your impressions of this activity in your journal using the Heartwood Path Follow-up Protocol found in the Appendix. Afterwards, consider sharing your interpretations with others.

Heartwood Path Axioms

Key Assertions From Waypoint 5.31

5.31.1.

The way a culture sees the world determines what it becomes.

5.31.2.

Meditation results in the internalization of good habits and the strengthening of the will.

5.31.3.

Any attempt at transformation without the three legs of view, mediation, and action will be both short-sided and short-lived.

Nocturnal Pilgrimage 5.31

For best results, write down your impressions of each night's dreams in your journal using the Heartwood Path Dreaming Time Protocols found in the Appendix. Afterwards, consider sharing your Dream Tending with others.

We all know...

The (Un)Natural Law Of The Just Beyond:

The location of the itch
is always just beyond the reach.

And

The (Un)Natural Law Of Severity:

The severity of the itch
is inversely proportional to
one's reach.

Pertinent And Instructive Gems From My Dream Tending Journal

We have the tent set up but, as is usual on our float trips, we are sleeping outside, on the sand, under the stars. The glow of the campfire is shimmering on Kim's face and body. As Orion watches, Kim, naked atop our sleeping bag, asks an important question.

Kim:

"I gotta know something. You have protected rivers and wilderness. You have led efforts to stop all sorts of dumb development, even a nuclear power plant. How do you overcome laziness?"

Don:

"I never waste time, for even when I'm taking time off, as we are now, I focus on what brings me joy."

Kim:

"Do I do that for you?"

Don:

"Do ya, do ya, do ya, ever!"

Kim:

"Seriously, how can I overcome my laziness?"

Don:

"Are you a procrastinator?"

Kim:

"I sometimes put things off for no good reason, yes."

Don:

"Do you habitually indulge in contrary behavior."

Kim:

"Who talks like this? What do you mean?"

Don:

"You don't spend a lot of time doing inappropriate stuff just to avoid the important stuff."

Kim:

"Correct."

Don:

"And you don't seem discouraged."

Kim:

"Correct again, Deepak!"

Don:

"You are confident. Look how you took the canoe out by yourself."

Kim:

"Okay?"

Don:

"You don't underestimate your actual capacity. Do you tend to have admiration, trust, and confidence in your teachers?"

Kim:

"Yes!, Noble Canoeing Teacher!"

Waving her arms to illustrate her understanding:

"Turn the boat with a 'C-stroke.' Keep the boat straight with a 'J-stroke.'"

Laughing at her suggestiveness, Kim announces:

"We gonna practice our 'F-stroke' as soon as you answer my question: what's the best way to avoid laziness?"

Don:

"Okay, six ways, quickly: One, deep awareness of the pros and cons and the cost-benefit ratio. Two, clarification of values. Three, cultivation of strong aspirations. Four, assessing your own capability. Five, putting in the required effort, including the effort to knock out selfishness. And sex, I mean six, suppleness."

Kim:

"Ooooh, let me help you with that last one."

Trying to focus, Don:

"Suppleness means, in short, being flexible, having room enough to counter-act laziness with joy. There is always room for joy."

Kim:

"Gotcha, Fine Teacher, Now show me how we do that 'F-stroke' again!'

By the time the fire was down, Kim—hot and satiated—exposed her body to the night air. Her beads of perspiration were so fine, when the moonlight hit her body it dispersed in a smooth silvery glow. With a post-orgasmic giggle, she said:

"I'm so, so grateful that I am not holding back any grainy sediment, if you know what I mean. The below-tide people of New Orleans need all of the alluvium they can get to protect themselves from the rising seas. They can have it, especially those fearsome errant specks. Just one of those babies,

deeply embedded in the wrong place, would really squash my oceanic
surges."

Don:

"'Errant specks!' 'Alluvium!' 'Oceanic surges!' I can't decide if I want to call
you Emily or Edna, but you sure are a poet."

Kim:

"You're funny! Just don't make it 'Edna St. Vincent Malaise.' Come over
here. Give Edna some more quantum healing, Deepak!"

Lesson Learned: Never trade away your joy. Use the six ways to overcome laziness: awareness, clarification of values, cultivation of aspirations that lead to inspirations, matching your goals to your capabilities, sufficient effort, and flexibility.

Sleep. Dream. Tend to your dreams, When ready, go on an agenda-free walk in nature or turn to the next waypoint, entitled "Encouragement to Consume."

32

Encouragement To Consume

BE WARY OF ADVERTISEMENTS

We see the good life on television and paper ads. Advertising makes us see that our lives do not measure up. Such comparisons make us suffer. To overcome what we feel we lack we consume. We chase for happiness by consuming. But this is never satisfying, so we buy more. Collectively, all of this extra consumption is destroying the environment. The alternative is stillness.

Without moments of quiet meditation we do not know who we are or what we want out of life. Pointlessly, we move from one distraction to another. We buy this, and then we buy that.

We do not have time to contemplate the need for change. And we are unable to monitor the transformations that are sure to emerge, whether or not we are paying attention.

To counter the ongoing rush to consume, cultivate stillness. Do it as often as possible.

Do nothing but monitor your bodily sensations. This action will prepare your mind for the second of our three steps towards individually being the change you seek for the word: meditation (which is preceded by accurate awareness of the view and followed by action).

To Continue On The Pathway Of Love...

HumaNatureConnect Activity

Start-up Protocol

If this is not a day when you prefer to spend time in nature without an agenda, do the Heartwood Path Start-up Protocol found in the Appendix. Then return here to do the remaining portion of this activity:

Walking On The Path Of Love, Part Four

Before you begin your nature communing, read the following ideas for what you can do to stamp out humanity's addiction to fossil fuels:

1. Clean up litter.
2. Stop using foam food containers.
3. Help protect the rainforest by not using palm oil.
4. Attend a meditation retreat. And
5. Join a community group.

Then look for ways that natural beings are inspiring you to put your head, hands and heart to use in the effort to smother the fossil fuel inferno. Focus most on solutions that are more pleasurable than your present daily fossil fuel-guzzling actions. And, remember that the components of a plan amount to who is going to do what by when.

1. I can do something kind for a neighbor. My plan for bringing this solution to fruition is...
2. I can plant a fruit tree. My plan for bringing this solution to fruition is...

3. I will go without predetermined solutions to a natural area and use my natural senses to glean valuable inspiration and information. Once a nature-inspired solution becomes evident, here is my plan for bringing it to fruition.

Follow-up Protocol

For best results, write down your impressions of this activity in your journal using the Heartwood Path Follow-up Protocol found in the Appendix. Afterwards, consider sharing your interpretations with others.

Heartwood Path Axioms

Key Assertions From Waypoint 5.32

5.32.1.

Be wary of advertisements.

5.32.2.

We chase for happiness by consuming.

5.32.3.

The alternative to extra consumption is stillness (attention to bodily sensations).

Nocturnal Pilgrimage 5.32

For best results, write down your impressions of each night's dreams in your journal using the Heartwood Path Dreaming Time

Protocols found in the Appendix. Afterwards, consider sharing your Dream Tending with others.

Through dream incubation, I am able to continue my dreams night after night. I can, more or less, predetermine my dreams. Despite this level of control, my dreams remain their own and are always full of surprises. And mysteries, like the following:

We all know...

The (Un)Natural Law Of The Wandering Screw:

Drop a screw
and it will roll
to the least accessible spot
in the galaxy.

The Natural Law Of Acceptance:

Balance
responding and taking action
with listening and being passive.

Pertinent And Instructive Gems From My Dream Tending Journal

Kim wakes up early and goes to her place at the down-river tip of the sand. I build up the fire and prepare breakfast. She meditate and does some yoga. When she returns, she adds to my satisfaction in the moment by offering a big, long smile. Then she says:

Kim:

"I love how we have not used fossil fuels and cell phones for this entire trip. It's motivating me to become, among other things, a vegetarian."

Don:

"If everyone does that, what would we do with all the boy cows?"

Kim:

"I'll have to think about that one?"

Don

"Wanna eat fish next time?"

Kim:

"I'm not gutting any slimy catfish, if that's what you mean."

Don

"Salmon, then?"

Kim:

"Only if their numbers don't dwindle?"

Don:

"I think the wild ones have. So, what shall we eat next time?"

Without looking up from her plate of bacon, eggs, and scrambled veggies,

Kim says:

"Cake."

Lesson Learned: There will always be trade-offs. Try to reduce your impact but not to the point of suffering. Keep your life joyful.

Sleep. Dream. Tend to your dreams. When ready, go to the next waypoint, entitled "Sensual Awareness."

33

Sensual Awareness

FOLLOW THE BREATH AND SCAN
FOR SENSATIONS

Vipassana is keeping your attention on your breath. It is a vital practice for becoming the change you seek for the world. It helps one see things as they really are. Following your breath will bring you out of the suffering that promotes the false remedies that prevent happiness and result in environmental destruction. Vipassana washes away stress and anxiety. Following the breath helps one become less concerned about outcomes. One is able to separate oneself from one's work. Work habits and decision-making becomes improved. What others think of you will become less burdensome. With an increase in the accuracy of observations, cravings, jealousy, and negative self-talk fade away. You will know you are doing vipassana correctly when your sense of equanimity (composure) and your sense of harmony in relationships go up.

To Continue On The Pathway Of Love...

HumaNatureConnect Activity

Start-up Protocol

If this is not a day when you prefer to spend time in nature without an agenda, do the Heartwood Path Start-up Protocol found in the Appendix. Then return here to do the remaining portion of this activity:

Walking On The Path Of Love, Part Five

Before you begin your nature communing, read the following ideas for what you can do to stamp out humanity's addiction to fossil fuels:

1. Unplug electrical devices when not in use.
2. Cut back on water usage.
3. Install downspout flower boxes and barrels to catch rainwater.
4. Insulate your home.
5. Downsize your home and car. And,
6. Lower your thermostat in the winter and raise it in the summer (even two degrees will help).

Then look for ways that natural beings are inspiring you to put your head, hands and heart to use in the effort to smother the fossil fuel inferno. Focus most on solutions that are more pleasurable than your present daily fossil fuel-guzzling actions. And, remember that the components of a plan amount to who is going to do what by when.

1. I can spend time following my breath. My plan for bringing this solution to fruition is...
2. I can cultivate loving-kindness towards others. My plan for bringing this solution to fruition is...
3. I will go without predetermined solutions to a natural area and use my natural senses to glean valuable inspiration and information. Once a nature-inspired solution becomes evident, here is my plan for bringing it to fruition.

Follow-up Protocol

For best results, write down your impressions of this activity in your journal using the Heartwood Path Follow-up Protocol found in the Appendix. Afterwards, consider sharing your interpretations with others.

Heartwood Path Axioms

Key Assertions From Waypoint 5.33

5.33.1.

Vipassana—keeping your attention on your breath—is a vital practice for becoming the change you seek for the world.

5.33.2.

Following your breath will bring you out of the suffering that promotes the false remedies that prevent happiness and result in environmental destruction.

5.33.3.

You will know you are doing vipassana correctly when your sense of equanimity (composure) and your sense of harmony in relationships go up.

Nocturnal Pilgrimage 5.33

For best results, write down your impressions of each night's dreams in your journal using the Heartwood Path Dreaming Time Protocols found in the Appendix. Afterwards, consider sharing your Dream Tending with others.

We all know...

The (Un)Natural Law Of Befuddlement:

Every car has its own Black Hole—
that space between the front seats
where things fall
but can never be retrieved.

The veiled view given to us by our industrial culture was leaving us blind to the total picture of our lives. We saw the way we are told to see. As cogs in the industrial machine, we were befuddled. We were not encouraged to see beyond our jobs and consumption patterns.

With the help of the Heartwood Path and its HumaNatureConnect Activities, your veil is by now at least partly removed. With what you can now see and your newly acquired or boosted valued traits, you are well suited to go into action, in earnest. Choose your involvement and go. Watch for positive changes in yourself and your environment.

Pertinent And Instructive Gems From My Dream Tending Journal

Just as we were finishing our meal, in flies one of the largest wading birds in North America. His approach brings to mind a large flying dinosaur. He lands at the upstream tip of our island, arranges his feathers, and seems to be waiting for Kim.

Kim, while sponge bathing in the open air:

"Look! Orange pantaloons. It's Great Blue!"

She doesn't bother dressing. She immediately walks slowly in her bird
friend's direction.

"So good to see you, pretty boy. What brings you my way?"

His up and down neck movement is reminiscent of a salute. Kim focuses on
Great Blue. Asks for permission to approach and, noticing his continued
dusk-infused radiate beauty, assumes she has his content. As she approaches
she scans the space around her avian friend. Her softer gaze seems to relax
Great Blue, who actually takes a few steps in her direction. Kim pauses on a
log as a way not to be intimidating. She puts thoughts out of her head,
focuses her attention, breathes in appreciation and breathes out gratitude.
They remain together until the lack of light sets Great Blue on his way
back to his rookery, the location of which is still a mystery. As he flies out
of view. Kim, feeling changed by Blue's gentle, quiet, and insightful
guidance, walks back to camp, turns to the fire, and announces, much to
her own surprise:

"You and I will soon fly overseas to help some indigenous women with a
regeneration project."

Lesson Learned: In numerous dreams Kim—always sexy and impressive—delivered many helpful realizations. Watching her reactions to the experience of canoeing on the Missouri River was both pleasurable and rewarding. She provided an excellent example of how book learning need not supersede direct experiences as sources of trustable truths. Her growth from submissive girlfriend to equal partner demonstrates how communing with consenting natural beings can foster transcendent growth.

Sleep. Dream. Tend to your dreams. Move to the next book in the Heartwood Path series: **Volitos**. In it, you will learn how to fortify and better your individual Will.

374 | DON PIERCE

Use what you learn in Volitos to grow and go into action as an individual. You will see in Volitos how manipulation occurs when there is Will without Love. You will also see how Love without Will is overly sentimental. Without the Will, thoroughly presented in Volitos, one could not function optimally as a human being.

Don't sell yourself short. Keep heading towards happiness and the regeneration of nature by reading Volitos as soon as possible. It contains the most potent suggestions for individuals on the Heartwood Path.

References

Abram, David. (1987) The perceptual implications of Gaia, Revision, 9(2), 7-15).

Access to Insight Website: http://www.accesstoinsight.org/lib/authors/silananda/bl137.html

Aizenstat, Stephen, Ph.D. (2009). Dream tending. New Orleans, Louisiana: Spring Journal, Inc.

Barrett, Julie Langdon. Website: http://julielangdonbarrett.com/2011/08/11/how-to-tell-the-difference-between-intuition-and-your-imagination-or-ego/

Babauta, Leo. (2009) The power of less: the fine are of limiting yourself to the essentials . . . in business and in life. New York, New York: Hyperion.

Barasch, Marc, Ian. (2000). Healing dreams: exploring the dreams that can transform your life. New York, New York: Riverhead Books.

Beck, Larry and Cable, Ted (2002). Interpretation for the twenty-first century. Urbana, Illinois: Sagamore Publishing, Incorporated.

Beck, Martha (2012). Finding your way in a wild new world. New York, New York: Free Press

Bernard, Patrick. (2004). Music as yoga: discover the healing power of sound. San Rafael, CA: Mandala Publishing.

Borden, Richard, J. (2014). Ecology and experience: reflections from a human ecological perspective. Berkeley, California: North Atlantic Books.

Bosnak, Robert. (1986). A little course in dreams. Boston, Massachusetts: Shambala Publication, Inc.

Bosnak, Robert. (1996) Tracks in the wilderness of dreaming. New York, New York: Delacorte Press

Boston, John Website: (https://www.american.edu/spa/cep/upload/jonathan-boston-lecture-american-university.pdf).

Bowden, Jonny, Ph.d, C.N.S. (2009). The 150 most effective ways to boost your energy. Beverly, Massachusetts: Fair Winds Press.

Buddy, Cathal Br. ofm. Website: www.praying-nature.com.

Buechner, Frederick. (1993). Wishful thinking. A theological abc. San Francisco, California: Harper.

Buhner, Stephen Harrod. (2004). The secret teaching of plants. Rochester, Vermont: Bear and Company, Inner Traditions International.

Bunzl, John M. (2004). Evolutionary Biology and Simultaneous Policy: Vision-Logic for the Next Stage in our Evolutionary Future, Website: http://www.integralworld.net/bunzl.html

Byzant Kabblah Website (www.byzant.com/mystical/kaballah/Path.aspx?number=31)

Care2.com

Cairns, John Jr. (2001) Equity fairness, and the development of a sustainability ethos. Blacksburg Virginia : Ethics in Science and Environmental Politics, February 1., Blacksburg Virginia. www.mnfor-sustain.org/cairns_j_equity_and_a_sustainability_ethos.htm

Cameron, Julie. (2006). Finding water: the art of perseverance. New York, New York: Jeremy P. Tarcher.

Cannon, Walter B. (1963). The wisdom of the body. New York, New York: W.W. Norton & Company, Inc.

Cengagesites Website: http://www.cengagesites.com/academic/assets/sites/4713/Chapter%2015.pdf

Capra, Fritjof. (1996). The web of life. New York, New York: Anchor Books, Random House.

Castro, Dr. Anthony J. (2009). Creating space for happiness: the secret of giving room. Amherst, New York: Prometheus Books.

CGJungPage Website: http://www.cgjungpage.org/learn/articles/technology-and-environment/683-robert-romanyshyn-on-technology-as-symptom-a-dream

Chakra Tones and Notes Website: http://www.wingmakers.co.nz/Chakra_Tones_and_Notes.html

Chalquist, Craig, editor (2010). Rebearths: conversations with a world ensouled. Walnut Creek, Caliifornia: World Soul Books.

Chapman, Alan. (2003) website: http://www.businessballs.com/maslowtest.pdf

Childre, Doc and Martin, Howard. (1999). The heartmath solution. San Francisco, California: Harper Collins Publishers, Inc.

Chopra, Deepak. (2000). How to know god: the soul's journey into the mystery of mysteries. New York, New York: Harmony Books.

Chopra, Deepak. (2004). The book of secrets: unlocking the hidden dimensions of your life. New York, New York: Three Rivers Press.

Millaka Chopra Website: http://www.huffingtonpost.com/mallika-chopra/finding-serenity_b_868151.html

Cialdini, Robert B. (2009) Influence: science and practice. Boston, Massachusetts: Pearson Education, Inc.

Clark, Rawn. (2002) Journal of Wester Mystery Tradition, No. 3, Vol 1 (Website www.jwmt.org/v1n3/32 paths.)

Cohen, Michael J. Ecopsych Website: http://www.ecopsych.com/iupsmswaiver.html.

Cohen, Michael J. Ecopsych/Ecopsychology Journal Website: http://www.ecopsych.com/ecopsychologyjournal.html.

Cohen, Green Wave, ecopsych.com

Cohen, Michael J. Ecopsych/Lifeweb Website: www.ecopsych.com/lifeweb.html.

Cohen, Michael J. Ecopsych Thesis Quote Website: www.ecopsych.com/thesisquote.html.

Cohen, Michael J. (1993) Integrated ecology: The process of counseling with nature. Humanistic Psychologist, 21(3), 277-295.

Cohen, Michael J, Ed.D. Personal email dated December 23, 2010.

Cohen, Michael J, Ed.D. Project NatureConnect Website: http://www.ecopsych.com/insight53senses.html.

Cohen, Michael J, Ed.D. Project NatureConnect Website: http://www.ecopsych.com/earthstories101.html).

Cohen, PNC Website: www.ecopshych.com/universealive.html

Cohen, Michael J, Ed.D. Green Wave Information: (Project NatureConnect Website: http://www.ecopsych.com/journalaliveness.html and personal email June 8, 2016)Comaford-Lynch, Christine. (2007). Rules for renegades. New York, New York: McGraw-Hill.

Cohen, Michael J. (2018). Principles of Organic Psychology. The Eco-Arts and Science of Unconditional Love Friday Harbor, Washington: Project Nature Connect

Cook, Charles. (2001). Awakening to nature: renewing your life by connecting with the natural world. New York, New York: Contemporary Books, MacGraw-Hill

Cope, Stephen. (1999) Yoga and the quest for the true self. New York, New York: Bantam Books.

Copenhagen Qabalah Website: www.qabalah.dk/paths.html.

Csikszentmihalyi, Mihaly. (1993) The evolving self: a psychology for the third millennium. New York, New York: HarperCollins Publishers, Inc.

Csikszentmihalyi. http://psychology.about.com/od/PositivePsychology/a/flow.htm)

Dangerfield, Dr. J. Mark Website. https://www.smashwords.com/.../how-to-love-nature-when-you-live-in-the city.

Delaney, Gayle, Dr. (1994) Sexual dreams: why we have them, what they mean. New York, New York: Fawcett Columbine.

De Stefano, Matias, Three Earth Chakra Videos on You Tube. https://m.youtube.com/watch?v=IcfOwlVQGec.

Discovery Fit and Health Website. http://health.howstuffworks.com/wellness/stress-management/finding-serenity-in-your-life2.htm

DreamTending Website: http://dreamtending.com/naturedreaming.pdf

Dyer, Wayne, Ph.D. (2005) The power of intentions: learning to co-create your world your way. Carlsbad, California: Hay House.

Dwoskin, Hale. (2009). The Sedona Method. Sedona, Arizona: Sedona Press.

Eat, Taste, Heal: an Ayurvedic Guidebook website: http://www.eat-tasteheal.com/ETH_6tastes.htm

Edge Magazine Website: http://www.edgemagazine.net/1995/11/robert-sardello/

E-How. http://www.ehow.com/how_2338305_develop-character.html.

EnglishClub.com Website: http://www.englishclub.com/vocabulary/fl-making-request.htm

Evernden, Neil. (1985). The natural alien. Toronto, Canada: University of Toronto Press.

Ewolt, Dave and Weeks-Ewolt, Alison. (2001) Rational spirituality: evidence of the web of life, Attraction Retreat Website: http://www.attractionretreat.org/Writings/RationalSpirituality.html

Farley, Kent M. (2002) Developing character traits through sport/athletic participation. The Sport Digest- ISSN: 1558-6448. The United

States Sports Academy Website: http://thesportdigest.com/archive/article/developing-character-through-sportathletic-participation

Ferlic, K. (2007). Tapping and sustaining the source. Website: http://ryuc.info/common/creation_process/tap_sustain_source.htm

Ferlic, K (2009) A bottom line about sex and our creativity. Website: http://ryuc.info/creativesexuality/bottom_line_about_sex.htm

Fitness Health Zone Website: http://www.fitnesshealthzone.com/meditation/walking-meditation-and-its-benefits/

Fiorenza, Nick Anthony (2010). Planetary harmonics & Neurobiological resonances, Website: http://www.lunarplanner.com/Harmonics/planetary-harmonics.

Flickstein, Matthew. Online Website: Swallowing the River Ganges: http://innerself.com/Meditation/mindfulness.htm?phpMyAdmin=1IAC4WZXEVp9XvKgNokyjpr3el1.

Franden, Nathaniel. (1996). Taking responsibility, New York, New York: Simon and Schuster.

Franklin Institute Website: http://www.fi.edu/learn/brain/exercise.html.

Gallup, Inc: (http://www.gallup.com/poll/190916/americans-identification-environmentalists-down.aspx)

Gardner, Howard. (1999) "Intelligence reframed: multiple intelligences for the 21st century." New York: Basic Books.

Garon, Henry A. (2006). The cosmic mystique. Maryknoll, New York: Orbis Books.

GDRC Website: https://www.gdrc/uem/ee/Tbilissi.html.

George, James. (1995) Asking the Earth. Saftsbury, Dorset; Element Books Limited.

Goldman, Jonathan. (2002) Healing sounds: the power of harmonics. Rochester, Vermont: Healing Arts Press.

Goodreads Website: www.goodreads.com. Alan_Wilson_Watts

Grand, David, (2001) Emotional healing at warp speed. New York, New York: Harmony Books.

Gunther, Folke, and Folke, Carl, "Characteristics of Nested Living Systems," Journal of Biological Systems, 1:3, Stockholm: Sweden. Website: http://library.uniteddiversity.coop/Systems_and_Networks/Nested%20Living%20Systems%20(Holons)%20.pdf

Hargrove, Eugene C. (1988) Foundations of environmental ethics, Englewood Cliffs, New Jersey: Prentice Hall.

Hawkes, Joyce Whiteley, Ph.D. (2012) Resonance, nine practices for harmonious health and vitality, Carlsbad, California: Hay House, Inc.

Henning, Sequoia. Website: http://www.feelingsoulgood.com/index.php?id=2

Howerton, Mari and Sorensen, "Maya." Website: http://www.singand-hum.com/educational-development/humming-for-health.html

Inner.org. The Gal Einai Website: http://www.inner.org/Institute of HeartMath. Online Website. Global Coherence Initiative. http://www.glcoherence.org/about-us/about.html

Hauser, Marc D. (2006) Moral minds: the nature of right and wrong. New York, New York: Harper Collins.

Helm, Russell Buddy. (2001). The way of the drum. St. Paul, Minnesota: LLewellyn Publications.

Hindu Temples and Gods Website: http://hindutemplesandgods.blog-spot.com/2013/03/sri-yantra.html

Hubbard, Barbara Marx. (2001). Emergence: the shift from ego to essence. Charlottesville, Virginia: Hampton Roads Publishing Company

Huning, Barb. (2-28-11) Personal email: "Re: Editorial Help with Instructions and Marketing."

InnerVision Yoga Website: http://www.innervisionyoga.com/what-is-my-sacred-work/

Institute of Human Conceptual and Mental Development. Online Website. Experiences and Feelings: http://www.ihcmdonline.com/mentalproblems/experiences.htm.

Institute for Social Ecology Website: www.social-ecology.org/199.

Jackson, Brooks and Jamieson, Kathleen Hall. (2007). Unspun: Finding Facts In A World Of Disinformation. New York, New York: Random House Trade Paperbacks

Jensen, Derrick. (2000) A language older than words. White River Junction, Vermont: Chelsea Green Publishing Company

Jensen, Derrick. (2006) Endgame volume I: the problem of civilization. New York, New York: Seven Stories Press.

Jensen, Derrick. (2006). Endgame volume II: resistance. New York, New York: Seven Stories Press.

Jung Atlanta: http://www.jungatlanta.com/articles/winter02-decoding-hillman.pdf

Jurado, Anthony. (2010) Cracked.com Website: http://www.cracked.com/article_18405_7-insane-ways-music-affects-body-according-to-science_p2.html

Kahn , Pete3r H Jr. and Hasbach Patricia H. (2012) Ecopsychology: science, totems, and the technological species, Cambridge, MA: MIT Press.

Kawasaki, Guy (2004). The art of the start. New York, New York: the Penguin Group.

Kawasaki, Guy. (2012). Enchantment. New York, New York: Penguin Group.

Kaza, Stephanie. (1993) The attentive heart: conversations with trees. New York, New York: Fawcett Columbine.

Kittleswon, Mary Lynn. (1996). Sounding the soul: the art of listening. Einsiedeln, Switzerland: Daimon.

Kohn, Alfie (1990). The brighter side of human nature. New York, New York: Basic Books, Inc.

Kroeber, Theodora. (1961) Ishi: in two worlds. Berkeley, California: University of California Press.

Krutch, joseph Wood. (2009) The voice of the desert. New York, New York, General Books.

Kundalini Yoga Info Website: http://www.kundalini-yoga-info.com/humming.html.

Lachance, Albert (1997). "The Architecture of the Soul: Sacred Process Ecopsychology," from the book The Greening of religion: god, the environment, and the good life, edited by Carrol, John E., Broclelman, Paul, and Westfal, Mary. Hanover, New Hampshire: University Press of New England

Lama Dalai. (2011) How to be compassionate. New York, Neew York: Atria Books..

Lame Deer and Erdoes, John. (2009). Lame deer: seeker of visions. New York: New York: Simon and Schuster.

Leopold, Aldo. (1949) . A sand county almanac. London, England: Oxford University Press.

Leopold, Aldo and Flader, Susan L. (editor). (1991) The river of the mother of god and other essays by aldo leopold. Madison, Wisconsin: University of Wisconsin Press.

Lesser, Elizabeth. (2009). The seeker's guide. Website: www.oprah.com/ spirit/10-Signs-of-Progress-on-Your-Spiritual-Path/10 - God is Optimistic - Oprah.com.

Lessmann, Kevin. (2004) Emotions of the Musical Keys Website: http://www.gradfree.com/kevin/some_theory_on_musical_keys.htm

Lewis, Dennis. Website: http://www.authentic-breathing.com/breathing_tips.htm

Levey, Joel and Michelle. (2003). The fine arts of relaxation, concentration & meditation: ancient skills for modern minds. Somerville, Massachutsetts: Wisdom Publications.

Levi, Renee. (2003). Group magic; an inquiry into experiences of collective resonance, doctoral dissertation executive summary: http://resonanceproject.org/execsum.cfm

Lovelock, James. (2010) The vanishing face of gaia. New York, New york: Basic Books.

Luks, Allen and Payne, Peggy. (1991). The healing power of doing good.   New York, New York: Fawcett Columbine.

Luskin, Fred and Pelletier, Kenneth R. (2005) Stress free for good. San Francisco, California: Harper Collins Publishers.

Maathai, Wangari. (2010). Replenishing the earth. New York, New York: Random House.

MacGregor, Catriona. (2010). Partnering with nature: the wild path to reconnecting to the earth. New York, New York: Atria Paperback.

Macy, Joanna and Johnstone, Chris. (2012) Active home: how to face the mess we're in without going crazy. Novato, California: New World Library.

Mander, Jerry (1979) as quoted in the website: http://www.eco-action.org/dt/elimtv.html

Marc and Angel Website Practical Tips for Productive Living: http://www.marcandangel.com/2013/04/21/8-effective-ways-to-let-go-and-move-on/

Mayo Clinic/Ranges of Self-Esteem. www.mayoclinic.org

McCraty, Rollin Ph.D., Atkinson, Mike, Tomasino, Dana and Bradley, Trevor Raymond, Ph.D. (2006). The coherent heart: heart-brain interaction, psychophysiological coherence, and system-wide order. Boulder Creek, California: Institute of Heartmath.

McCraty, Rollin Ph.D. and Tomasino, Dana. (2006). Emotional Stress, Positive Emotions and Psychophysiological Coherence, Institute of HeartMath Website: alternativeworldwidehealth.com, Heartmath_Stress_chapter.pdf

McKay, Kim and Bonnin, Jenny. (2007) True green. Washington D.C: National Geographic Society.

McKay, Pip. (2009). Website: http://www.evolvenow.com.au.

McIntosh, Steve (2007) Excerpt from Integral consciousness and the future of evolution. Website: http://www.stevemcintosh.com/books/integral-consciousness/chapter-five-integral-politics/

McTaggart, Lynne. (2002). The field: the quest for the secret force of the universe. New York, New York: HarperCollins Publishers, Inc.

Mellick, Jill. (1996). The art of dreaming. Berkeley, California: Conari Press.

Michigan Online Website. http://web1.msue.msu.edu/4h/char-coun.html

Mindbodygreen Website: mindbodygreen.com

Montgomery, Pam. (2008) Plant spirit healing. Rochester, Vermont: Bear and Company.

Morris, Jill. (1985). The dream workbook: discover; the knowledge and power hidden in your dreams. Boston, Massachusetts: Little, Brown, and Company.

Murray, William H. From the website: http://innerself.com/content/social-a-political/environment/3934-for-those-who-would-save-the-earth.html

Myersbriggs.org

Myth-Dream-Symbols Website: http://www.mythsdreamssymbols.com/432.html

Nahko Bear (Medicine for the People). Song lyrics to "Aloha Ke Akua," (Onecommunityglobal.org).

Naiman, Rubin R. Ph.D. (2006). Healing night: the science and spirit of sleeping, dreaming, and awakening. Minneapolis, Minnesota: Syren Book Company.

National Catholic Reporter Website: http://ncronline.org/blogs/eco-catholic/fr-thedreamoftheearth.

Neubauer, Joan, R. (1985). Dear diary: the art and craft of writing a creative journal. Nashville, Tennessee: Turner Publishing Company.

New Oxford American Dictionary. Online Edition.

Noll, Doug. Website: http://lawyertopeacemaker.com/heartmath.html

Norbu, Namkhai. (2002). Dream yoga and the practice of natural light. Ithaca, New York: Snow Lion Publishing.

Nordhaus, Ted and Shellenberger, Michael. (2010). Break through: why we can't leave saving the planet to environmentalists. New York, New York: First Mariner Books.

Oelschlaeger, Max. (1991). The idea of wilderness. New Haven, Connecticut: Yale University Press.

Oestreich Associates. www.teamtrustsurvey.com

Oktar, Adnan. website: http://www.secretbeyondmatter.com/our-brains/theworldinourbrains3.html

Orloff, Judith (2003) Website: Trust your hunches: 5 steps to develop your intuition - Intuitive Advice: http://findarticles.com/p/articles/mi_m0NAH/is_8_33/ai_108786014/

Ortiz, John M., Ph.D. (1997) The tao of music: sound psychology. York Beach, ME: Samuel Weiser, Inc.

Ortner, Nick. (2013). The tapping solution: a revolutionary system for stress-free living. Carlsbad, California: Hay House, Inc.

Ouderkirk, Wayne and Hill, Jim editors. Land, value, community: Callicott and environmental philosophy. State University of New York Press. Internet: Callicott_My_Reply_to_Land_Value_Community.pdf

Parker, Jonathan (2011). The soul solution: enlightening meditations for resolving life's problems. Tiburon, California: H J Kramer.

Partridge, Ernest, Ecological morality and nonmoral sentiments. Internet: 60477.pdf.

Partridge, Ernest and Holmes, Ralston III. (1984 ad 1996) The Online Gadfly: http://gadfly.igc.org/papers/values.htm

Peaceful Mind. (2011) Website: http://www.peacefulmind.com/music_therapy.htm

Peaceful Rivers Online Website. Eckhart Tolle Quotes: http://peacefulrivers.homestead.com/EckhartTolle.html

Pearson, Carol S. (1991) Awakening the heroes within: twelve archetypes to help us find ourselves and transform our world. New York, NY: HarperCollins Publishers.

Peat, F. David. Nature and Ethics. http://www.paricenter.com/library/papers/peat23.php

Plotikin, Bill (2008). Soul craft: crossing into the mysteries of nature and the psyche. Novato, California: New World Books.

Plotkin, Bill. (2010). Nature and the human soul: cultivating wholeness and community in a fragmented world. Novato, California: New World Books.

Plotkin, Bill (2013). Wildmind: a field guid to the human psyche. Novato, California: New World Books.

Pratt, Vernon (Unknown) website: http://www.vernonpratt.com/211/

Reverso Online English Dictionary and Thesaurus: http://dictio-nary.reverso.net/english-cobuild/linear

Ricard, Matthieu. (2006) Happiness: A guide to developing life's most important skill. New York, NY: Little, Brown and Company.

Robbins, Stephen P. Organizational behavior, Chapter Six: website: http://www.gobookee.net/organizational-behavior-stephen-p-robbins-14th-edition/

Root-Bernstein, Robert and Michele. (1999). Sparks of genius. Boston, Massachusetts: Houghton-Mifflin Company.

Rudd, Vols, Aaker Website: http://faculty-gsb.stanford.edu/aaker/pages/documents/TimeandAwe2012_workingpaper.pdf

Scull, J (n.d.) Eco-psychology: Where does it fit in psychology? Web-site: http://www.island.net/~jscull/ecopsych.htm

Scully, Matthew. (2002), Dominion. New York, New York: St. Martin's Press.

Second Journey Website, "Itineraries:" http://www.secondjourney.org/newsltr/NDX/Sullivan_frameset.htm

Selhub, Eva M. and Logan, Alan C. (2012). Your brain on nature: the science of nature's influence on your health, happiness, and vitality. Ontario, Canada: John Wiley and Sons Canada Ltd.

Seligman, Martin E.P. (2011). Flourish: a visionary new understanding of happiness and wellbeing. New York, New York: Free Press, Simon and Schuster.

Sewell, L. (1995). The Skill of ecological perception, In T. Roszak, M.E. Gomes, & A.D. Kanner (Eds.). Eco-psychology: Restoring the earth, healing the mind (pp. 201-215). San Francisco, California: Sierra Club.

Sewall, Laura Ph.D. (1999). Sight and sensibility: the ecology of perception. New York, New York: Jeremy P. Tarcher/Putnam.

Shannahoff-Khalsa, David S. (2006) Kundalini yoga mediation. New York, New York: W.W. Norton & Company

Sharp, Jonathan. (2002). Diving your dreams. New York: Simon & Shuster.

Silva Therapy Website: http://www.silvamindbodyhealing.com/articles/mind-body-healing/healing-colors/

SingingToThePlants Website: http://www.singingtotheplants.com/2014/01/dreaming-with-open-eyes/

Songwriting-guide.com Website: http://www.songwriting-guide.com/basic-music-theory.html

Sound Essence Website: http://www.soundessence.net/chakras.php

Sound-PHYSICS.com: http://www.sound-physics.com/Sound/Resonance-NaturalFrequency/

Spoto, Donald (2003). Reluctant saint: the life of francis of assissi. New York, New York: Penguin Books

Spurgeon, C.H. (1871) http://www.spurgeon.org/sermons/1005.htm

State of California, Department of Education, Regional Occupation Centers, and Department of Developmental Disability. (2014). Student Resource Guide: Direct Support Professional Training. http://www.dds.ca.gov/DSPT/Student/StudentYear1_FullVersion.pdf

Steep Path Online Website: http://www.steeppath.com/article.php?ID=6

Sun Bear. (1980). Medicine wheel: earth astrology. Austin, Texas: Touchstone.

Sunstein, Cass, R. and Nussbaum, Martha C. (2004) Animal rights. Oxford, England: Oxford University Press.

Székely, Edmond Bordeaux. The Essene Gospel of Peace. International Biogenic Society, 1981.

Tebra's Writer's Blog Website: http://www.thepensters.com/tebra/secular-saints-philosophy.html.

Templin, Steven, D.O.M Website. http://www.innerbalanceconsulting.com/wp-content/uploads/2011/11/HeartMath-Guide.pdf

Tharp, Twyla. (2003). The creative habit. New York, New York: Simon and Schuster.

Thomashow, Mitchell. (1996). Ecological identity: becoming a reflective environmentalist. Cambridge, Massachusetts: MIT Press.

Thompkins, Peter and Bird, Christopher. (1973) The secret life of plants. New York, New York: Harper and Row, Publishers.

Thoms, Justine. (2008) Small pleasures: finding grace in a chaotic world. Charlottesville, Virginia: Hampton Roads Publishing Company.

Thornton, James. (1999). A field guide to the soul: down-to-earth handbook of spiritual practice. New York, New York: Bell Tower

Thoreau, Henry David. (1965) Walden and on civil disobedience. New York, New York: Harper and Rowe.

Thoreau, Henry David. Excerpt from Journal, quoted from online website: http://www.mothwingarts.com/waldenvisionquest/excerpts.html

Thorncraft, Sylvan. 2006. Website: http://www.emeraldspritestudio.com/articles_toning_and_sacred_sound.htm.

TotalWellnessWorldwide   Website: www.totalwellnessworldwide.com/ions.html

Twenge, Jean M. and Campbell, Keith, W. (2009). The narcissism epidemic. New York, New York: Free Press, Simon and Schuster. United States Conference of Catholic Bishops, Themes from Catholic Social Teaching" Washington, D.C., 2005. Website: http://www.cchdbaltimore.org/soc-teach-color-inst.pdf

Uphanishads. Uphanishads quotes and sayings. Website: http://spiritquotes.com/quotes/upanishadsquotes/upanishads_quotes1.htm.

Van Dyke, Deborah.Mantras Sacred Sounds Website: http://www.kirtancommunity.com/html/mantras_sacred_sound.html

Vedicyagyacenter Website: http://www.vedicyagyacenter.com/mantras-chant/Devi-Khadgamala-Stotram-lyrics-with-meaning.pdf

Veracious.   Wikihow.com   Website: http://www.wikihow.com/Choose-the-Right-Life-Coach

W, Karen. How to overcome fear. Website: http://www.wikihow.com/Overcome-Fear.

Wallace, Alan B. (2012). Dream yourself awake. Boston, Massachusetts: Shambala Publications, Inc.

Webster's Online Dictionary. http://www.websters-online-dictionary.com/definitions/Ethos

Weissman, Darren, R. (2005). The power of infinite love and gratitude. Carlsbad, California: Hay House, Inc.

Whitfield, Charles, L., Whitfield, Barbara H., Park, Russell, and Pre-
vatt, Jeneane. (2006). The power of humility. Deerfield Beach, Florida:
Health Communications, Inc.

Whitworth, Laura, Kimsey-Shouse, Karen, Kimsey-House, Henry, and
Sandeahl, Phillip. (2007). Co-active coaching: new skills for coach-
ing people toward success. Mountain View, California: Davies-Black
Publishing.

Wholistic Healthworks Website: www.wholistichealthworks.com/
healing%20with%20colors.htm

Wilber, Ken. (1995). Sex, Ecology, and Spirit: the spirit of evolution.
Boston, Massachusetts: Shambala Publications, Inc.

Wilber, Ken, (1998). The essential ken wilber: an introductory reader.
Boston, Massachusetts: Shambhala Publications, Inc.

Wilber, Ken (2007) Chapter 14. Integral Politics, or Our of the Prison
of Partiality . . . KenWilber.com Website: http://www.kenwilber.com/
Writings/PDF/14-integral%20politics.pdf

Wilber, Ken; Patton, Terry; Leonard, Adam; and Morelli, Marco.
(2008) Integral life practice: a 21st –century blueprint for physical
health, emotional balance, mental clarity and spiritual awakening.
Boston, Massachusetts: Integral Books.

Williams, Ernest H. Jr. (2005). The nature handbook: a guide to
observing the great outdoors. New York, New York: Oxford University Press.

Wikia Website: http://synchromystic.wikia.com/wiki/432

Wiki-How. http://www.wikihow.com/Strengthen-Character

Wikipedia. David Hume. website: http://en.wikipedia.org/wiki/David_Hume

Wikipedia. Theory Z: webssite: http://en.wikipedia.org/wiki/Theory_Z

Wilderness Survival Sills for Save Wilderness Travel Website: http://www.wilderness-survival-skills.com/how-to-predict-weather.html

Wilson, Carol. (1997) Online Website. Mindfulness: Gateway Into Experience: http://www.dharma.org/ij/archives/1998b/carol_wilson.htm

Wilson, Edward O. (2002). The future of life. New York, New York: Vintage Books.

Winter, Deborah Du Nann and Koger, Susan M. (2004) The psychology of environmental problems. New York: Psychology Press

Wohlforth, Charles. (2010). The fate of nature: rediscovering our ability to rescue the earth. New York, New York: Thomas Dunne Books: St. Martin's Press.

You Tube: Caposiena, Nicholas. (2011) You Tube Podcast: https://www.youtube.com/watch?v=o-r_sMYzW_w

Zclcski, Incssa. North Star Wellness Center Website: http://www.calmness.com/chakras.htm

Zohar, Dana and Marshal, Dr. Ian. (2000). Spiritual intelligence: the ultimate intelligence. New York, New York: Bloomsbury Publishing.

Appendix

Online Resources

Your senses and the Heartwood Path will all come alive as you use the following online resources:

Read the **Glossary** and watch your sense of reason come alive. (www.heartwoodpath.com/glossary)

Use your sense of language when you connect online with other EartHearts at a variety of locations:

- **EartHeart Networking Forum** (www.heartwoodpath.com/connect)
- each **online waypoint** (learning station)
- our **Instagram** account (@heartwoodpath)
- our **Facebook** Page (Heartwood Path)

Your sense of light and sight will be activated when you watch our informative and visually appealing podcasts on **YouTube** (www.youtube.com/user/heartwoodpath).

Inside or outside, online or offline, the Heartwood Path helps you overcome any breaches in your well-being that hinder increasing your happiness and the sustainability of the natural environment.

HumaNatureConnect Activity Protocols

The full meaning of each protocol is revealed as you progress, waypoint by waypoint.

Start-up Protocol

- Read The Text — Use your literary sense, your mind sense, and your reason sense to move towards happiness and sustainability by reading the Heartwood Path text but also go outdoors to the backyard or to the backwoods, where the higher levels of negative ions in the air will improve your mood and well-being.
- Attention Restoration —With a pen and journal in hand, go to a natural area that is attractive, has a variety of plants and animals, and is tranquil enough to leave room for reflection.
- Source — Spend time wandering without an agenda in nature or, if you don't have time to receive nature's magic in this way, follow the instructions in the text at each learning station.
- Attractive Natural Being — Once you are in a natural area (the wilder, the better), look to find a natural being that is attractive to you and remain near that being until the end of the activity.
- Appreciation And Gratitude — While communing with your chosen natural being, appreciate it as you inhale and show it gratitude as you exhale.
- Consent — Once you find an aspect of nature that is attractive to you continuously for at least ten seconds, think of your continued attraction as your consent to have a connection experience that will help you function optimally; receive information, guidance, and healing; and establish in your mind a more helpful egalitarian relationship with the natural being.
- The Natural Senses — Beyond seeing, hearing, and the three other commonly recognized senses, use as many of the fifty-four Natural Senses as you see fit and prepare to document the ones that you use in your journal.

- Great Trustable Truth — Experience what is happening at the present moment in nature, paying particular attention to the role of both beauty and balance; remember that the impressions you form about attractive natural beings and natural areas, coming from your experiencing of them in the Now, are trustable; and recognize that the natural processes and features witnessed are a source of special, substantial, and irreplaceable truthfulness about both nature and yourself.
- Recall — Place the great trustable truth and any other insights that you discover in a mental lock-box so you can later record them in your journal.

Follow-up Protocol

- Date —Write down the date of your outdoor nature-communing experience.
- Activity —Write down the waypoint title and number each time each you do an activity.
- Location —Write down the location of your outdoor nature-communing experience.
- Natural Being Indicator — Draw a picture or write down in your journal a nameless way to remember your chosen attractive Natural Being; for example, call it your "____ ____ Connection Experience."
- The Natural Senses Used — Write down all of the Natural Senses you used for this activity.
- General Description — Write a general description of how you did the activity and what happened.
- Freeform — Write, in freeform, what you found attractive about your natural being.
- Three Qualities — Write down three qualities you found attractive about your natural being.
- Three Learnings — Write down three things you learned from this activity.

- Self-esteem & Trust — Write down how, if at all, this activity changed your self-esteem or trustfulness of NNIAAL (Nameless-ness, Now, Intelligence, Alive, Attraction, and Love).
- Changes To Self — Write down what aspects of your Self, if any, were changed by this activity.
- Honor Yourself — Praise yourself and your commitment to making another stop along the Heartwood Path good for yourself and the world.
- I'm A Person Who. . . — Write down three different so-called "G/G Statements" using the following format: "This connection experience tells me that I am a person who_____."
- Feelings If Activity Taken — Write down a sentence about how you would feel if you lost your ability to experience this connection.
- Nature Compared To Self — Create a sentence that reads: "I love this (insert words that identify the attractive natural being) because it is (insert words that refer to the qualities you like about the natural being); then, create a parallel sentence that reads: "I love (insert the word "myself") because I am (insert the same qualities as before)."
- Ride The Green Wave — Determine whether you understand and agree with **all** of the Ten Green Wave Validation Statements.
- Name Your Discomforts — Make a list of aspects of your negative emotional residue, if any, that lifted simply by being in nature.
- Goethean Phenomenology — Write down impressions after observing a natural being over time and indicate the starting and ending dates for the observation.
- Defocalization — Write down impressions after using good blurry vision to observe a natural setting.
- Integral Immersion — Improve your journal writing by addressing what is, what could be, and what ought to be.
- Adding Suffixes — add "ing" or "ness" to the end of your name and the natural being on your bridge of your awareness, and

note how references such as "Don*ing*" or "Sycamore*ness*," if at all, add unity or any other value to your experience.
- Love Letter — Write a letter of gratitude to a natural being and another love letter from a natural being.
- Two-word Summary — Write down two words that summarize your response to this activity.

Heartwood Path Exchange

- Comment — Post your impressions and photos in the Comments section of this waypoint—the place for on-going discussion regarding this waypoint.
- Join — Engage with others in a Heartwood Path course or salon.
- Create — Start your own Heartwood Path salon that meets regularly online, by phone, or in person.
- Talk — Share your impressions with trusted family members and friends.
- Network — Post your impressions and photos on our EartHeart Networking Forum.
- Post — To see what conversations you can ignite, upload on social media your photos and impressions about anything pertaining to your journey down the Heartwood Path.
- Connect — Follow our account on Instagram, Like our Page on Facebook, Subscribe to our Channel on YouTube, and use hashtags such as "#heartwoodpath", "#eartHeart", and "#waypoint(insert book)(insert waypoint number) i.e."#waypointecos5").

Dreaming Time Protocols

The full meaning of each protocol is revealed as you progress, waypoint by waypoint.

Before Dreaming Protocol

- Perform A Reality Check — At least daily, during your waking hours determine whether you are dreaming as a way to develop lucid dreaming skills.
- Dream Prep — Prepare yourself for productive dreaming by de-cluttering your mind before sleeping.
- Set An Intention — Repeat the affirmation: "I remember my dream."
- Incubate A Dream — Decide what lucid dream you are going to have by using visualization.
- Journal Ready — Prepare to record your dream impressions by placing your journal so that you can make initial recordings in it without changing your dreamtime sleeping position.

Dreaming Protocol

- Remember This — Look to your dreams to tell you what you need to remember.
- Open To Dream — Be receptive, fluid, interactive, and grounded as you dream.
- Lucid Dreaming — Be aware that you are dreaming and have an impact on what happens in the dream.
- Wake-Back-To-Bed — Wake up after six hours of sleep, staying awake for twenty minutes, then go back to sleep.
- Look For Dream Signs — Stay on the lookout for recurring elements of your dreams that let you know you are dreaming.
- Stabilize Your Dreams — Prolong your lucidity by making your dreams stable like the real world.
- Shape-shifters — Watch characters that change in your dream to see into the possibilities of your own transformation.
- World Dreams — Consider that your dreams may be tapping into the dreams of your chosen attractive natural beings or the wholeness of Nature.

After Dreaming Protocol

- First Off — Recall your dream by staying in your sleeping position as you make your first attempt to remember your dream.
- Book Of Dreams — Create an entry in your dream journal using the following linguistic tools: 1) talking in the present tense, 2) using verbs ending in "ing," 3) removing articles such as "an" or "the," and 4) using capital letters when naming the Dream Characters—which can be any notable people, places, or things that show up in your dream.
- Title — Give your dream a memorable title.
- Date — Write down the date of your dream.
- Description — Write down a short, general summary of your dream.
- Mood — Write down how the dream affected your mood upon waking.
- Life Event Affecting Dream — Write down any events in your life that may have influenced your dream.
- Dream Characters — List all remembered notable "actors" in your dream, whether they are people, places, or things.
- Setting — Describe the location of your dream.
- Statement Of Problem — Write down the complication, challenge, predicament, situation, obstacle, plight, quandary, or misadventure presented in your dream.
- Culmination Or Response To The Problem — Describe what you or another Dream Character did in your dream to respond to the problem presented in the dream.
- Conclusion — Describe how your dream ended.
- Beings Revealed — Write down how your dream seemed to be, if at all, linked in some way to your chosen attractive natural beings.
- Freud's Approach — Associate the actions of your Dream Characters with latent, infantile, repressed, or sexual drives.

- Jung's Approach — Amplify your Dream Characters into Archetypes that are global in scale, symbolic, pervasive, positive, and helpful.
- Hillman's Approach — Recognize your Dream Characters as animated, living beings by honoring their presence, place, and body.
- Right Information — Ask yourself the two main questions for Dream Tending: "Who is visiting now?" And "What is happening here?"
- The Richest Treasures — Do not force narrow interpretations upon the natural being impressions that reappear in your dream by condensing them into limited signs when it is more fruitful to simply engage with them as living beings that reside in your dream, possibly with infinite symbolic value.
- Dream Keywords — Write down single words that seem to solidify what you are thinking about your dream and then process these words using association, amplification, and animation.
- Privacy — Store your dream journal in a safe place and, where appropriate, share your dream with others.

Dream Council Protocol

- Create Dream Figures — Periodically create physical representations of select Dream Characters using natural materials, give them some form of identification, and gather them together.
- Pick Dream Council Members — Designate eight to fifteen of your most revered Dream Figures to serve on your Dream Council, which is your most honored dream advisory group.
- Convene A Dream Council Meeting — Whenever you desire, ceremoniously hold conversations with the Dream Figures that make up your Dream Council and write down any guidance you receive.
- Listen Deeply — If what you come across during your occasional interactions with Dream Figures does not make sense to

you, write down your impressions so you can consider them at another time (when more experience can be brought to bear).

Natural Senses

The Radiation Senses

- Sense of light and sight, including polarized light.
- Sense of seeing without eyes such as heliotropism or the sun sense of plants.
- Sense of color.
- Sense of moods and identities attached to colors.
- Sense of awareness of one's own visibility or invisibility and consequent camouflaging.
- Sensitivity to radiation other than visible light including radio waves, X rays, etc.
- Sense of temperature and temperature change.
- Sense of season including ability to insulate, hibernate, and winter sleep.
- Electromagnetic sense and polarity which includes the ability to generate current (as in the nervous system and brain waves) or other energies.

The Feeling Senses

- Hearing including resonance, vibrations, sonar, and ultrasonic frequencies.
- Awareness of pressure, particularly underground, underwater, and to wind and air.
- Sensitivity to gravity.
- The sense of excretion for waste elimination and protection from enemies.

- Feel, particularly touch on the skin.
- Sense of weight, gravity, and balance.
- Space or proximity sense.
- Coriolis sense or awareness of effects of the rotation of the Earth.
- Sense of motion, body movement sensations, and sense of mobility.

The Chemical Senses

- Smell with and beyond the nose.
- Taste with and beyond the tongue.
- Appetite or hunger for food, water, and air.
- Hunting, killing, or food obtaining urges.
- Humidity sense including thirst, evaporation control and the acumen to find water or evade a flood.
- Hormonal sense, as to pheromones and other chemical stimuli.

The Mental Senses

- Pain, external and internal.
- Mental or spiritual distress.
- Sense of fear, dread of injury, death or attack.
- Procreative urges including sex awareness, courting, love, mating, paternity and raising young.
- Sense of play, sport, humor, pleasure, and laughter.
- Sense of physical place, navigation senses including detailed awareness of land and seascapes, of the positions of the sun, moon, and stars.
- Sense of time.
- Sense of electromagnetic fields.
- Sense of weather changes.
- Sense of emotional place, of community, belonging, support, trust, and thankfulness.
- Sense of self including friendship, companionship, and power.

- Domineering and territorial sense.
- Colonizing sense including compassion and receptive awareness of one's fellow creatures, sometimes to the degree of being absorbed into a superorganism.
- Horticultural sense and the ability to cultivate crops, as is done by ants that grow fungus, by fungus who farm algae, or birds that leave food to attract their prey.
- Language and articulation sense, used to express feelings and convey information in every medium from the bees' dance to human literature.
- Sense of humility, appreciation, and ethics.
- Senses of form and design.
- Sense of reason, including memory and the capacity for logic and science.
- Sense of mind and consciousness.
- Intuition or subconscious deduction.
- Aesthetic sense, including creativity and appreciation of beauty, music, literature, form, design, and drama.
- Psychic capacity such as foreknowledge, clairvoyance, clairaudience, psychokinesis, astral projection, possibly certain animal instincts, and plant sensitivities.
- Sense of biological and astral time, awareness of past, present, and future events.
- The capacity to hypnotize other creatures.
- Relaxation and sleep including dreaming, meditation, and brain wave awareness.
- Sense of pupation including cocoon building and metamorphosis.
- Sense of excessive stress and capitulation.
- Sense of survival by joining a more established organism.
- Spiritual sense, including conscience, capacity for sublime love, ecstasy, a sense of sin, profound sorrow, and sacrifice.
- Sense of homeostatic unity, of natural attraction aliveness as the singular essence-diversity attraction dance of all our other

senses (NNIAAL). (Cohen, website: http://www.ecopsych.com/insight53senses.html).

Acknowledgments

I would like to thank everyone who helped me blaze the trail that has become the Heartwood Path. Initially, David Brower got me going, after asking me to "write a piece" to combat "burnout" in environmentalists. Roger Fritz helped me with my conversion from corporate executive to author. Paula Badger was a good listener on our frequent walks. Michael J. Cohen helped me to add nature's intelligence to the methodology. "Forest Maiden" Sylvia Shelton served as my "muse"—always with humor, tenderness, intelligence, and love. I started out thinking I was writing traditional books. My daughter Courtney Logue converted my text into an interactive website. Without her efforts—in editing, in creating the format, and in providing important encouragement—there would not be a Heartwood Path. To these people, and many more, I am forever grateful.

About The Author

Pierce has spent nearly his whole life working to protect the environment. After decades of work as a professional environmentalist, Pierce concluded that a new approach—one focused on the environmentalist and not just the environment—was needed.

When famed conservationist David Brower asked him to write "a piece" to show environmentalists how to persevere, the result was a series of books and courses that are good for both environmentalists and anyone seeking happiness and the preservation of nature. This series—the Heartwood Path—helps people to develop spiritually, helps people discover the benefits of communing with nature, and helps people find the abundant, abiding, and authentic happiness that comes from helping others, including natural beings.

Pierce formed his first environmental group—a tree planting club—when he was nine. After that, he was president of both his high school and college environmental organizations. After a few years as a professional river conservationist, he was hired by Brower to be the Midwest Representative of Friends of the Earth. Pierce has led numerous conservation groups, including the Illinois Chapter of the Sierra Club. He was a governor-appointed member of the Illinois Nature Preserves Commission.

He has a Bachelor's Degree in environmental science, a Master's Degree in political science, and Master's Degree in social work. When he was not working to protect the environment or guiding people down the Heartwood Path, Pierce—a qualified life coach and mental health practitioner—served those who needed his care—including those who are young, aged, mentally ill, or mentally disabled.

Currently working on his PH.D in eco-psychology, Pierce divides his time between Santa Barbara, California and St. Louis, Missouri. He is a professional drummer, an avid canoeist, and a photographer. He loves to walk in nature. He has two grown daughters (one, the mother of his two granddaughters, in Missouri and another one somewhere on a sailboat that is often close to Santa Barbara).

Heartwood Path One-On-One Guidance

(30 minute or 60 minute sessions)

Don Pierce will move you to an extraordinary awakening of personal happiness and ecological sustainability.

"Make a difference, happily."

To do so, go down the Heartwood Path under the skilled guidance of its creator, Don Pierce. Don's education and experience will help you turn your advocacy into a source of abiding, abundant, and authentic happiness. His years as an active environmentalist will enable him to teach you how to become both happy and effective in your own causes. His years as a social worker will help you fit better into your own environment. His experience as a life coach will help you set your own agenda towards meeting your goals. His years as a mental health practitioner will enable him to help you achieve the integrity that comes when your inner world enables you to be "glad" as you endeavor to make the outer world "green." By signing up for guidance, you will have Don at your side to answer questions, provide encouragement, and avoid wrong turns.

In productive and easy-to-afford steps, Guidance moves you to an extraordinary awakening of personal happiness and ecological

413

sustainability. Guidance moves you beyond a common state of separation to an extraordinary awakening of oneness that is experienced as personal happiness, ecological sustainability, and spiritual maturity.

Sessions, which are purchased in thirty minute and one hour segments, occur online, on the phone, or in person with Heartwood Path creator Don Pierce. Elements of Heartwood Path guidance include:

- making checklists of topics or actionable items
- establishing guidelines
- setting and reviewing deadlines
- explaining and reviewing practices
- responding and questioning journal entries
- instructing
- providing individualized templates of models
- supporting individuals and teams in the field
- defining terminology and elaborating on Heartwood Path text
- mentoring on related subjects and
- assistance in interpreting signs and symbols.

Complementary Guidance sessions are available when you sign up for any Heartwood Path course.

Further Action

REVIEWS APPRECIATED AND OTHER HEARTWOOD PATH BOOKS

If you enjoyed reading **Ethos,** the Heartwood Path book on the development of positive personal traits, please leave a review on Amazon. I would appreciate any comments you may wish to share. Positive reviews go a long way in spreading our important message.

For further reading, see **Kosmos,** the Heartwood Path book that prepares you at the onset of your journey of spiritual growth, and **Logos,** our book on universal principals and the structure of integrity.

The third book is **Egos: Connecting with the Individual Self.** Here you will learn of the important personal preparations necessary for the creation of happiness and a sustainable environment.

Another book is **Ecos: Connecting with the Ecological Self.**

All Heartwood Path books are available on Amazon.

In recognition for all that you do along the Heartwood Path regarding the development of your own happiness and the sustainability of the world, I say "thank you" and "Great Work!"